MANSERVANT AND MAIDSERVANT

IVY COMPTON-BURNETT'S life was, on the surface, uneventful. One of the twelve children of a homeopathic doctor, James Compton-Burnett, she spent her childhood in a huge and ugly Victorian house in Hove and continued to live there until she was twenty-seven, except for a period as a student of classics at Royal Holloway College. At the outbreak of war she moved to London, and from the end of the war until her death in 1969 she lived there, sharing a flat with her friend Margaret Jourdain. But this bald summary conceals in its first part an upbringing of claustrophobic family tension on which she was to draw for the subject matter of her novels throughout the whole relatively tranquil second part of her life. Her biographer, Hilary Spurling, has said "Ivy used her early experience as other writers have used a body of myth, selecting from it images and archetypes...": the tyranny and the rages of her mother, the oppression by her of the five older step-children (offspring of James Compton-Burnett's first marriage), the rigidly segregated and hierarchical household, the prolonged and exaggerated mourning into which the family was plunged after their father's death—all this was to become the substance of the nineteen novels. It was a tragic family: both Ivy Compton-Burnett's beloved brothers died young—Guy of pneumonia, Noel in the war—and her two youngest sisters committed suicide. By 1919 the family was dead or dispersed, but its effect on Ivy was total; she remained, as a novelist, locked in the period before the First World War. Ivy Compton-Burnett was made a Dame Commander in 1967 and Companion of Literature in 1968.

PENELOPE LIVELY was born and grew up in Egypt. She is the author of five novels (of which *The Road to Lichfield* was shortlisted for the Booker Prize and *Treasure of Time* received the Arts Council National Book Award for fiction) and a collection of short stories. She has also written a number of children's books.

ALSO AVAILABLE IN
TWENTIETH-CENTURY CLASSICS

IVY COMPTON-BURNETT

Manservant and Maidservant

Introduced by
PENELOPE LIVELY

Oxford New York
OXFORD UNIVERSITY PRESS

Oxford University Press, Walton Street, Oxford OX2 6DP

London Glasgow New York Toronto
Delhi Bombay Calcutta Madras Karachi
Kuala Lumpur Singapore Hong Kong Tokyo
Nairobi Dar es Salaam Cape Town
Melbourne Auckland

and associates in

Beirut Berlin Ibadan Mexico City Nicosia

First published by Victor Gollancz Ltd 1947
First issued as an Oxford University Press paperback 1983
Reprinted 1983

British Library Cataloguing in Publication Data

Compton-Burnett, I.
Manservant and maidservant.—(Twentieth-century
classics)
I. Title   II. Lively, Penelope   III. Series
823'.912[F]   PR6005.03895
ISBN 0–19–281380–3

Library of Congress Cataloging in Publication Data

Compton-Burnett, I. (Ivy), 1892–1969.
Manservant and maidservant.
(Twentieth-century classics) (Oxford paperbacks)
I. Title.   II. Series.
PR6005.03895 M3 1983   823'.912   82–19031
ISBN 0–19–281380–3 (pbk.)

Printed in Great Britain by
Richard Clay (The Chaucer Press) Ltd
Bungay, Suffolk

INTRODUCTION
BY PENELOPE LIVELY

IVY COMPTON-BURNETT'S nineteen novels occupy a curious position in the spectrum of English fiction: maverick, *sui generis*, they are as remarkable for what they are not as for what they are. Detached both from public events and from recognizable landscapes, they concentrate on a Sartrean world: the enclosed torments of family life. The standard situation of a Compton-Burnett novel involves oppression, exploitation and rebellion. Violence predominates—mainly verbal, sometimes actual. In a world stripped of the intrusions of public existence, husbands and wives, parents and children, masters and servants perform a subtle, comic and horrifying ceremony of insult and manipulation. It is like nothing else; her voice is unique, though echoes of its manner can be heard in Henry Green and of its accuracy in Barbara Pym. She has always been a special taste, attracting irritation from some quarters and passionate advocacy from others. But the extraordinary wit and force of her style are undeniable; she creates a world of her own, a world that is a luridly distorted and at the same time disconcertingly apt reflection of the real one.

The families who provide the casts of the novels exist in a state of detachment from the processes of history and the evocations of place. Public events are never mentioned; locations are seldom specified. Nearly all the books have the same setting: a large country house occupied by a family of disparate generations and complex relationships in the late Victorian period. The subject matter is the exercise of power. Various interpretations of Ivy Compton-Burnett's choice of so restricted a stage have been put forward, but the most potent one seems to be the absolute appropriateness of its attributes for her purposes. The extended Victorian family offered opportunities for the use and abuse of power unequalled since the baronial system: an emphasis on primogeniture, an attendant serf class by way of children and servants, concentration of economic resources in a single hand. Exclude distractions by way of wider social comment or the demands of employment, suspend the characters in time, and the way is open for an exact scrutiny of what they then say and do to each other. The weapons of personality and language are brought to bear against those of money and position. The result is tragedy—and comedy.

Ivy Compton-Burnett died in 1969, aged seventy-five. Her last novel, *The Last and the First*, was published posthumously; her first, *Dolores*, had appeared in 1911. *Dolores*, though, is an unsatisfactory book, generally regarded as outside the main body of her work, which begins with the publication of *Pastors and Masters* in 1925. Although the novels are seldom specific about time, they are all sternly late Victorian or Edwardian in atmosphere. She herself is quoted as having said, "I do not feel that I have any real or organic knowledge of life later than about 1910."

The masterly first volume of Hilary Spurling's biography (the second volume appears in 1984) discusses the relation of the novels to the early circumstances of Ivy Compton-Burnett's life: enormous family, offspring of different mothers, the oppressive widowhood of Ivy's own mother, Ivy's tyranny over her younger sisters. "I think that actual life supplies a writer with characters much less than is thought" she later said, ". . . people in life hardly seem to be definite enough to appear in print. They are not good enough or bad enough, or clever or stupid enough, or comical or pitiful enough." And indeed the essence of her characterization is exaggeration, that dramatizing and formalizing of personality that has led some critics to find her people unreal. If members of her own family appear in the novels, they do so with the poetic licence of distortion; more importantly, she drew, for ever after, on the traumas and claustrophobias of her own youth for the basic subject matter of her fiction—the ways in which people live with those from whom they cannot escape.

The quintessential Compton-Burnett scene is a meal-time—most likely breakfast or tea—at which the members of the family, with delicate savagery, perform the daily ritual of verbal attack and counter-attack and establish for the reader the power structure of the household. The family will probably include two or three generations, servants engaged in prurient participation, and its composition will embrace situations of inherent unease such as second marriages, step-children, penniless resident dependants and precarious financial circumstances. The stage thus set, the drama unfolds, and may well include actual as well as emotional violence, implications of adultery, homosexuality and incest, all taking place off-stage and recounted by means of the formal and startling dialogue which is the crux of Ivy Compton-Burnett's literary style. The theatrical analogy is not only apt but essential; in many ways the books—especially those such as *A Heritage and its History* and *A Father and his Fate* in which the manner is pared down to its most bleak and unadorned—are more like plays than novels. There is a deliberate sense of scene, of entrance and departure, and above all of the dominance of voice. To read them is to have an eerie sense of disembodied voices, as powerful and disturbing as a radio play can be, without the distractions of visual description. Furnishings and landscapes are rarely described; props may appear from time to time—a piece of crockery, an ivy-covered wall—but are there simply as that, adjuncts to the plot. The characters are often granted a minute physical description; the curious thing is that none of these descriptions stays in the head, as you read on. Horace and Mortimer, the cousins in *Manservant and Maidservant*, have respectively "thin, wrinkled cheeks, eyes of a clear, cold blue" and "a round, full face, rounded, almost blunt features, a mobile, all but merry mouth"—but as the book progresses we are aware only of their distinctive voices, petulant and self-justifying, humorously resigned. The structure of each book is a symphony of voices; the narrative advances through the words of the participants. The reader is left with a sense of eavesdropping; when the book is closed the voices will carry on, remorseless.

vii

Ivy Compton-Burnett characters speak with studied precision. Here are Horace and Mortimer Lamb, at the opening of *Manservant and Maidservant*.

"Is that fire smoking?" said Horace Lamb.
"Yes, it appears to be, my dear boy."
"I am not asking what it appears to be doing. I asked if it was smoking."
"Appearances are not held to be a clue to the truth," said his cousin. "But we seem to have no other."

In the briefest of exchanges she establishes pedantry and a position of command in one character, while allowing another a wry hint at circumstances not yet revealed.

The form of her dialogue is at the heart of the matter of the books. Towards the end of *Manservant and Maidservant* Mortimer, writing to his cousin, thanks him for a letter: "It has broken my heart, but that is the natural result of the use of words. When human speech developed, it was a foregone thing. It allowed people to communicate their thoughts, and what else could come of that?" Her characters are in constant, dangerous and frequently fatal communication and to this end she constructed a form of speech which is quite removed from reality but demonstrates all the subtle ways in which people use language as a weapon. Each line of a Compton-Burnett exchange needs to be carefully examined; people may be lying, dissembling, speaking as they think, or concealing their real meaning. Few of the novels demonstrate this as satisfactorily as *Manservant and Maidservant*.

First published in 1947 it is, by Compton-Burnett standards, positively discursive. She allows herself an unusual amount of authorial intrusion and comment and, above all, she indulges to the full her talent for conversations of barbed humour which are also masterpieces of pace and dramatic effect. The servants—Bullivant the butler, Mrs. Selden the cook, Miriam the skivvy and George the young manservant—are given scenes of wonderful hilarity in which the hierarchy and oppression of the servants' hall both mirror and caricature the tyrannies and hypocrisies of the drawing-room. But it is the children who have all the best lines in *Manservant and Maidservant*: Sarah, Jasper, Marcus, Tamasin and Avery, ranging in age from thirteen to seven.

Ivy Compton-Burnett children are a special creation: totally unchildlike and at the same time endowed with all the ruthless and more usually unspoken perceptions of childhood. There are other memorable groups of children in the novels—notably in *Elders and Betters*—but the Lamb children are given a peculiarly effective role as a kind of Greek chorus, commenting, with unswerving accuracy, on the actions of their elders. We first meet them stoically enduring the cold of their schoolroom (the alternate heaping up and banking down of fires is a potent symbol of the state of the household).

"They all pretend to be cold," said Horace. "It becomes a monotonous pose."

"We don't pretend," said Marcus. "If we were not cold, we should not think about it."

Horace Lamb is a tyrant, oppressor of his offspring, his wife, his cousin, his servants. He married Charlotte for her money—"hoping to serve his impoverished estate, and she had married him for love, hoping to fulfil herself. The love had gone and the money remained, so that the advantage lay with Horace, if he could have taken so hopeful a view of his life." Thus, with one swipe, Ivy Compton-Burnett establishes the relationship; the scene is set for the unfolding of its consequences. A second and subsidiary family is introduced— a typical Compton-Burnett device—whose pressures and machinations complicate the existing tensions. Ivy Compton-Burnett always had a patrician disregard for the niceties of plot and a robust taste for the techniques of melodrama; *Manservant and Maidservant* demonstrates both these tendencies to a fine degree. There is a fortuitous and slightly gratuitous departure (of Charlotte) enabling the events to be set in train, matters of an intercepted letter, a secret passion and a thwarted marriage (all favourite Compton-Burnett ingredients) while the central drama—the two alleged assassination attempts on Horace—must be quite the most improbable narrative device that she ever proposed. An unreliable bridge, a concealed notice, a stolen knife and other props—not to mention a ravine, an unlikely landscape feature for eastern England—are produced as vehicles for what is the real matter of the book: the study of the manipulation of power.

And it is in their observation of and comment on its use and abuse that the children come into their own. They behave with a mixture of suppressed exuberance—despite their father's severity—and resignation, using the restrictions of their experience to make swingeing points about the customs of the adult world. Kept short of fuel, food and clothes by their father's parsimony, they draw on what appears to be their habitual reading matter for the occasional apt comment.

"Be of good cheer, Master Jasper, and follow the example of Mistress Sarah," said Marcus, in a forced, deliberate tone. "For she this day has lighted a candle that shall point our way."

"Who talks like that?" said Jasper.

"The people in Foxe's Book of Martyrs."

Children, in all the novels, are used as symbols of powerlessness, in bondage not only to their parents but also to their condition: "We are waiting for time to pass", says Tamasin. But the rules of warfare allow to the weaker the right of comment; one of the subtleties of Ivy Compton-Burnett's investigation of the function of language is that she allows the oppressed characters in her books to make most effective use of it. The weapons of position and money rest in the hands of heads of household, the classic tyrants of the books, but it is the poor relations, the dependants, the children who are given the most elegant and crushing verbal skills. Horace Lamb, in response to the orchestrated criticism of his family, is in a constant state of self-defence: "Has none of you any sympathy except with children and servants?" He hectors and bullies but it is the children who have the last word—or the delicately ambiguous word—in reply to his justifications.

"They must learn it is meaner to be selfish. That sort of lavishness is self-indulgence, and that is the meanest thing of all. It has to be extirpated, rooted out, by whatever method is soundest."

"It is a dreadful thing," said Avery, with his eyes on Horace's face.

"What is?" said Jasper.

"What Father said," said his brother.

Discussion of Ivy Compton-Burnett's status has continued ever since the publication of *Pastors and Masters*. Her stylistic austerity has offended some critics, along with the "unreality" of her situations and her characters. She has never achieved popularity as a novelist and probably never will, but to base rejection of her work on its manner is to be impervious to its purpose. Like all major writers, she is performing at several levels: what is said, what appears to be said, what is not said. The richness and craft of her language give it an after-effect; it is often only when you arrive at the next page that you realize what has been conveyed on the previous one. The real meaning of the novels—the outraged sensibilities, the griefs, the stoicisms—lies beneath the language. Perhaps the best analogy to be drawn is the way in which actions, whether trivial or momentous, frequently take place behind a conversational exchange. Thus, the setting of the scene in the first chapter of *Manservant and Maidservant*—the introduction of the characters and the explanations of their position in the household hierarchy—takes place against the activities of Bullivant and George who are engaged in dislodging from the chimney a dead jackdaw which has been causing the fire to smoke. It is a piece of writing of the utmost elegance and economy: informative, dramatic and extremely funny.

The other singularity of her work is its lack of development, and this perhaps is the feature against which criticism can more fairly be levelled. There is a remarkable consistency of both style and matter from *Pastors and Masters* (1925) to *The Last and the First* (1971); there are variations in theme and treatment but not the sense of the imaginative progress which is usual in the work of a major novelist. Nevertheless there are significant differences of approach; all Ivy Compton-Burnett addicts have their favourite novel, but to my taste her powers were at their greatest in the central group, which includes *Manservant and Maidservant*. Here her wit was at its sharpest, her characterizations most memorable, her dramatic sense at its peak. Above all, it is a book which is inexhaustible; each new reading prompts fresh insights. This is the strength of her extraordinary command of language; the set-piece conversations—whether they take place in the servants' hall, the schoolroom or the drawing-room—have the depth and resonance of a piece of music. Different emphases are revealed at every hearing. It is the height of her art: precise, disturbing and original.

MANSERVANT AND MAIDSERVANT

CHAPTER I

"Is that fire smoking?" said Horace Lamb.

"Yes, it appears to be, my dear boy."

"I am not asking what it appears to be doing. I asked if it was smoking."

"Appearances are not held to be a clue to the truth," said his cousin. "But we seem to have no other."

Horace advanced into the room as though his attention were withdrawn from his surroundings.

"Good morning," he said in a preoccupied tone, that changed as his eyes resumed their direction. "It does seem that the fire is smoking."

"It is in the stage when smoke is produced. So it is hard to see what it can do."

"Did you really not understand me?"

"Yes, yes, my dear boy. It is giving out some smoke. We must say that it is."

Horace put his hands in his pockets, and caused an absent sound to issue from his lips. He was a middle-aged man of ordinary height and build, with thin, wrinkled cheeks, eyes of a clear, cold blue, regular features unevenly set in his face, and a habit of looking aside in apparent abstraction. This was a punishment to people for the nervous exasperation that they produced in him, and must expiate.

"Has that fire been smoking, Bullivant?"

"Well, sir, not to say smoking," said the butler, recoiling before the phenomenon. "Merely a response to the gusty morning. A periodical spasm in accordance with the wind."

"Will it put soot all over the room?"

"Only the lightest deposit, sir. Nothing to speak about," said Bullivant, keeping his eyes from Horace, as he suggested his course.

Bullivant was a larger man than his masters, and had an air of being on a considerable scale in every sense. He had pendulous cheeks, heavy eyelids that followed their direction, solid, thick hands whose movements were deft and swift and precise, a nose that hardly differentiated from its surroundings, and a deeply folded neck and chin with no definite line between them. His small, steady, hazel eyes were fixed on his assistant, and he wore an air of resigned and almost humorous deprecation, that suggested a tendency to catch his masters' glance.

Mortimer Lamb liked Bullivant; George, his subordinate, disliked and feared him; and Horace merely feared him, except in his moods of nervous abandonment, when he feared nothing and nobody.

George was an ungainly, overgrown youth, whose garb still indicated a state of juvenile usefulness, who shuffled, started and avoided people's eyes, but managed to present a pleasant appearance, and could not avoid presenting a pathetic one. He made every movement twice under Bullivant's eye, as though doubling his effort proved his zeal, and the former continued to observe him until he went with a suggestion of flight on some errand to the kitchen. Bullivant relaxed his bearing and turned to Horace almost with a smile, being an adept at suggesting a facial movement without executing it.

"It is to make them do it, sir, not to do it yourself. I should never call doing things myself the harder part."

"Then why don't you do them yourself?" said Mortimer, in a reckless manner.

Bullivant turned his eyes on him, and Horace turned his eyes away.

"I cannot understand anyone's choosing the harder part," said Mortimer, on a humbler note.

"Well, sir, we have to think of the future, when our own day will be done," said Bullivant, taking his revenge by including Mortimer in this prospect, and just drawing back before an eddy of smoke.

"I do not have to. I should not dream of doing such a thing."

"We must not think that the world stops with us, sir, because it stops for us."

"Bullivant, you did not think I meant you to do things yourself, did you?"

"Does that chimney want sweeping?" said Horace, not pretending to abandon his own line of thought.

"No, sir, not until the spring," said Bullivant, in a tone of remonstrance.

"Might it be as well to light the fire earlier?" said Mortimer, not looking at his cousin.

"Well, sir, for one morning like this, there may be a dozen with the grate drawing as sweet——" Bullivant broke off before his simile developed, and again recoiled.

"There must be some obstruction in the chimney," said Horace.

"Well, sir, if that is the case, it is not for want of enjoinder," said Bullivant, referring to his latest encounter with the sweep, and keeping his face immobile in the face of another gust. "George, ask Mrs. Selden to retard the breakfast. There is a matter that calls for investigation."

George despatched the errand and returned. Bullivant made a dumb show of his requirements, as though spoken directions would be beneath himself and difficult for George. The latter, after a moment of tense attention, disappeared and returned with a pole, which he proceeded to thrust up the chimney.

"Is the fire too hot?" said Horace.

"No, sir," said George, with simple truthfulness.

"It seems to lack most of its natural characteristics," said Mortimer.

Horace kept his eyes on the operations, as if he did not hear. George conducted them with no result, became heated without aid from the fire, and finally glanced at Bullivant. The latter took the pole, gave it an easy, individual twist, and caused a dead bird to fall upon the hearth. George looked as if he were witnessing some sorcery, and Bullivant returned the pole to him without word or glance, but with an admonishing gesture with regard to some soot upon it.

"Well, the grate is not at fault," said Horace, as if glad to exempt his house from blame.

"The bird is a jackdaw," said Mortimer. "A large, black bird. Did you put it there, Bullivant?"

Bullivant indicated the bird to George with an air of rebuking omission, and when the latter had borne it away, turned gravely to Mortimer.

"So far am I, sir, from being connected with the presence of the fowl, that I was not confident, when I took matters into my own hands, of any outcome. I merely hoped that my intervention might lead to a result."

"The mistress is late," said Horace, "but she prefers us not to wait for her."

"That is understood, sir," said Bullivant. "She has spoken to me to the effect."

He moved to a door and returned with an air of having met the situation. When George reappeared with the dishes, he took them from him and set them on the board, turning the implements for serving to the convenient angle, as though people accustomed to full attendance might not be certain of their use. When Horace had served them, he replaced the covers, and gave the coffee pots a suggestive adjustment.

"The ladies do not mind their breakfast cold," said Horace.

Bullivant just raised his shoulders over feminine indifference to food, and motioned to George to place a dish by the fire. He kept his eyes on him, as he was intercepted by smoke, to see he gave no signs, and frowned as he gave somewhat dramatic ones.

"So the jackdaw was not responsible," said Mortimer. "We were too ready to blame what could not defend itself."

"Yes, sir, I think it was," said Bullivant, in a low, smooth tone, as though willing to keep the matter between Mortimer and himself. "A proportion of soot has been dislodged, and is having this momentary result."

"Well, ham is supposed to be smoked," said Mortimer.

"How do you mean? Supposed to be?" said Horace. "Is it not smoked?"

"Yes, I should think so by now, my dear boy. I meant that a little extra smoking would do no harm."

"Will you have coffee?" said his cousin.

"Why, is there tea?"

"No, I asked if you would have coffee."

"Well, I must have it, mustn't I?"

"How do you mean? Must? There is no compulsion."

"Of course there is. To have one or the other in the morning."

"We have given up having our choice, sir," said Bullivant, in an easy and distinct tone.

"Then you will have coffee?" said Horace.

"Yes, yes, so I must, my dear boy. So I will."

Bullivant walked on a wide circuit to Mortimer's place, and set the cup at his hand, meeting his abrupt stirring of it as his natural behaviour.

"I have lived in this house for fifty-four years," said Mortimer. "Fifty-four years to-day. I was born in eighteen hundred and thirty-eight."

"Do you mean it is your birthday?" said Horace.

"No, no, not that, my dear boy, nothing like that. Just that I was born in this house fifty-four years ago."

"Many happy returns of the day," said Horace.

"May I also offer my congratulations, sir?" said Bullivant, his tone striking a subtle degree of initiative and intimacy.

"Thank you very much. It is unusual to have all one's experience under one roof. And I have really had none outside it. I cannot imagine anything happening to me anywhere else, or anything happening to me at all. Not that I mean anything; I do not much like things to happen, or I should not much like it. I am content to live in other people's lives, content not to live at all. Whatever it is, I am content."

Mortimer Lamb had a short, square figure, a round, full face, rounded, almost blunted features, a mobile, all but merry mouth, and dark, kind, deep-set eyes, that held some humour and little hope. He would have been disappointed not to have a profession, if he had thought of having so expensive a thing. He gave his time to helping Horace on the place, or rather gave part of his time, and did nothing with the rest. His chief emotions were a strong and open feeling for his cousin, and a stronger and necessarily less open feeling for his cousin's wife.

"I also was born in this village, sir," said Bullivant, "and have also spent the major part of my life under this roof."

"And where were you born, George?" said Mortimer.

"In—in the institution—in the workhouse, sir," said George, with a startled eye, giving Bullivant an almost equal glance, in recognition that the worst had come to pass.

"Well, but in what place?" said Mortimer, as if this were the point of his question.

"At the workhouse in our town, sir."

"And were you brought up there?" said Mortimer, while Bullivant gave a slight shrug, in acceptance of George's past being thus in keeping with him.

"Yes, sir, until I was old enough to work."

"And were you unhappy there? That is, were you happy?"

"No, sir. Yes, sir. Not unhappy," said George, causing Bullivant's shoulders to rise again over his finding the experience to his mind.

"So it was not like Oliver Twist?" said Mortimer.

"No, sir, not often, sir," said George, evidently used to the question. "It was only no home life, sir."

"And did they teach you there?"

"We went to the local school, sir, with other boys."

8

"And was it all right for you there?"

"We were scorned up to a point, sir," said George, in simple comprehension.

Bullivant glanced at George, but went no further, as though he himself knew where to stop.

"Well, we carry no sign of our history," said Horace.

Bullivant gave George another glance, feeling this was a point on which opinions might differ.

"You can keep your own counsel," said Horace. "You owe no one your confidence."

"I have never sailed under false colours, sir," said George, causing Bullivant to frown at the needless personal touch.

"What made you think of being a house servant?" said Horace.

"I was put out as houseboy, sir, because a place offered, and then one keeps on with it."

"Do you regret it?" said Mortimer.

"No—no, sir," said George, with a glance at Bullivant, who did not countenance belittlement of the calling.

"So you have no home in the neighbourhood?" said Mortimer.

"No, no home at all, sir."

"He has places to go to, sir," said Bullivant, in a tone that deprecated exaggerated concern. "The lad has met with kindness. He is on his feet."

"The ladies are on the stairs," said Horace, as though the private lives in question at the moment were hardly George's.

Bullivant pointed sharply to the hearth. George, in concordance with his master's view, sped to lift the dish and place it on the board. Bullivant himself walked forward and drew out a chair.

"Good morning," said a rather deep voice, as the mistress of the house entered and took the seat opposite to Horace, something in their way of meeting without words showing them husband and wife. "There is nothing to justify my being late. The morning is no damper and colder for me than for anyone else, though I felt it must be."

"It was for us it was that," said Mortimer. "But we were glad to bear it for you."

"This room is never damp. It could not be in its situation," said Horace, who saw in his family house the perfection he had not found in his family. "And cold is too strong a word."

"What word should be used?" said his wife, with her glance about the wide, bleak room coming to rest on the grate.

"A slight contretemps with the fire, ma'am," said Bullivant in a low tone, bending towards her.

Charlotte Lamb was a short, broad woman of fifty, ungraceful almost to ungainliness. She had iron-grey hair, so wiry that it appeared unkempt, though it was not always so; clothes that were warranted to defy any usage, but hardly did so in her case; a rather full colour, features somewhat poorly formed, and eyes of a strong, deep blue, that showed anger, mirth or emotion as occasion called; and occasion called a good deal.

Horace had married her for her money, hoping to serve his impoverished estate, and she had married him for love, hoping to fulfil herself. The love had gone and the money remained, so that the advantage lay with Horace, if he could have taken so hopeful a view of his life.

Horace had inherited a house and land, and Mortimer had inherited nothing, save an unspoken right to live under the family roof. Horace's father, who was uncle and guardian to Mortimer, had assured the young men on his deathbed that he left no debts. They had expressed at the moment their appreciation of the inheritance, and had found later that his description of it was just. Mortimer took what money was given him, without even formal gratitude, feeling it enough to harbour no grievance. Horace saw the possession of money with a rigid and awed regard, that in the case of his wife was almost incredulous.

That the money belonged to Charlotte rather than to anyone else, was a problem he had never solved, though the solution was simply that she came of a substantial family and was the only surviving child. He laid his hands on the balance of her income, and invested it in his own name, a practice that she viewed with an apparent indifference that was her cover for being unable to prevent it. She had put off remonstrance until it had become unthinkable. Horace held that saving the money, or rather preventing its being spent, was equivalent to earning it, and he pursued his course with a furtive discomfiture that clouded his life, though it could not subdue his nature.

"Has the fire been smoking?" said Charlotte, unconscious of the effect of her words.

"Yes, but not of its own accord. There was a jackdaw in the chimney," said Mortimer.

"A what?"

"A jackdaw. Bullivant brought it down."

"How did he know it was there?" said another voice, as an elderly woman entered the room, and paused with an air of humour and weight.

"There was palpably an obstruction, ma'am," said Bullivant, as he placed a chair.

"Was it a dead jackdaw?"

"Yes, and a stage beyond that," said Mortimer. "George did what was necessary. I don't know what it was."

George paused in readiness to supplement the account.

"No, George, no. Not before the ladies," said Bullivant, making a gesture with his hand.

"And did the fire stop smoking then?" said Miss Lamb.

"Well, it had formed the habit," said Mortimer. "It did not break it all at once."

"Some soot had been dislodged, ma'am, and caused the later ebullition," said Bullivant.

Emilia Lamb was aunt to Horace and Mortimer, and had also spent her life in the house. She was a tall, large woman of seventy-five, with a marked, individual face, a

11

large, curved mouth, grave, pale eyes, obtrusive hands and feet, and the suggestion of imperfect control of movement, that accompanies unusual size. She was seen as a rare and impressive personality, and as she saw herself as others saw her, had one claim to the quality of rareness.

"It is a very cold day," said Charlotte, looking again at the grate. "They say there is no smoke without flame, but it does not seem to be true."

"A jackdaw might lead to the one rather than the other," said Mortimer.

"Why was it a jackdaw rather than any other bird?" said Emilia, bending her head with her slow smile.

"I don't think another bird would have done. There was a good deal of smoke. A sparrow would have been no good."

"Breakfast seems to get later and later," said Horace, looking at the clock.

"No, it keeps to its time," said Charlotte. "It is Emilia and I who do that. In the winter eight o'clock might be the middle of the night."

"Many people get up earlier."

"Yes, those who do all manner of work."

"At what time do you rise, Bullivant?" said Mortimer.

"Well, sir, the foundations of the house have to be laid."

"And you, George?" said Mortimer.

"Well, sir, there is no hardship here, that I did not get used to in the workhouse."

Horace glanced up in question of this word for George's experience, and the latter, in relief that his secret was out, moved about rapidly, without encountering anyone's eye.

"George was born in the town," said Mortimer. "The workhouse is on the market square. We are all natives of the place."

But a silence ensued, and Bullivant, feeling that George was unsuitably the cause of it, put something into his hands and motioned to him to withdraw.

"So that was George's start in life," said Charlotte,

"Yes, ma'am," said Bullivant, in a tone in which regret and acquiescence had an equal part.

"I had not heard of it before."

"No, ma'am. I thought the boy had his feelings about it, and of a nature to be respected. He drew no veil over it with me."

"I wonder how it has served him as a background for his life," said Emilia.

"Oh, well, ma'am, it has to serve some people."

"What happened to his mother?" said Mortimer.

Horace looked a question.

"Well, George had to be born of woman, my dear boy, even in a modern institution."

Bullivant gave a slight, involuntary sound, and answered as if it had not occurred.

"I have understood that his mother died in his infancy, sir."

"Poor George!" said Emilia.

"Oh, well, ma'am, he knew nothing better."

"That is what I mean."

"Yes, ma'am," said Bullivant, in submission to her feeling.

"How about the father?" said Mortimer.

Bullivant did not lift his eyes and busied himself with something on the table.

"Well, so much for the parents," said Mortimer, finding himself speaking for Bullivant's ears, or rather for the ears of the women as Bullivant regarded them. "The only problems for George concern himself."

"He would have no problems, sir," said Bullivant, as though George would hardly be up to these.

"What made you engage him?" said Horace.

"Well, sir, the lad wished to better himself. And I was not averse to a piece of plastic clay. It takes one's own mould. It is better than having someone who knows everything and can learn nothing. And the first can hardly be said of George."

"And you find he shapes, do you?"

"Oh, well, sir, shapes!" said Bullivant, lifting his shoulders and then glancing at the women and lowering his voice. "But we have to think of our wages, sir."

"He takes the rough work off you, doesn't he?" said Mortimer.

"Well, sir, I give him what chance I can," said Bullivant, piling some china on a tray and bearing it to the door on one hand, in illustration of his personal standard.

"It is true that George is underpaid," said Charlotte, "though it is not like Bullivant to refer to it almost aloud. And he has lived down the workhouse stigma by now."

"We knew nothing about the workhouse," said Horace.

"Bullivant knew," said Mortimer, "and kept it in his heart."

"We cannot ask Bullivant about it," said Charlotte, "because he is not paid quite enough himself. Of course we do not dare to pay him much too little. We only oppress the weak."

"From him that hath not, shall be taken away," said Emilia.

"Not everyone would engage a man of Bullivant's age," said Horace. "I remember him in George's stage when I was a child. He must be years older than I am."

"His years of service here have put him beyond serving anywhere else," said Mortimer. "It must happen, if we give it time. The same thing is true of me, though I have not his footing in the house. And talking of time reminds me that today is my birthday. If there is any money to spare, Charlotte, do not give it to—to anyone but me."

Bullivant, whose return had determined this conclusion, resumed his duties without sign of having heard it. This was no indication that he had not done so, but he did not concern himself with the material affairs of the family. Such things, as they managed them, were beyond his range, and so outside his interest. He knew that Mortimer was dependent on his relatives, but did not know the unusual nature of the situation, saw it indeed as another form of private means, and had no idea how it differed from other forms.

"Mrs. Selden is hoping to see you this morning, ma'am," he said to Emilia.

"I will come to the kitchen at the usual hour."

"It is good of you to relieve Charlotte of the house-keeping," said Horace.

"I have done it since the day of your birth and your mother's death. A habit is formed in that time."

"There is no time left for me to form it," said Charlotte. "And I admit the housekeeping does not attract me. It seems so frugal and spare and plain. And if my children are to be unwarmed and poorly fed, it shall not be my arrangement for them."

"We are all very well," said Horace.

"But hardship is known to mean that people are never ill."

"You had a letter that seemed to trouble you, Charlotte. Can I be of any help?"

"My father is feeling his age, and wants me to go and see him. And he lives on the other side of the earth."

"Does he ask you to pay him a visit?"

"No. He says it is my duty to do so."

Charlotte's father had made over money to her, in view of the expense of her family, and his son-in-law could not ignore his claim.

"I could take you, if both of us could leave the children."

"It is I who cannot do that, and I who shall have to. That is the beginning and the end."

"We will all do our best," said Emilia, who had heard with grave eyes. "But the news is not good."

"Bullivant, are you going to be all day, lifting that cloth off the table?" said Horace.

Bullivant took up the cloth by the corners to preclude the escape of crumbs, and bore it to the door, his manner acquiescing in the occasional propriety of his absence.

"We must not think Bullivant has no sense of hearing," said Horace.

15

"I thought you did think so," said Mortimer. "But he will not accuse you of it on this occasion."

"He has so much, that it is no good to reckon with it," said Charlotte.

"Now I do not know why I should be belittled and left out of account, as if I were a nonentity in my own house," said Horace, taking enough advantage of Bullivant's absence to explain his desire for it. "What children have a better father? Do I ever forget them for a day? Do I ever spend time or money on myself? Do I ever think of the life I could lead, if I had no family?"

"Why could not Bullivant tell you, my dear boy?" said Mortimer. "Why should he be the one to go?"

"Why should I not be granted the position that is mine?"

"It is assumed that it goes without saying," said Emilia.

"That is a dangerous line to take. You might estrange anyone by acting on it."

"Why, so we might," said Mortimer. "So it appears we have."

"What is my life but sacrifice of myself?"

"What is anyone's life?" said Charlotte. "We all owe so much to each other, that no life can be anything else."

Horace fixed his eyes on her face with a conscious, questioning look that repelled and angered her.

"A woman is not the creature that cannot bear to be stared at," she said.

As Horace withdrew his eyes, they happened to fall on the grate, and he was carried away on a more instinctive emotion.

"Now how often have I forbidden this piling up of a fire, that is to be of no use until the afternoon? I have said it and said it until I am weary of the words. What a waste of fuel that might be of use to somebody! What a coarse and common thing to do! It savours of ostentation, of display for its own sake. I could not have believed that anyone in this house would stoop so low. Now who was it who did the thing? It must have been somebody."

"Why, so it must," said Mortimer. "You might have thought of that."

"It was Bullivant," said Emilia, keeping her mouth grave.

Horace walked to the bell and stood with his hand upon it, and withdrew it only as steps approached the door.

"Who made up the fire, Bullivant?"

"Either George or myself, sir."

"But which of you?"

"Well, there were various dealings with it this morning, sir. I could not definitely say who was the last to be in contact."

"You were *seen* to make it up," said Horace, in a deepening tone. "Miss Emilia can bear witness to it."

"Then it was I, sir," said Bullivant, turning to Emilia with a slight bow, in acknowledgement of her aid to the position.

"But what possessed you to go counter to my wishes? Have you not heard me say a hundred times that this fire is to be low in the morning? What moved you to build up this great, showy pile?" Horace, who had removed some coal from the grate, restored it to show its previous condition.

"Well, sir, the ladies remarked upon the cold, and I felt I had perhaps overstressed economy in postponing the putting of the match until so late. And I hoped by some extra attention to redress the balance."

"I thought you did not remember making it up."

"It has been recalled to me, sir," said Bullivant, with another bow towards Emilia, who would have felt inclined to return it, if she could have accepted his view that she had served him.

"But there was no need to overdo things like this."

"No, sir, overdo is perhaps the word. But there were matters to contend with in various shapes this morning."

"And one of them took the shape of a jackdaw," said Emilia, with a smile, but disappointed of an answering one from Bullivant.

"See that it does not occur again," said Horace.

"No, sir, the circumstances would hardly repeat themselves," said Bullivant, in an acquiescent tone, as he went to the door.

"You informed against your aunt, my dear boy," said Mortimer. "And she informed against Bullivant. He comes out better than either of you."

"Oh, he was going to blame it all on to George, a helpless orphan from the workhouse," said Horace. "There is not much to choose between us."

"It was a bad hour for George, when he told the truth about himself," said Mortimer. "It was sad to see him thinking that honesty was the best policy."

"Well, he cannot learn too soon that it is not," said Charlotte. "He should leave the workhouse training behind."

"Honesty does not involve a complete lack of reticence," said Horace.

"George thinks that is what it does," said Emilia.

"There are things he could reasonably keep to himself."

"He was asked a question and answered it truthfully," said Mortimer. "We know we should not ask questions, but the reasons given are wrong. I asked him where he was born."

"Why did you want to know?" said Horace.

"I don't know, my dear boy; I don't think I did want to. But Bullivant had told us where he was born, and I had told people where I was; I don't know if they wanted to know. So when George did not tell us, I asked him. I think it was just to include him as a fellow creature. And then the poor lad had to confess that he was not one. It was sad to see him thinking how much credit the confession did him."

"I wonder who began this treating of people as fellow creatures," said Charlotte. "It is never a success."

"Once begun, it is a difficult thing to give up," said Emilia.

"We shall lose interest in it, when the novelty wears off," said Mortimer. "It seemed such an original idea."

"We can see how unnatural it is, by what comes of it," said Charlotte.

"I wonder if George regards us as fellow creatures," said Emilia.

"I believe he does," said Mortimer. "But I do not think Bullivant would approve of it."

"Are you really thinking of leaving us, Charlotte?" said Horace.

"I am thinking of visiting my father, which will involve my doing so."

"And we can do nothing," said Mortimer. "Only count the hours to your return."

"That will hardly be of help to her," said Horace.

"I think it will be a little help, my dear boy. It is nice to be missed."

"We had better not tell the children until just before she goes," said Emilia.

"They should face the truth," said Horace. "It is a sounder preparation for the future."

"We can never prepare for that," said his wife. "We know too little of it. And facing things is not a good habit; it causes needless suffering."

"Coming events very seldom cast their shadows before them," said Emilia. "But in this case we see the event itself. Perhaps they should be told while it is still ahead. Then they will be spared the shock."

"Of course that is how it is," said Horace, as if this had been his thought all the while.

"It was not the account you gave," said Charlotte.

"Well, no, it was not, my dear boy," said Mortimer.

Horace rose and left the room in an abstracted manner, and Emilia glanced at the other pair and followed.

"So you are deserting me, Charlotte," said Mortimer.

"I am deserting the children and am thankful to leave you with them."

"I will serve them because they are yours. But I wish I were your child."

"I do not wish it. I have enough children. I often wonder how much harm I have done. Would it be better for them, if they had not been born?"

"The change for them is coming. Your return must be our sign. If we hesitate longer, we shall lose our time and theirs. We must break from Horace and live apart and at peace. We will marry, if he makes it possible. It will be easier for him after this break in his life; the parting will smooth the way. How we find ourselves considering him! Is it a sign of some nobility in us?"

"Not unless there is a touch of nobility in every human creature, as I have heard it said."

"Is there something in Horace that twines itself about the heart? Perhaps it is his being his own worst enemy. That seems to be thought an appealing attribute."

"The trouble with those who have it," said Charlotte, "is that they are bad enemies to other people, even if not the worst."

"Will he be able to remain in this house, without your income?"

"He can live in a corner of it, with Cook and Bullivant."

"That will bring back his early days. And of course home is where Bullivant is. But still, the poor boy! A poor thing but mine own."

Bullivant returned to the kitchen and to conversation with the cook. The latter was engaged in supervising her underling, a work in which she and Bullivant were equally versed.

"Fire too large, Mrs. Selden," he said, taking a seat with a view of George in the distance, in order to maintain this usefulness. "And the master as heated as the fire, if you ask my opinion."

"As seems to increase in frequency," said Cook. "Was it you or George?"

"Myself, as I freely admitted, Mrs. Selden."

Mrs. Selden was really Miss Selden, but Bullivant followed the address of the cook observed in formal households, deprecating the modest fashion of basing it on her calling. George did the same, whether by reason of precept or example was not known. Cook showed indifference on the matter, and thereby showed her dignity as dependent on itself.

"More can be asked of no one than admitting it," she said. "It is at once the most and the least that can be done. Miriam, are you attending to your work or listening to me?"

Miriam, who was doing the latter, gave the start she was accustomed to give when addressed, and proved the bracing effect of the words by proceeding to do both.

"It emerged about George and the workhouse this morning," said Bullivant, lifting one knee over the other. "All of it out in the open! And where was the need? It had better have remained where I had consigned it, in oblivion."

"How did it transpire?" said Cook.

"There was talk about our places of birth, and we all made our contribution," said Bullivant, with a note of complacence. "The master and Mr. Mortimer and I had spent the major part of our lives under this roof. With George, as we know, it has been otherwise."

"And what was made of it?"

"Nothing much on the surface, Mrs. Selden. But I suspect there was consternation beneath. But, as I hinted to the master, wages such as ours can hardly preclude slurs of the venial kind."

"And how did George bear himself under the ordeal?"

"As well as could be asked of him," said Bullivant, craning his neck as the name recalled its possessor. "They were not circumstances calculated to bring out any latent advantage in him, if such there be. But he was equal to owning the truth."

"It is to his credit that he did not have recourse to invention."

"Well, Mrs. Selden, the boy would hardly have it in him."

"Miriam, are you working this morning or observing an occasion of leisure?" said Cook.

Miriam started and resumed her employment.

"I suppose all this about George is highly interesting to you," said Cook, with a note of belittlement that Miriam could not explain.

"The world is new to you, is it not, Miriam?" said Bullivant.

Miriam remained transfixed for a moment, her habit when addressed by Bullivant. She was a stolid-looking girl of sixteen, on whom the plumpness incident to this age had fallen in excessive measure. She had a round, red face, large, startled eyes, round, red arms, a mouth that, as it was generally open, may also be described as round and red, and a nose that must be described in this manner. Mortimer had met her on the stairs and asked if she enjoyed her life, and had not suspected that her reply that she did not know, was a true one. She had no standard by which to form her judgement. Cook showed her no unkindness, and Bullivant was almost kind, though he would hardly have noticed if she had appeared with another face, and had no idea how much she would have liked to do this. Cook acted towards her as her conscience dictated, and Bullivant felt that she was female and was not George.

Two housemaids, whose d· ·es lay upstairs, completed the household, and seemed . .ave little to do with the others, as they accepted no dealings with George and Miriam, and were permitted none with Bullivant and Cook.

"Are you a native of this district, Mrs. Selden?" said Bullivant, with courteous interest.

"Well, I was born in the county, though in a part that would make this section look very bare. It was on the more luxuriant side."

"And you, Miriam?" said Bullivant, after a moment of humming with some tunefulness.

Miriam did not reply.

"Did your family live about here?" said Cook, translating for her benefit.

"I don't know," said Miriam.

"Did they know?" said Bullivant, smiling.

"You must know where you were born," said Cook.

"No. I was six months old when they took me."

"When who took you?"

"The orphanage. They could tell I was about that."

"The orphanage beyond the town?" said Bullivant.

"Did you not know she had passed her life under those conditions?" said Cook. "Something of that nature seems to emerge?"

"Dear me, so we are all natives of the district," said Bullivant, who had an example to guide him in the circumstances.

"Surely they told you as much as where you were born," said Cook, who was without this advantage.

"No, I was found."

"On a doorstep?" said Bullivant.

"Yes," said Miriam.

"On a doorstep where?" said Cook.

"The orphanage," said Miriam, looking surprised by the idea that there might have been a choice of such resting-place.

"But your parents must have given you your name."

"No. It was the name of the baby who died, the one whose place I took."

"Dear, dear, a sad little tale," said Bullivant, on a musical note.

"Well, the name does as well as any other," said Cook. "What is your other name?"

"She can't have one clearly, Mrs. Selden," said Bullivant, in a lower voice.

"Yes, I have. It is Biggs, the baby's name," said Miriam.

"Miriam Biggs," said Bullivant, as if he hardly congratulated the baby. "Well, I expect you like your first name, do you not?"

"No."

"And why do you not like it?" said Bullivant, who had felt it was rather above its bearer. "What kind of name do you like?"

"A name like Rose," said Miriam, with a sort of glow in her voice.

"Well, perhaps you would like to be called a lily as well," said Cook.

Miriam's eyes showed that this was the case.

"What resemblance do you bear to either of these blossoms?" said Cook, causing a slight, sensitive recoil in Bullivant.

Miriam had not words to explain that she would appreciate a single point in common.

Cook, recalled to the matter of appearance, stepped to a glass to smooth her hair, and glanced at her tight, shiny forehead, the nose that rose towards it, her sallow complexion and clear, shrewd, grey eyes, with the encouraged air that tends to result from such a survey, as though people are relieved to find no feature as yet missing.

A look that can only be described as roguish, flitted over Bullivant's face. It occurred to him to ask Mrs. Selden what blossom *she* resembled, but he was deterred by propriety and a regard for their future relation, if not by the consideration that he resembled no blossom himself.

"You were well and happy at the orphanage, Miriam?" he said.

"I am always well," said Miriam, on a rather unexpected note.

"And do you not like that?"

"No, not much."

"And what is your reason for desiring poor health?" said Cook.

"I have never had an illness," said Miriam, on a wistful note.

"Well, let me tell you that it is not an object for aspiration," said Cook, in a tone of some personal affront. "I have been laid prostrate more often than most, and am in a position to testify."

"I should like to have a real illness. It seems as if it might pull me down and make me different."

"But your recovery would build you up again," said Bullivant, as if the question of stoutness or the opposite were a light one.

"I presume that you would not wish your indisposition to become a chronic state," said Cook. "I should never call my recovery, even from the most lenient of my onsets, complete. And it adds to what has to be contended with."

"And we are none of us the worse for a covering on our bones," said Bullivant.

"We can't all belong to the lean kine," said Cook, veiling by the phrase her pride in being of these.

"Do not aspire to be ill until you must, Miriam," said Bullivant.

"And some constitutions do not tend to illness," said Cook, almost in a tone of threat. "They are not susceptible."

Miriam could not dispute this.

"And I like to see a good, wholesome girl," said Bullivant, bringing no comfort to Miriam, who had been told before that she gave people this pleasure, and had found it increased their demands of her rather than their opinion.

"What an amount of charity origin there is in the house!" said Cook. "It is my first contact with it. My family looked down on no one, but we had our bounds."

"Our wages, Mrs. Selden, our wages," said Bullivant, in a low tone that seemed designed to elude the ears of Miriam, and did elude her attention.

"Well, they did not teach you much at the orphanage," said Cook, surveying the latter's handiwork.

"We learned from books until we were sixteen," said Miriam, in an explanatory tone.

"And were you a promising scholar?" said Bullivant.

"In which case the promise has hardly led further," said Cook.

"No, I didn't get on," said Miriam, in a tone of assent.

"Now you know the next thing to be done, after the times you have been told," said Cook.

Miriam knew, as the result of this method, and left the room to accomplish it.

"I always say that not the least thing I have done, is the number of girls I have trained," said Cook.

"I say the same, Mrs. Selden, both of you and of myself."

"Boys are not the same demand."

Bullivant shook his head and rose, under the necessity of acting on the opposite assumption. He did not pursue George with success, for the latter presently edged round the door, saw Cook by herself, and looked round to assure himself that his eyes had not deceived him. Then he betrayed the turmoil of his spirit by taking Bullivant's chair, while Cook looked on with an equivocal eye but without prejudice. She could always feel that George was male and was not Miriam.

"My secret is out, Mrs. Selden."

"Well, as long as you had no recourse to deception, you have no reason to bow the head."

"There was one that spoke to me like a father, and that was Mr. Mortimer."

"I always said a heart beat under that exterior."

"But I did not like the master's eye."

"The eye may be colder than the heart," said Cook.

"This will always stand in my way, Mrs. Selden. It will prevent my advance."

"It might tend to militate against it. But you are leaving it behind," said Cook, who supposed that George was satisfied with his progress.

"People are fortunate to be born into a respected place."

"I admit that my family would eat bread for respect," said Cook.

"I could feel to you as to a mother, Mrs. Selden," said George, on an impulse.

"Then behave to me as a son and hand me those forks," said Cook, regarding this as the right way to meet excess of feeling. "What with Mr. Mortimer your father, and me your mother, your orphan days are numbered, as far as I can see. And an ill-assorted pair Mr. Mortimer and I should be, as regards worldly station, if not in other points. It was an arbitrary combination."

There was a pleasure in Cook's tone, for which George could hardly claim the credit. He was spared the demand of the situation by the entrance of Bullivant, who fixed on him eyes of concentrated feeling.

"Are you the mistress or Miss Emilia, George, that you elect to spend your morning in an easy chair?"

George rose and sped to the fulfilment of his own character, and Bullivant succeeded to the chair, without specifying which of these ladies he personified.

George gained an adjoining scullery, where Miriam was employed at the sink.

"Now get along with your business and leave the place clear for something better. And don't let me have to tell you twice, because I don't speak a second time to such as you."

Miriam recognised an enjoinder to haste, and slightly accelerated her movements.

"And don't be all day getting hold of what I say," said George, continuing to prove he was right in regretting his origin, "because I have other things to do, and higher people to listen to me."

Miriam took this speech to repeat the first, and paid it no heed.

"Whom am I to understand that you are addressing, George?" said a voice from the door, where Bullivant stood with his head thrown backward, so that he seemed to look down on his hearers.

"Miriam," said George, with a note of triumph, supposing that Bullivant assumed him to be addressing some other person.

"And when have you heard the master or Mr. Mortimer address a woman in that manner?"

George cast his mind over his employers' deportment, and waited for more enlightening words.

"Miriam," said Bullivant, in a distinct tone, "will you have the goodness to be as expeditious as possible, in order that George may succeed you at the sink? There are matters requiring his attention, when those that claim your own, are disposed of. I am much obliged to you, Miriam."

There was a pause while Miriam recognised the same injunction in these words as she had in George's.

"May I never again, George, be called upon to witness such an exhibition of unmanliness. A woman of whatever standing is always a woman, as the dealings of the master and Mr. Mortimer would prove. There are things that stamp a man as unworthy of the name, and no one of us, of whatever origin, need emerge as that. I will leave you to mention your regret to Miriam."

Bullivant retraced his steps; Miriam resumed her work; George stood in silence broken by no contrite word.

"I have finished now," said Miriam, in her usual tones, disregarding an interlude that stood apart from life. "You can have my place."

George took it and found himself framing with his lips some words that he did not utter: "I am much obliged to you, Miriam."

Miriam stood doing nothing, her natural state when she was not urged to modify it, and George was seized by one of his sudden impulses.

"I shall always be rough, Miriam."

"Well, a good deal of the work to be done is rough," said Miriam, feeling that George had his place in the scheme of things.

"I should like to rise above it."

"There would be nobody to do it, if everyone rose," said Miriam, who was more articulate with her equals, and saw George as among these.

"But he who does high things, has people as much indebted to him, as he who does low ones. Wouldn't you like to rise?"

"No, not very much," said Miriam, who saw the height of her calling as exemplified in Cook.

"You might rise by marriage," said George, seeking some means of elevation that had no personal basis.

"I would rather not be married. I like to be by myself. Here I have a room to myself," said Miriam, in a tone of hardly crediting her situation. "It has a chest of drawers and a looking-glass on a table."

"And do you look at yourself in the glass?" said George, echoing a note of Bullivant's.

"I see myself. No one could help it."

"Well, wouldn't you like to rise?" said George, as though such a survey must lead to a mood of aspiration.

"Well, I should like to be different."

"And you would not want to be lower?"

"I hardly could be, to stay respectable."

"I am only as you are," said George, in another tone. "I want to rise, without knowing what I could rise to, indeed knowing it is nothing."

"You might be like Mr. Bullivant."

"Yes, that must be my object, but it was not my hope."

"You did not want to be like the master and Mr. Mortimer?" said Miriam, breathing the words rather than uttering them.

"No, there are things I am content to live beneath. But there are points between. Not that there is any disgrace in honest work," said George, ending on a sardonic note.

"No real disgrace," said Miriam, as if she had perceived a resemblance to it.

"And servants are as good as anybody else," said George in the same manner.

"Well, other people know about things more. And talk and behave better."

"And think better too," said George. "Compare the cast

of Mr. Mortimer's mind with Bullivant's. I know the real thing. I know when it goes right through. I have no use for the copy."

"We could never be anything but that," said Miriam. "I should like to be good of my own kind. It would be a real thing, even if it was not much."

"You are not so bad," said George, considering her aspect.

"I am worse than you are," said Miriam, in simple statement.

"Well, I should not think about it."

"It is what I do think about," said Miriam, recognising that everyone had some ground for thought.

Bullivant returned to the kitchen with a preoccupied, responsible air, that, though unwitnessed, was not wasted, as his mind's eye was on himself. He did not broach the matter to Cook, being unsure of her attitude to Miriam's claims to chivalry, and she glanced at him and said nothing, preferring not to solicit information, and not anticipating the need to do so.

Bullivant sat down and seemed to make an effort to throw off his preoccupation.

"I doubt if the young ones will attain to our standard, Mrs. Selden."

"Well, some must remain subordinate."

"But those are the ones that do not act accordingly. The boy is above his calling, if you will believe it."

"Shame in the wrong place is a characteristic of youth."

"It is not much that George should be above. And he is not without personal grounds for shame. He need not seek further ones."

"They are not of a kind to be cast up against him."

"I am the last person, Mrs. Selden, to take that line with matters that are misfortune rather than fault. But it was not those to which I referred."

Cook waited to hear the others.

"There is something, Mrs. Selden, between you and me,

between the master and the mistress, between any man and woman, that I would not countenance any breach of. Rather would I check it in the bud, and be the last to grudge the effort."

Cook glanced at Bullivant's recumbent form, and her rejoinder that he should have some effort to spare, was not less swift that it was silent.

"Where is the girl now?" she said, not incommoded by Miriam's name not having been mentioned.

"It was not Miriam herself, but womanhood in general, that I was regarding, Mrs. Selden."

"Well, Miriam has not much claim to be considered as a member of that community as yet," said Cook, mollified by the disclaimer of personal feeling. "We had better go and see how they are engaged. Your having spent your time well does not ensure their having done the same."

The sight of George and Miriam together seemed to lend support to Cook's words.

"What is your reason, Miriam, for regarding George as in need of your superintendence this morning?"

Miriam did not answer the question, indeed could not, as she was not sure of its meaning.

"And what is yours, George, for withholding Miriam from her correct employment?" said Bullivant.

"And what is yours, for prying into other people's business while you neglect your own?" said George, with his face to Miriam and the sink.

"We began to talk," said Miriam, as if this were dawning on her.

"And what was the subject of your discourse?" said Cook.

"We talked of what might be before us," said George, as if he had every right to do this.

"And are we to hear the contents of your castles in the air?"

"They will not be much, if you cannot keep your mind upon mundane matters," said Bullivant. "You will be sinking back to your original point, which was hardly a castle, as we know."

"You get to your work and keep your mind on it, Miriam," said Cook. "Picturing yourself a lily or a rose will not take you far. They are more for ornament than use, and with you the obligation is different."

Miriam went her way with an air of acquiescence.

As Cook returned to the kitchen, she broke into religious song, and maintained it with unself-conscious fervour and a full rendering of such word and phrase as generally command a modified delivery. Cook's faith was the foundation and the excitement of her life, and her life fell short under neither of these heads. Her reason for choosing her place had been that no stipulation was made for conventional worship. Charlotte did not seem to know that she had any control over her opinions, and though Emilia was not equally unaware, she did not exercise it.

Bullivant began to polish some plate, with automatic movements but swift and sure result. Now and then he lifted his voice in support of Cook's, in passages she had especially familiarised, taking care to subdue his tones to hers, but finding little scope for this exercise in gallantry.

CHAPTER II

"Fire piled right up the chimney! Who is responsible?" said Horace, opening the door on his children. "And on a day when many people would not have a fire at all."

"Some poor little children can't have one," said the youngest child, looking up in a tentative manner.

"And who has been spilling water?" said Horace, on a deeper note.

There was a pause.

"Answer me," said the father, striking the table.

"I have," said another boy, in an even tone.

"And why were you playing with water? You know that it is forbidden."

"I was pouring some into a saucer, to see if it would freeze."

"You know better than that. We are not at the North Pole."

"No one has ever been there. But we are only fifty miles from the east coast of England," said the boy, as if mentioning a point that was not so different. "Some water froze in this window last night."

"But then there was no fire."

Marcus glanced at the grate, as if he would hardly give this name to its contents at the moment.

"And what do you want with frozen water?"

"It takes up more room than ordinary water," said Marcus, not enlarging on his grounds for interest, but placing the saucer by the window. He was a short, strong boy of eleven, with a round, innocent face, a large, dark head, and wide-open greenish eyes, clad in a worn sailor suit, that also accommodated sundry personal possessions.

His shabbiness transcended even the convention of his day, but he appeared unconscious of it.

"Why do you not keep better order, Sarah?"

"They don't want me to tell them what to do, and they are not doing anything wrong."

"They do not appear to be doing anything. And people should never sit about doing nothing. I have told you that scores of times."

Sarah did not dispute the assertion. She was a childish-looking girl of thirteen, with a small, spare figure, straight, dark hair, her mother's indifferent profile, Emilia's large, curved mouth, and beautiful, clear, grey eyes. Her shabby, best dress, handed down for daily use, was scanty on her frame, and she wore her mended stockings and shoes as if they were on her mind. Her look at her father might have been one of aversion, if it had been possible; and it was possible.

"And why is not Nurse with you?"

"She went out of the room some time ago. I don't know where or why," said Sarah, forestalling the questions.

"Where or why, where or why," chanted a boy of twelve, jumping up and down to the refrain.

"Do not behave like a clown, Jasper; you are not a baby," said Horace, with an open mind on the characters suggested by his eldest son.

Jasper stood in a mood of simple goodwill, his short, soiled fingers seeking the possessions in his suit, that were less numerous than his brother's, owing to the garment's precarious hold. He and Marcus were growing old for such attire, but a change would have meant attention and expense, and had not been suggested. Jasper was unaffected by his almost pitiful aspect. His small, light eyes sought his father's in question of his mood, and there was no trouble on his simple, comely face.

"Why do you sit reading by yourself, Tamasin, instead of playing with the others?" said Horace.

"People have to read by themselves," said a girl of ten,

keeping her hands on her open book. "And people do nothing by themselves too. We are waiting for time to pass."

"What a way to talk about time, the most precious thing there is! Those are terrible words to use."

"There seems to be plenty, and it is not much good. We don't know what to do with it."

Tamasin turned her face to her father and kept it towards him. She knew that her mother's eyes were meeting his own, and almost knew that he found himself awaiting their judgement.

"What is your book?" he said, with the suspicion that accompanies this question.

"A tale I know by heart. The cold takes most of my attention."

"Cold, cold, cold. I must have an end of this talk about cold. I must teach you the meaning of the word. Why do you not have a romp together, instead of sitting about in this lackadaisical way? I do not like to see it."

The youngest child, a boy of seven, the first to be divided by more than a year from his predecessor, ran up to engage in the pursuit. He had Sarah's grey eyes and indefinite features set in Tamasin's oval face, and wore the dependent, appealing air that dies so hard in the last of a family. It was an air that Sarah had lost at half his age, that Jasper and Tamasin had never worn, and that Marcus still wore in intervals of sickness or distress, but did not wear as he moved to the window to see if the change he awaited, had taken place.

"Do not be foolish, Marcus," said his father. "Water cannot freeze in a few minutes."

"Sometimes it must freeze in less than a second. You can see where the drops have frozen while they were falling off a house."

"But that is out of doors."

Marcus glanced at the open window and again at the water, as though it might respond to conditions at any moment.

35

"Here is Cousin Mortimer," said Horace. "He will not find you an interesting family. When you have so much done for you, you might show a little life and gratitude sometimes. It is disheartening to have anything to do with you."

Sarah looked about for signs of these benefits, confronted the objects of her forbears' childhood, and turned to the hearth for signs of contemporary attention.

"If the fire is what we are grateful for, it was wise to try to improve it," said Tamasin, whose constraint before her father took the form of speaking for his ears.

"A fire is not a thing to be taken for granted," he said.

"It is always taken like that in the winter," said Marcus.

"Oh, a fire is not a matter of course to everyone," said Horace, as though correcting a wrongheaded conception of life.

"A sad word, my dear boy," said Mortimer, "and one that has a hard-hearted sound. Well, my dears, I do not know why I am here, except that the nursery is the pleasantest spot in the house; or is it the kitchen?"

"There would be some difference in the heat," said Tamasin.

"They all pretend to be cold," said Horace. "It becomes a monotonous pose."

"We don't pretend," said Marcus. "If we were not cold, we should not think about it."

"All up together! Heads up, hands at your sides, quick march!" said Horace, clapping his hands and using a martial tone that also held a domestic note. "That is the way to be warm; that is the way to get the sluggish blood to flow. There is no need to pile up the fire and brood over it. There are quicker and better ways than that."

The children obeyed as a matter of course, and Horace kept their limbs in motion until signs of fatigue rewarded him and relieved his feelings.

"Well, are you all warm now?"

"Yes, Father."

"Are you warm, Sarah?" said Horace, uncertain if his daughter's voice had swelled the chorus. "If you are not, you can go on with the exercises by yourself."

"They are not of that kind, my dear boy," said Mortimer, "as you seemed to know."

"I said I was warm, Father."

"Now who made up the fire?" said Horace, as if he had been postponing the question to an opportune moment. "Now let me have the truth."

"It was made up by common consent," said Mortimer. "Everyone has the benefit of it."

"I did," said Sarah, after a moment's pause. "The room was too cold for the children."

"And too cold for a certain young lady, eh, Sarah?"

"It was too cold for anyone," said Marcus.

"I was speaking to Sarah, Marcus."

"Yes, the room was too cold to sit in, Father."

"But why need you sit? Why did you not stand, walk, run? How often have I told you that exercise is the thing, when the blood is congealed or sluggish? You can surely get up and move about. Had anyone tied you to your chair?"

"No, Father," said Sarah, not mentioning that the rigour of cold had rendered human agency superfluous.

"People have to rest sometimes, and then the cold keeps them in one place," said Jasper, with some exercise of imagination, as this was not the case with himself.

"Was I speaking to you, Jasper?"

"No, but he spoke to you," said Marcus. "Anyone is allowed to speak."

"You can wait to speak to your father, until he speaks to you."

"But suppose there was something we had to say to you?"

"Then say it," said Horace, sending his voice to a higher note. "Say it, say it, say it. I am not preventing you. I await your pleasure. What is the important communication? I am all attention; I am all ears. Say it, say it."

Marcus did not obey.

37

"So it did not exist," said Horace.

"There was no suggestion that it did, my dear boy," said Mortimer.

"Did it exist, Marcus?" said Horace.

"No," muttered Marcus, his eyes filling with tears.

Horace felt that an argument ended in his favour, when his opponent wept, and as he always pursued one to this point, had no experience of defeat in words.

"Now, Sarah, get up and take that coal off the fire. Use the tongs and put it back in the scuttle. It is not alight."

"Perhaps it will start a fire in the scuttle," said Jasper.

"Perhaps it will," said Mortimer.

"We should all be warm then," said Tamasin.

Avery fell into laughter that passed beyond his control, but felt his father's glance and knew that mirth was dead.

Charlotte opened the door, surveyed the situation and advanced to deal with it. She stayed Sarah's hand, restored the fire, took a seat by it, and drew her daughter into her lap. Sarah leaned against her and fixed her eyes on the grate, while Avery took a breath and looked about him, as if at a different world.

"Have you never seen a fire before, Sarah?" said Horace.

"Not often one as worthy of regard as this," said his wife.

"It is not a cold day, and coals cost money."

"I find it cold, and chills cost other things as well."

Charlotte beckoned Marcus to her other side, and held him in her arm with his sister. These two of her children struck her as the most pathetic. This was the condition she was most alive to in them, and such things as their pleasure or success took a second place, and perhaps deserved it. They showed their feeling of safety in her presence, and Avery approached the fire and leaned over the guard.

"Peering into the fire! Is that allowed?" said Horace.

"Just for a few minutes. Until he is warm," said Charlotte.

"Peering into the fire! Is that allowed?" said Horace, repeating his tone as exactly as his words.

"Just for a few minutes. Until he is warm," said Charlotte, smiling as she followed his example.

"A game that two can play at," said Jasper.

"What do you mean?" said Horace.

"Both of you saying the same thing over again."

"I wish that were not necessary," said Horace, with a sigh. "It never should be. I should like Avery to answer me, Charlotte."

"I have answered you for him this time. I thought you were speaking to me."

"Did you think so, Avery?"

"Yes. Speaking to Mother," said Avery, in a light tone.

"We shall have to instigate a fine for making up the fire without leave," said Horace.

"Fire was the chief cause of human progress," said Mortimer. "But it seems to have ceased to be that."

"We will not have any more fines," said Charlotte, playing with Sarah's hair with her eyes upon it. "We see too many things in terms of money."

"Most things have to be bought and paid for," said Horace. "Coals certainly do."

"And they should indeed be an exception. Mere warmth ought to be free."

"Many people cannot afford a fire at all. It does not do to forget that."

"Why do you like to remember it?" said Mortimer. "So as to feel that, if you can bear the cold, they can?"

"It is better to forget it, if we are not going to do anything about it," said Charlotte. "Remembering it and doing nothing seems so bad."

Tamasin laughed, and Jasper came up to his mother.

"Shall we have our whole sixpence every week? Sarah as well?"

"Yes, you will; and why should one of you be an exception?"

"Sarah is too old to be exempt from the consequences of her actions," said Horace.

39

"Then she is old enough to be given the means of meeting them."

"That is a veiled threat," said Mortimer. "I am interested in it. In real life threats are so seldom veiled."

"It is not a crime to be twelve months older than the next child," said Charlotte, with a flash of her eyes, "and it shall not be visited as such. Indeed it is not often avoided."

Tamasin sat with her eyes on her mother and sister, accepting the preference of another to herself, but finding it hard to believe in it. Tamasin was the person she was always to be, as Marcus was still the child he had always been.

"Do we give the coals we save, to the people who don't have any?" said Avery.

"I don't know what we do with them, my dear child," said Mortimer. "I don't think we should call that saving them."

"They must be mounting up," said Tamasin.

"Charlotte, do you realise that the children will waste half a crown a week?" said Horace.

"I had only realised that they would spend it."

"And that that will come to six pounds, ten shillings in a year?"

"The money is sixpence a week, my dear boy," said Mortimer. "What has it to do with a year?"

"What can the children need, that requires such a sum?"

"They do not need much that it would pay for," said Charlotte.

"No rubbish is to be bought," said Horace. "I put my foot down there." He made the actual movement, and Avery unconsciously copied it, as he stood with his eyes upon him.

"Shut that book, Tamasin, and come and join the others. Do not sit apart, just putting in a word when you choose."

Tamasin came to the fire and stretched her hands towards it, as if fulfilling a desire.

"Why do you make things sound wrong, that are not wrong?" said Marcus.

"Get off your mother's knee, Sarah," said Horace, not looking at his son. "You are too heavy to sit there for so long."

Sarah's mouth took a set line, and she did not move.

"Do you hear me speak, Sarah?"

The latter gave no sign.

"Now we see the use of fines," said Horace looking round.

"Or we see the result of them," said Charlotte.

"The result of discontinuing them. We shall have to instigate the use of the rod. If we may not use one method, we must find another."

"Mother wouldn't let you use the rod," said Marcus.

"I am not subject to anyone's control."

"Well, she would not let us have it."

"That is a better way of putting it," said Charlotte. "You are under my control, are you not?"

"Yes, under Mother's," said Avery.

"Spare the rod and——" said Horace, looking round and using a tone that demanded an answer.

"Spoil the child," said Jasper, with a note of success.

Charlotte put Sarah off her knee, as though to discountenance rebellion, and the latter slid to the floor and leaned against her.

"Move away from your mother, Sarah. Do not put your weight upon her in another way."

Sarah seemed not to hear.

"Are you deaf, Sarah? Oh, you evidently are," said Horace, speaking with contempt for this infirmity. "What are you laughing at, Jasper?"

"If you call people deaf, you can't expect them to hear, and then you can't blame them for it."

"Oh! That is a simple thing to be amused at. Do not stand in the centre of the fire, Tamasin. You are keeping the heat from other people."

"If the fire is too large, that does not matter," said Marcus.

Horace gave him a look and nodded to himself, as though confirmed in his ideas.

"It is a nice fire now," said Avery, "but it need not be so big, if we all stay near it."

"Perhaps there will be a rule that no one is to move away from it," said Tamasin. "It might save more in the end."

"If you are not ashamed of what you have to say, Tamasin, say it so that we can hear."

"I said it might be cheaper to have a smaller fire, and keep near to it, Father."

Horace made no answer, as his heart had said the same thing.

"Coal would not cost very much," said Jasper. "Miners are not men who would earn a great deal."

"How much does it cost, Father?" said Tamasin.

Horace seemed not to hear.

"You have the most extraordinary ideas about money," he said. "I cannot think how you come by them."

"Children are born with lavish ones," said Mortimer. "Economy strikes them as petty and mean. And it seems to me to have that side. Perhaps I have the heart of a child; I certainly have the experience."

"They must learn it is meaner to be selfish. That sort of lavishness is self-indulgence, and that is the meanest thing of all. It has to be extirpated, rooted out, by whatever method is the soundest."

"It is a dreadful thing," said Avery, with his eyes on Horace's face.

"What is?" said Jasper.

"What Father said," said his brother.

"Nurse is coming with the tea," said Charlotte. "So the afternoon has drifted away."

"That is what it has done," said Horace. "I have seen no sign of employment."

Marcus glanced from his father to Mortimer, as if seeking such evidence in them.

"Yes, I am a warning, my dear child," said Mortimer, who took the general view that Horace led a life of usefulness. "But they say that a change of occupation is rest; so I may not rest as much as other people."

"Have you recovered your hearing, Sarah?" said Horace.

"Yes, Father," said Sarah, before she thought.

"And how did you come to lose it?"

"I don't know, Father."

"I do know," said Horace, advancing towards her and shaking his finger before her face. "I do know, Sarah. Through obstinacy, temper, sullenness, a dislike of not being thought perfect. I do know, and you will see that I do. Do you understand me?"

"Yes, Father," said Sarah, shrinking back.

Nurse took in the scene without appearing aware of it, her methods of observation being sharpened to vanishing point. She summoned the children to prepare themselves for a meal. Sarah was glad of an excuse to escape; Jasper unobtrusively remained, his dislike of ablution being insurmountable; Tamasin also lingered, with an instinct to remain under her parents' eyes.

"You are in a strange mood, Charlotte," said Horace.

"I am allowing myself to be in a natural one. My children must know me as I am, before I leave them."

"Civilised life consists in suppressing our instincts."

"Or does all life consist in fulfilling them?"

"The maternal instinct may be left to itself," said Mortimer.

"It has to be adapted to civilisation, like all instincts common to—all nature," said Horace, conquering an impulse to other words.

Avery ran into the room, wiping his hands down his suit. Marcus followed, similarly occupied. Sarah approached her mother's chair as a point of protection.

43

"My hands are clean," said Tamasin.

"They should be," said her father; "they have not been of much use."

Jasper glanced at his own hands, as if they suggested employment.

"I will make some buttered toast," he said.

"No, no, that means a waste of butter," said Horace, struck simply by this aspect of the matter.

"You must not be extravagant, Jasper," said Charlotte, taking this way of giving her sanction.

Horace rose and left the room, as if to remain would be useless. Mortimer felt a compulsion to follow. Nurse looked after them with a complete lack of expression. Charlotte remained in her seat.

Nurse was a spare, upright woman of forty-five, with small, quickly tearful eyes that seemed to reserve their comment on what they saw, a jutting jaw and chin, a long, nondescript nose, and an expression at once resolute and emotional. She was an estimable rather than an appealing character, self-righteous and righteous, critical and merciful, ready to judge others and also to judge herself and act on her judgement. The children hardly loved her, but they trusted and depended on her, and felt she was theirs for better or worse, if on the whole for the latter.

"Are you always going to be against Father now?" said Marcus to his mother.

"Only where I think he is making a mistake. He has been so careful with my money for so long, that he forgets that I like to spend some of it on my children. Mothers do like to do that."

"It is a good thing it is your money, isn't it?" said Avery.

"It usually belongs to the man," said Tamasin.

"What do you do with the money that is saved?" said Marcus.

"It would be invested in Mother's name," said Sarah.

"I expect Father keeps it for himself," said Jasper, with no real idea that Horace followed this course.

"Then are things going to be different?" said Marcus.

"Yes, just a little. I want you to have more change and freedom."

Jasper flung a piece of bread into the air, in accordance with this spirit.

"You won't die until you are much older, will you, Mother?" he said, wishing the new position to be securely based.

"No, I hope not. I do not think you could spare me."

"How old are you?" said Marcus.

"I am just fifty-one."

"Don't ask questions, Master Marcus," said Nurse, disconcerted by the question's being answered rather than asked.

"That is very old, isn't it?" said Avery.

"No, of course it is not," said Sarah, sharply.

"Fifty is like a grandmother's age," said Jasper.

"It is not; a grandmother is often eighty-five," said Tamasin.

"My poor little girls!" said Charlotte.

"Why are they poorer than the boys?" said Marcus.

"I don't think they are," said Avery. "I think boys are poorer. No, I think they are both the same."

"Your tea-table looks so nice, that I should quite like to sit down at it with you," said Charlotte, in a tone of suggesting an impossible situation, and causing no surprise by going to the door as she spoke.

"You have used a pound of butter," said Nurse; "I do not know what the master would say."

"You should by now," said Tamasin.

"Shall I tell you?" said Marcus.

"I should like some stale cake," said Jasper, saying the two words in one, as staleness was the condition of their having it.

"Who would dare to go down and ask Father for some?" said Tamasin.

"We could ask Mother," said Avery.

"No, no, the mistress has been kind enough to you to-day," said Nurse, who knew at what cost to herself Charlotte showed the kindness.

"I don't mind going down," said Jasper. "What he says can't do any harm."

"Hard words break no bones," said Tamasin.

"They may do other things," said Sarah.

"But not to Jasper, do they? Father does sometimes give us things, when he has been especially cross," said Avery, in an excited, clamorous manner. "Doesn't he, Sarah?"

Jasper descended to the dining-room, where Horace and his cousin were alone. The drawing-room was used by the women, and a third fire in the library was not considered. Jasper walked up to his father and spoke without following his words.

"Is there any stale cake, Father?"

"Cake?" said Horace, looking up over his glasses. "Why, do you want some?"

"Yes, please, if we may have some, Father."

Horace went to the sideboard and produced a slab of cake in the state described.

"You must not have anything else to-day," he said, as he gave it to his son, his manner suggesting that his discipline was a matter of duty and did not extend into his leisure hours.

"Oh, no, Father; thank you," said Jasper, turning away without pretence of further object, and causing Horace to smile at Mortimer over his singleness of purpose.

"Shut the door after you," he called in a tone of rough indulgence.

Jasper was greeted by a grateful chorus and took his seat with the smile of a willing benefactor. As Nurse apportioned the cake, she looked at it rather narrowly.

"Come here, Master Jasper."

Jasper readily approached.

"I cut mine off as I came upstairs," he said as she sought

in his pockets with an inscrutable expression. "The rest is for the others."

Nurse laid a piece of cake on the table in a silence that said more than words.

"How did you guess, Nurse?" said Tamasin.

"One side of the cake is newly cut, and it is only used for guests."

"Jasper meant to have two pieces," said Avery, in the tone of one impressed by the enterprise.

"Well, he had the risk of going to get it," said Sarah.

Horace entered the room, and Jasper's face showed its first anxiety. His father had been known to listen at a door before opening it. But the latter's expression reassured him.

"Well, am I in time to see the lions fed? Or rather in time for their last titbit? Is it a good one, children?"

"Yes, thank you, Father."

"They like a little treat sometimes," said Horace, smiling at Nurse. "But we could not have buttered toast and cake every day."

"We don't have them even every week," said Marcus.

"Oh, so that is the result of a little bit of spoiling. I must see it is not repeated. It is easy to see when indulgence suits people."

There was a silence.

"Did Nurse have some cake?" said Horace, feeling an impulse to approach a point of danger.

"I did not want any, sir. I had some bread and butter and a cup of tea. That is my meal," said Nurse, adjusting Avery's collar, as if she did not give her attention even to these. "And there was only enough for the children."

"There was plenty for you all. I had no thought of anything else. I am quite ashamed of all of them, especially of Sarah."

"Why is it more to do with Sarah?" said Marcus.

"Surely you can see as much as that?"

"I can't see why Sarah should think of it any more than anyone else."

"I shall have to send you to Coventry, young man," said Horace, giving him a cursory glance. "If you were older and your words meant more, I would do so. Where are you going, Sarah?"

"To Mother in the drawing-room. She said I could go when I liked."

"She is a difficult child, Nurse," said Horace with a sigh.

"She gives me no trouble, sir, and she is very good with Master Avery."

"He does not look to you then?" said Horace, raising his brows.

"I have many things to do for them, sir, and cannot always be with them."

"I like Sarah," said Avery.

"Well, don't you like all your brothers and sisters?" said Horace.

"No," said Avery, looking at him. "I only like Sarah, and rather like Tamasin. I don't like Jasper and Marcus; I only don't mind them. And of course I like Nurse and Mother and Aunt Emilia."

"It all comes to much the same thing, I should think," said Horace, checking the elimination in time.

"No, it is different things," said Avery, after a moment's thought.

"Why don't you want people to like Sarah?" said Marcus.

"Naturally I want them to. That is why I try to teach her to be likeable."

"I like her the most of us all," said Tamasin.

"So do I," said Jasper.

"She is the oldest and the best," said Avery.

Sarah, returning at her mother's word, heard the speeches with tears coming to her eyes, and turned and disappeared.

"Why does Sarah cry?" said Avery.

"She was touched by what she heard," said Nurse, blinking her own eyelids.

"What is touched?"

"Her heart was touched," said Nurse.

"There is no need to elaborate the matter," said Horace, sharply. "There is no occasion to pity anyone, because she hears a pleasant word of herself."

"She doesn't always," said Avery.

"It is when people don't, that they are made to cry when they do," said Marcus.

Horace left the room, and Sarah at once returned, as if she had been waiting for the moment. She went to the fire and sat down with her eyes upon it. Avery came and sat close to her, as if there were comfort in his presence.

Horace, overtaken by the compunction that dogged his path, glanced back through the door in apparent recollection.

"I had a piece of news for you, but it went out of my mind."

"I know. We are to have a tutor," said Jasper.

"How did you know?" said Horace, his mood already different.

"Oh, I heard somebody say something about it."

"You did not repeat what you heard?" said Horace, his tone revealing his sense of the unlikelihood of such reticence.

"No, Father," said Jasper.

The others looked at their brother in question of his opportunities, and Avery kept his eyes on him, as his hand moved amongst his toys.

"So none of you knew?" said Horace.

"No, Father," said Sarah.

"I didn't know," said Avery, in a perfunctory, dutiful tone.

"Did not you take any interest in the matter, Jasper?" said Horace, betraying that the course he approved, hardly appealed to him.

"I wasn't quite sure what I heard, Father, and I did not think it could be true, and girls don't have tutors."

49

"Well, it is true," said Horace, in a tone of making a staggering statement, and looking round on his children. "Jasper may have heard something, and girls do sometimes have tutors, and both the boys and the girls here are to have one very soon."

"Are we going to have him always?" said Marcus.

"Is he coming every day?" said Tamasin.

"Will the lessons be more difficult?" said Sarah.

"Natural questions," said Horace, almost with approbation. "And the answer to all of them is 'yes'."

"I shan't have him?" said Avery, in a tone that asked for support rather than information.

"No. Aunt Emilia will still teach you."

"Why doesn't she do for all of us?" said Jasper.

"She does 'do'," said Horace, with a disapproving note. "But she feels you are passing beyond her, or that it is time you were."

"We are not beyond her," said Marcus.

"I do not suppose you are, but it is usual for boys to have a man to teach them."

"It would begin to look too different from other people," said Jasper.

"That is a small matter. But the change seemed to be best on various grounds."

"Will it cost a great deal?" said Sarah, thinking of more pressing needs.

"Well, we do not talk about the cost of people who are clever enough to teach you."

"Aunt Emilia did not cost anything," said Marcus.

"Did you hear what I said?" said his father.

"Doesn't the tutor do it for a living?" said Jasper.

"You would think he would want to do other things with his cleverness," said Tamasin.

"A lady would be nice to teach them," said Avery.

"Of course these things are not done for you, except at trouble and expense," said Horace.

"It would be Mother's expense, wouldn't it?" said Avery.

"When two people make a partnership, things are in common between them."

"So you can say about them too."

"Well, I will leave you to digest the news with your cake and toast," said Horace.

Avery turned to his own concerns, as one who had no part in the change.

"I wonder where we shall have the lessons," said Sarah, looking round the room.

"Here, to save an extra fire," said Tamasin.

"It is a better room than you think," said Nurse. "The old furniture is coming into fashion."

"And the new does not exist," said Tamasin, "and so need not trouble us."

"Aunt Emilia teaches us in it," said Marcus.

"Aunt Emilia teaches us in it," said Avery, running up to Sarah and speaking these words of comfort, before returning to his own affairs.

"Is there a candle?" said Marcus. "I need one for my private purposes."

"You may fetch one from your room," said Nurse, "if you are not going to waste it."

"It will melt," said Avery, as his brother set the candle near the fire, and Nurse watched him without confidence.

Marcus took the candle and moulded the wax, and a recognisable image of a man took shape in his hands.

"Now where are the pins?" he said, with a twitch of his lips. "They will not be wasted. It is an honourable purpose for them."

Jasper drew near at the sight of a practical measure.

"Why are you doing it?" said Avery.

"If you put pins into an effigy of someone, the person feels pain."

"But you don't know who this is," said Tamasin.

"It is Father," said Marcus, in an incidental manner.

"No, no, that is not a nice joke," said Nurse. "You make me quite ashamed."

"What is effigy?" said Avery to Sarah.

"An image of someone, like a statue."

"Father doesn't feel it," said Avery, with his eyes on the figure.

"It is really a little like Father," said Sarah, with her slow smile.

"Press down the wax, and it will be more like him," said Tamasin.

"Now it *is* Father," said Avery, in a grave tone.

"Put pins round the head," said Jasper, bending down with his hands on his knees.

"Not *quite* so many pins," said Avery.

A housemaid opened the door.

"Nurse, could you give the master your lotion? He has a return of rheumatism with the change in the wind."

Nurse rose without a movement of her face.

"What is rheumatism?" said Avery.

"Pains in your arms and legs," said Marcus, with his eyes down.

"No, no. Poor Father! Take them out. Take them out," said Avery.

"Take them out, or he will begin to scream," said Sarah.

Marcus drew out the pins, flung the image on the fire and watched it blaze.

"Is it Father now?" said Avery to his sister.

"No, of course not. It is a lump of melting wax."

"The candle is not wasted," said Marcus. "It has had a noble history and a martyr's end."

Nurse returned to the room, and Avery ran up to her.

"It is not Father any more."

"He is burned alive," said Jasper.

"No," said Avery, shaking his head wisely. "It is not Father now. It was him for such a little while. It is only the candle that had the martyr's end."

Horace descended to join his family at dinner. They sat at one end of the family board, and occupied four chairs out of the two dozen that surrounded it. There were occasions when all came into use, but as these involved the building of the fire, the unearthing of stores of china and plate, and the revival and even the rehearsal of formalities fallen into disuse, they tended to be rare. Horace believed that the austerities of his home were unknown, and that periodical hospitality disposed of doubt, an opinion that showed how far the wish can be father to the thought. The children knew the view taken of their lot, though they could not have said how they knew it. Charlotte saw the matter as one where ignorance was bliss, and left it as one of the few grounds for this feeling in their lives, and they followed the same course with her own real unawareness.

"Six cutlets would have been enough," said Horace. "They know we do not eat seven. One cold cutlet does not serve any purpose. It means that one of the servants will eat it for supper."

"And is that quite a useless end for it?" said Mortimer.

"Of course it is, when other things are provided. It will be eaten as an extra, and that is pure waste."

"Not quite pure, is it?" said Emilia, smiling.

"I suppose Cook thought Emilia or I might take a second cutlet," said Charlotte. "It was not such an unnatural line of thought."

"I wish they would not think," said Horace, who tended to take both this view and the opposite. "Their thinking can be done for them."

"And other things cannot," said Emilia. "That is the strength of their position."

"I will have the cutlet," said Charlotte, "and prevent the end that is feared for it."

"But it will establish the custom of having one too many," said Horace.

"It is not so easy to mould the future. One cutlet will hardly do so much. They will only think we don't usually have quite enough to eat, and I dare say they already think that."

"They cannot," said Horace, sharply. "We are not large

eaters, and why should we supply the table simply for show?"

George entered to remove the plates, and cast his eyes over the empty dish.

"George had counted on that cutlet," said Horace, with grim comprehension.

"Do not expose the tragedies underlying daily life," said Charlotte. "We do not want George to come back and find me in tears. Though of course he would not know I was weeping for him."

"You are childish at times, Charlotte. You know that George is well fed."

"I know nothing about it. I somehow feel he is not. I cannot ask him if he has the same feeling."

"The housekeeping is not your province."

"No, it is a dark undercurrent that I do not dare to sound. That may be why I like to refer to it. Speaking of things robs them of half their terrors."

George returned with a pudding and carried it round, keeping his head bent over it in an almost protective manner, as though he would have liked to save it from its fate, as indeed he would. It was an occasion of ease and opportunity, as it was Bullivant's evening out. Horace's eyes were also watchful, though he disguised it better. When the pudding had been removed, he rose and went swiftly to the door that led to the kitchens. Before a table in the passage stood George, engaged in severing a portion of pudding with a knife, with an aspect that resembled Jasper's at a similar juncture, but with every emotion intensified.

"Is that what you are supposed to be doing, George?" said a voice that George took at first to be of divine origin, but recognised in a moment as of a more alarming source.

"No. No, sir."

"Then why are you doing it?"

"Because I am so plainly fed, that the dining-room pudding was irresistible," said George, but only in his heart.

"Do you want for anything?"

"No, sir," said George, taking the words to refer to the necessities of life.

"How old are you, George?"

"Eighteen, rising nineteen, sir."

"If you do things like this, we shall never be able to treat you as a grown man," said Horace, indicating the propriety of his present course.

"No, sir," said George, glad of any cover at the moment.

"Were you not ashamed of yielding to that sort of temptation?"

"Yes, sir," said George, agreeing that a greater sin would involve less of this feeling.

"Then why did you not withstand it? Surely it was not too strong for you?"

"No, sir," said George, almost feeling that this could not have been the case.

"Well, I can waste no more time for the present," said Horace, returning to the dining-room, but not neglecting to lead George's thoughts to the future, as he went.

"What do you think George was doing in the passage?"

"Something we shall soon know," said Emilia.

"Helping himself to the pudding from the table. There was a sight to meet my eyes."

"The sight of a great human need," said Mortimer. "What a dignified experience!"

"I wonder what made me get up and follow him," said Horace, with a note of excited interest.

"Something of guilty purpose in his aspect," said Mortimer.

"You did not notice it."

"No, I live on the surface, not in the depths."

"I thought he had his eyes on the pudding in a dubious way."

"So you kept your eyes on him in that way too, my dear boy."

"What led me to watch him in the first place?"

"George may feel it was some guidance from above. Do you take his view?"

"Probably some instinct from below," said Charlotte, "some impression of how you would feel in his place."

"I told him we could not treat him as a man, as long as he behaved like a child," said Horace, his tone seeming to draw attention to the moderation of his course.

"Perhaps the wages of a man would dispose of the need for such conduct."

"Do not be foolish, Charlotte. The pudding was not his."

"And the wages by rights are? What has happened to the pudding?"

"He has taken it to the kitchen. I hope his fingers were not all over it," said Horace, who shrank from the touch of those whom he engaged to prepare and serve the family food. "Some people might prosecute."

"No, not for a slice of pudding," said Emilia.

"They would hardly like it to be known that he needed it," said Charlotte.

"He did not need it; he merely wanted it," said her husband.

"Well, that has its own pathos. And courts are so easily moved to emotion. It leads to putting so much in brackets."

"Has none of you any sympathy except with children and servants?"

"They are helpless creatures," said Emilia. "Other people need it less."

"They will not thank you," said Horace.

"Servants could hardly feel gratitude," said Charlotte. "A feeling must have something to provoke it."

"They have a good home and good food and every comfort."

"They earn it; and it seems that pudding ought to come somewhere under those heads."

"What have you been doing to-day, Charlotte?" said

Horace, as though the other subject were exhausted.

"How seldom you ask me that! And this is the day when I do not want to tell you."

"Are you ashamed of it?"

"I think I am a little."

"I do not want to force your confidence."

"Surely you must, now that I have said I am ashamed. I have been making a change in my will, and people are naturally ashamed of that. It must mean they are taking something from somebody."

"Charlotte," said Horace, "it is nothing that I should be ashamed of for you?"

"I should think we are always ashamed of things for people, when they are ashamed of them for themselves."

"I have no wish to hear anyone's secrets."

"I can hardly believe that. I have a wish to hear everyone's. I thought people always had. When children want to bribe someone, they say they will tell him a secret. But those entrusted to a lawyer would not be the best."

"Or those entrusted to anyone," said Emilia.

"Does Emilia know?" said Horace.

"Yes, but no one else."

"Then it is not a secret," said Horace, in a tone that almost suggested that he would be justified in pursuing it.

"Nothing can be a secret from everyone. No, that is a mistake; of course it can."

"I think we all hope so," said Emilia.

"I think my wife is trying to tell me," said Horace, in a gentle tone.

"And I am not able to," said Charlotte. "Something is too strong for me."

"I have no idle curiosity."

"No, it is the other kind, the kind I have myself. I have never met an instance of the first kind. And I suddenly find I can tell you. I have divided my money between you and the children and Mortimer, instead of leaving it all to you. Of course I keep the proportions to myself, to observe the natural degree of secrecy. And it is a good deal in this case."

Horace was about to say that his own will was open to any eye, but recollected that it was on an unsuspected scale. He said nothing except to himself, and to this ear he said that economy was now doubly urgent. He always imagined himself as outliving his wife, though as the elder and a man, he was the less likely survivor. If he did not do so, he was saving to no purpose, and he might almost as well have lived to none. He was about to speak, when a voice came across the silence.

"So that is your game, my young master! That is how I get my blame and yours."

The sound was startling, new, familiar, and the listeners rose and followed it, and came on its source in the passage that was emerging as an ominous place.

"What is all this?" said Emilia.

"What is this, George?" said Charlotte.

"What is this, Avery?" said Horace.

"I too must ask what it is," said Mortimer.

"George, take your hand off Avery's shoulder," said Charlotte.

"I didn't do it; I didn't do anything," said her son. "No one took anything at all."

Charlotte looked at an open cupboard and an open comfit-box within it, and could not elude the truth.

"It is those boys that get people into trouble," said George. "I mean it is the young gentlemen, ma'am, who do things and are quiet about them. People think no one but me can lay a finger on anything."

"It wasn't ever me before; it is Jasper who takes things," said Avery, too lost in emotion for his principles to function. "I only opened the box and looked inside."

"What does it all mean?" said Horace.

"It is clear enough," said Mortimer, "and it is not much, my dear boy."

"Fetch Nurse and Master Jasper, George," said Horace.

"No, Jasper didn't do anything," said Avery, in a tone of despair. "I have not told anything: don't tell them that I did."

George departed with an air of some exultation. He did not find Avery unsuited to the character of adversary. He saw anyone likely to do him harm, in this light, and took his stand against him. Horace and his aunt kept their eyes on Avery, trying in their different ways to read his heart, and he stood with his face against his mother, a strange little figure in a dressing-gown handed down from Tamasin, and unsuited at once to his size and his sex.

Jasper joined the group in a garment worn only by himself, that in spite of this, or because of it, hardly retained its form. Nurse followed with a troubled and wary expression, as though she could say much, but would say nothing, Marcus came last, his figure the counterpart of Avery's, in a gown descended from Sarah.

Jasper was simply concerned with getting out of the dilemma. He had no rancour against Avery, no feeling against his elders. He took things as they came, and as they continued to come, maintained the course.

"Why are you here, Marcus?" said Horace, with a note of accusation.

"I have not done anything," said Marcus, answering the tone. "I came to say that there is no need for Jasper to come. He has nothing to do with this."

"You wish Avery to face the brunt of it alone?"

"It is nothing to do with anyone but him," said Marcus, with a note of patience under provocation. "You need not make the brunt any worse than you like. You know how small he is."

"You may all go upstairs," said Horace, after a pause. "I do not wish to see any more of you to-day. You may go, too, George. We do not suspect you of doing more than you did, but we find it quite enough. Your readiness to accuse a helpless child must show it to you in its proper light. I hardly thought you were as young in your mind as that."

George, clear that he would be young in the matter of his wages for an indefinite period, disappeared in the direction of the kitchen, intending to make no mention of the episode. He expected too much of Fate. In his path stood Bullivant, debarred from entering the dining-room by the clothes proper to his private life, that seemed to make a mysterious exposure of his personality, and to render it doubtful if his employers had ever seen the man he was.

He stood in George's path, with his eyes on George's face, his head shaking slowly to and fro, and full knowledge in his eyes. How he came by it George was never to know, though he had no sense of expecting him to be without it. George stood, poised for flight, his hands even spread for the purpose, but as he dared neither to return to the dining-room nor push by Bullivant, would have had to resort to the method in the literal sense.

"Just now—some trouble—Master Avery—the cupboard," he said.

Bullivant redoubled the shaking of his head, to include his deprecation of bringing in Avery's name, and turned, continuing the movement of a final headshake, and went towards the kitchen, motioning George to precede him. George knew that the women awaited them there, and that he faced the impossible. He prayed that he might swoon, indeed expected to do so under his stress of feeling, but found that his feet carried him onward. Cook and Miriam were standing at the table, and George felt for the first time a pang of envy of Miriam. Cook turned her eyes towards him, and Miriam did not, whether through apathy or delicacy George was not to know, or indeed again to consider.

Bullivant still stood and shook his head, while Cook waited in anticipation, and George began to move about uncertainly, with an instinct not to appear unoccupied.

"Well, is all the communication to be conducted by means of dumb show?" said Cook.

Bullivant explained his course.

"Words will not mend it, Mrs. Selden," he said.

"But there is no occasion for us to be condemned to silence, because of matters that do not relate to us."

"Have we heart for anything else, Mrs. Selden?"

"Well, I hope we are not all to lose heart and hope, because of an ill-judged action on the part of one, and that not the foremost."

"Not that, indeed, Mrs. Selden. Indeed that may be our trouble. It is these infantine tastes and temptations that cross our path! The pudding, if you will believe me, that was just taken from the dining-room! And George a tall young man of nineteen."

"I can believe it, as there is the proof on the table. And a piece cut with a knife! When a spoon was handed with it, as George must have been aware."

"George cannot even conform to habits," said Bullivant. "The pettiness of it all!"

"It would be worse, if it were not petty," said George. "I did not even eat the pudding. Petty it was indeed."

"Would you like to make good the omission?" said Cook, pointing to the dish on the table. "Then we can judge by your enjoyment if you attain the reward of your deeds."

"No, Mrs. Selden," said Bullivant, taking a step forward with a gesture. "That is not our level. And are we in any way responsible for this backward step? Is it to be referred to us?"

"No. George has been under influence that cannot be questioned, and that he knows as such. Nothing is gained by imputing matters erroneously."

"George, have you faced your position?" said Bullivant.

"Yes," said George, who had faced Horace and Cook, and felt the last effort to be a light one.

"And with resolve that you will make it a last occasion?" said Cook.

"Perhaps, Mrs. Selden," said Bullivant, waving his hand for a free scope for himself.

Cook became silent, her aspect suggested permanently so.

"Have you replied to Mrs. Selden's question, George?" said Bullivant, with a courtesy that was not directed towards the latter.

"No."

"But you do so in the affirmative?"

"Yes."

"Then perhaps, George, we may consign this matter to oblivion. Words on it being of a nature to degrade rather than to elevate. Mrs. Selden, I will ask you to respect my decision, and Miriam to follow your example."

"The girl is not given to gossip or to raking up of matters," said Cook. "That was quite a superfluous injunction."

"I am sure of it; I am glad of it; I depend on it, Miriam," said Bullivant, retiring behind his paper with a smile. "The master will not let fall another word on the matter. And like master, like man."

Horace returned with his cousin to the dining-room, and sat cracking nuts without mention of the recent scene, in tacit rehearsal of the one to come. The repression held through the sound of Avery's unrestrained weeping, and of steps descending the staircase and pausing at the cupboard, with a purpose that was hardly in doubt. The stilling of Avery's lament did not threaten it, and when Charlotte came to the table it was established.

"Walnuts from the tree on the west lawn," he said, as he offered them.

"How the children would like them!" said Charlotte, realising too late the untimeliness of her speech.

"Then I suppose they will take them," said Horace, with a sense of wasted effort, as his resolve failed.

"I do not know why you should think that."

"Do not know why?" said Horace, raising his brows.

"They live amongst so many forbidden things, and hardly ever touch them."

"Are hardly ever discovered to have done so. I gathered that George could open his mouth, if he chose. It seemed better not to encourage him," said Horace, suggesting a fatherly attitude that was hardly recognised.

"After all, there is nothing in their own home, that is not theirs."

"I suppose that is their view," said Horace.

"I did not know there was such a view," said Mortimer, "and I am sure they did not."

"One will be afraid to give them anything," said Horace, again throwing light on his own tendencies. "Is Emilia not coming down?"

"Not yet. She is reading Avery to sleep," said Charlotte.

"By way of a reward?"

"No, of necessity. He is upset."

"Well, I hope he is," said the father.

"Then your hope is fulfilled," said Emilia, as she came to the table. "He cannot listen to a book. They are playing with him, and Sarah will read to him later."

"Is he to keep them all up to attend on his pleasure?"

"On his needs. He has been frightened."

"Not by anyone here," said Horace. "We hardly spoke to him. Of course I do not know what has happened upstairs."

"Yes, I think you do," said his aunt.

"He was startled by George's pouncing on him and seizing his collar," said Charlotte.

"Should George have congratulated him?" said her husband.

"He knew he was a child of seven, only doing what he had done himself."

George, entering to clear the table, caught the last words and received the impression that the subject had not varied since his departure, and did not find the circumstances unnatural.

Horace frowned his wife to silence, with the usual result.

"George, the next time you find the children doing wrong, do not deal with the matter yourself. I am the person to judge of it."

"No, ma'am. Yes, ma'am," said George, putting plates rapidly together.

"Boys are only boys, as you know. You had just proved yourself no more than one."

"Yes, ma'am," said George, with a furtive glance at Horace.

"You will never grow up, will you, George?" said the latter, on an almost indulgent note, but taking an even darker view of his development than George had expected. "Well, I had better go and speak to Avery."

"No, no," said Charlotte, "he has borne enough."

"My dear Charlotte, he is a culprit, not a martyr. We shall do no good by confusing the issue for him. I must see that his mind is clear. I am his father, just as you are his mother."

"No, that is too large a claim," said Emilia.

Horace went into the hall without reply. Charlotte caught up with him, and they mounted the stairs abreast, neither giving place to the other. Sarah was seated on Avery's bed, reading from the Book of Job, not from any sense of fitness, but because it was her brother's choice. He lay with a convalescent air, his face responding as the words confirmed his memory. Tamasin blew soap bubbles, that he broke with a languid hand, and his brothers performed a series of antics, looking to see if he were attentive and entertained.

"It is too late for all these games," said Horace. "Is Avery keeping you up? Or are you just taking advantage of what has happened?"

"He has been upset," said Charlotte. "He needed something to make him forget it."

"I hope he will never do that."

"He wouldn't be able to," said Marcus. "Mother meant for to-night. She was afraid he would dream about it."

"I hope he will dream of it, think of it, dwell on it in every possible way."

Avery shrank back on his pillows, with his eyes on his father.

"You are not afraid of me, are you?" said Horace, putting a question that is seldom put, unless this is the case, and with the usual expectation of a negative reply.

"You know you are making him afraid," said Marcus.

Horace did not turn his eyes to Marcus, but kept them on Avery, as he went slowly to the door.

"Is Father gone now?" said Avery. "I don't want him to come here. He is always in all the places. I don't want him to come where I sleep. I don't like to think he might look at me in the night."

"He will not come here again," said Charlotte.

"Mother will forbid Father to come here," said Avery, looking round and using a note of discipline.

"We must not forget what began the trouble," said his mother.

"I said I would never do it any more."

"People always say that," said Jasper.

"Well, they can hardly say anything else," said Tamasin.

Avery broke into laughter and maintained it on a loud and artificial note.

"Hush. Father will hear you," said Sarah.

"But he is not coming here," said Avery, breaking off as consciously as he had begun.

"I wish we could always be as late as this," said Jasper.

"Mother says you always can," said Avery, in a voice that died away.

"He never wakes when once he is asleep," said Marcus. "Unless he has dreams later."

"He will have enough to dream about to-night," said Sarah, foretelling the truth.

CHAPTER III

"Good-morning," said Gideon Doubleday.

"Good-morning," said his four pupils.

"Has something happened to upset you?"

"Mother has just gone away," said Marcus. "That is why you were to come to-day. To take off our thoughts."

"The method has not been immediately successful."

Tamasin gave a faint laugh, and Jasper echoed it.

"Well, I need not feel that you will never smile again."

Sarah just gave a sign that this was not the case.

"Would a little reading distract you?" said Gideon, regarding them with his pale, prominent, spectacled eyes. "Here are some books for French translation, one for each of us."

"Five books all the same!" said Marcus, showing that the object was already achieved. "We always have only one."

"Does not that waste your time?"

"Time does not matter. Oh well, perhaps it does now."

Sarah frowned at her brother, and the action drew Gideon's eyes and brought them to his pupils' clothes. He suppressed an impulse to avert them, and continued to survey the pupils, as if he saw only themselves.

"So your great-aunt has taught you so far," he said as he distributed the books with his large, pale hands.

"Yes, but we call her aunt," said Marcus. "She is really aunt to Father. She will still teach Avery. She always used one book for us all."

"And so will still need the same number of books," said Sarah.

"I shall not shine as her successor."

"Five does seem a good many," said Jasper, "but of course one is yours."

"Yes, of course," said Gideon, who had meant them all to be Horace's until the end of the term, and then one to be his.

"Did you order ours and yours together?" said Marcus.

"Yes," said Gideon, realising that this was what he had done. "If I ask people to get books, they say there are enough in the house. They are not concerned about the kind."

Sarah gave a comprehending laugh.

"Did you want a new one for yourself?" said Tamasin. "Hadn't you read this book with anyone before?"

"Yes, but my copy was shabby and needed to be replaced."

"A shabby book does just as well," said Marcus, with a note of reproof. "Things should be put to their proper purpose until the end."

"What about Jasper's prayer-book, that fell in pieces and had to be replaced?" said Sarah, showing that replacement did play a part in the family.

"I wonder you did not choose a book that you had," said Tamasin.

"That would be a good plan," said Gideon, feeling that in future he might follow it.

"You are rather old for a tutor," said Marcus; "I thought they were generally young."

"Some young men begin by being tutors, and pass on to something else."

"Then are you a failure?" said Tamasin.

"I think I should be called one. I paid too much attention to my studies when I was young, and that does lead to people's being tutors."

"How old are you?" said Marcus.

"I am forty-one."

"Oh, quite a young man," said Tamasin.

"Does your wife think you are a failure?" said Marcus.

"I am not married. I live with my mother and sister. If they think so, they do not betray it. Women are so loyal."

"What do you do with the money you earn?" said

Jasper. "If you have no wife, you can't have children, and you don't seem as if you spent very much on yourself."

"Part of it I subscribe to the family expenses, and part to a fund that is to give me an income when I am old."

"Your hair is grey now," said Marcus.

"Yes, but that is premature. It merely gives me a personality."

"How do you know it does?"

"My mother tells me so."

"Does your mother know everything?"

"She knows this; she is in no doubt about it."

"You don't mind answering questions," said Tamasin.

"Not to-day. You must allay your curiosity before you give me your attention."

"Why should we take any interest in you?" said Marcus.

"I do not know, but you evidently do take it. I think you take the most."

"It is really for you to take an interest in us."

"In your studies; so it is. I am just about to begin."

"Do you do any work besides teaching?" said Sarah, in a social manner.

"People always regard teaching as a side line. Well, I am writing a book of essays."

"Oh, not a real book?" said Tamasin.

"No, not one with a beginning and an end."

"That would be more difficult."

"Yes, it would."

"Does a book of essays take very long?"

"Not the book itself, but I have come to putting in the charm. I put in so much, that I had to take some out; and that seemed a waste, and I put it back. And so it goes on."

"Like Penelope's web," said Sarah.

"Yes, like that."

"What are the titles of the essays?" said Tamasin.

"I could not tell you; they are too much involved with the charm. When that is the case, people do not talk about them."

"Because it would make them feel embarrassed?"

"Yes, that is the reason. I hope you will remember what I say."

"Do you earn much by being a tutor?" said Jasper.

"No, not a great deal."

"Isn't it skilled work?"

"I do not think that is the word."

"Does Father pay as much as other people?" said Marcus.

"People all pay the same," said Gideon, trying not to betray by his tone that Horace had hoped not to do this, and seeing from Sarah's eyes that he had failed.

"You know we don't talk about that sort of thing," she said to her brother.

"Father does, and he would not do what was wrong; or we ought not to think so."

"Things have to be discussed," said Gideon. "We have found that ourselves. And now we will get to work. Will you begin, Miss Sarah?"

Sarah read with some uneasiness, but also with success, and Tamasin with less of both; and Gideon corrected them in a spirit of suggestion.

"It is your turn, Marcus," he said.

"No, it is Master Jasper's."

There was a pause.

Marcus had taken the conventional address of his sister for a mark of deference to a higher class, assuming that someone who worked in the house might observe the form. His ignorance had so wide a range. Gideon perceived the truth of the matter, but was at a loss how to mend it. Sarah and Tamasin also saw, and the former's ease was threatened, and the latter's gravity. Gideon smiled at Tamasin, as though attributing her mirth to some personal cause. Marcus's face suddenly showed that he assigned it to the right one.

"Well, go on, Jasper," said Gideon.

"Be of good cheer, Master Jasper, and follow the

example of Mistress Sarah," said Marcus, in a forced, deliberate tone. "For she this day has lighted a candle that shall point our way."

"Who talks like that?" said Jasper.

"The people in *Foxe's Book of Martyrs*."

"So they do," said Gideon. "Well, follow the advice, Jasper. Your sister read very well."

Marcus relaxed and his flush gave way to pallor.

Jasper put his elbows on his book, as if to secure his attention to the page, a reasonable precaution, as it had a tendency to wander, but involving the exposure of points that hardly stood it.

"Our standard in clothes is our own," said Sarah. "We are a family who take our own way."

Marcus met her eyes, and a current of fellow feeling passed between them.

Horace entered the room and cast his eyes round the table.

"You are a tatterdemalion," he said to his son. "Well, you are all at the ragamuffin age."

Sarah smiled in support of the words, willing that the condition should appear voluntary.

"So you are reading French," said Horace, looking at the row of books. "Do they all read at the same time?"

"No, one at a time," said Gideon. "The others follow and hear the corrections."

"It was good of you to provide yourself with a book, but could you not have shared one of theirs?" said Horace, constrained to introduce the principle of sharing.

"I never hold up work for want of supplies."

"Are you a family man?" said Horace, feeling that this could hardly be the case.

"No, I live in my mother's house. I should like her to meet my pupils."

"I hope you will bring her to tea one day. With my wife away, I am grateful for interest in them."

Gideon accepted the invitation, surprising Sarah by

taking her father at his word, and also surprising Horace.

"You are warm enough, I hope?" said the latter, glancing at the grate, that had been supplied for the occasion.

"I hope I am not neglecting the fire," said Gideon, rising to replenish it.

"Mr. Doubleday's time is money in more than one sense," murmured Tamasin.

"What is that, Tamasin?" said Horace with a smile.

"Nothing, Father."

"The inevitable answer," said Horace, transferring the smile to Gideon.

"I am attentive to fires," said the latter. "You will not find this one an anxiety."

Horace could only contradict him in his own way.

"My children are not very used to large fires. They are brought up to be independent of them."

"I shall not leave it to them. I know what it is to trust fires to other people."

"I want my children to be hardy. It is a good foundation for the future."

"How can they be, when they are so young and weak? Older people are not, when they would be more equal to it."

"I flatter myself that I set an example."

"I do not call it flattery, and I hope they do not follow you. I cannot teach people who are cold. They cannot think of two things at once, and they waste my time and trouble."

"I hope you do not bring that charge against them to-day."

"By no means, but they are not cold; we have guarded against it."

"Well, I will not waste your time and your trouble and your fire and your row of books," said Horace, completing the summary of things that might be wasted. "I will hear your account of your pupils, when you have tried them further."

Gideon brought the session to a close, and took his leave

on the gentle, equal terms that ended any instinct to trouble him. But the instinct arose in Jasper with regard to anyone available.

"Well, Master Marcus!" he said.

Marcus gave him a glance and began to gather up the books.

"Well, Master Marcus!" said Jasper.

Marcus thrust his fist into his brother's face. The latter defended himself and found he must continue to do so. Tamasin drew away in alarm; Avery entered and called upon Nurse; Sarah tried to separate the combatants. The outcry brought Horace from the aimless tour of the house induced by his wife's absence.

"Brothers fighting!" he said, as though this relationship would preclude strife. "Brothers striking each other! And sisters compelled to witness such a scene!"

The victims of this compulsion stood with their eyes on the door. Gideon had heard the uproar and returned in concern.

"Now who began it? Who struck the first blow?" said Horace, concerned with the exact assignment of blame. "Did you see how it happened, Sarah?"

"Jasper did the first, and Marcus the second," said Sarah, using a light tone for the tutor's ears.

"Oh, six of one and half a dozen of the other," said Horace, perceiving the latter and following her example. "Well, there is an impression for Mr. Doubleday to take away."

"Jasper said something to make me angry," said Marcus.

"And achieved his object," said Tamasin.

"Well, and what was it?" said Horace, still true to himself.

"I only called him 'Master Marcus', Father."

Gideon noiselessly withdrew and closed the door.

"Well, I hope you are as ashamed of yourselves as I am of you. Why did you want to annoy your brother, Jasper? Tell him you are sorry for it."

"I only want him to promise never to say it again," said Marcus. "Not to me or anyone else."

"Oh, is that all?" said Jasper. "Well, I promise."

Marcus's face lightened, as he saw his future clear.

Gideon returned to his home, to find his mother and sister awaiting him as an employment. They did not think of filling the time, as they saw it as occupied. He came up to embrace his mother as a matter of routine.

"Well, how was the new family?" she said.

"It was new indeed, the newest I have met."

"Did they find you equally new?"

"I think they did, but many things would be new to them."

"Are they so much without experience?"

"Without the ordinary kind. I think they have their own."

"I have heard they are very old-fashioned children, and meet no one."

"They touched my heart," said Gideon, "and I think I touched theirs. They were kind about my position in the house. I have seldom had pupils so nice about it."

"Why do you not teach your pupils better?"

"I am not supposed to teach them that. I have to be seen as a warning. And the lesson would lack conviction, as of course it is humbling to be hired. And children exaggerate their own importance. They have so many people employed about them."

"I think that breaking the ice in a new house must be very tiring," said Magdalen Doubleday, bringing her brother a restorative with an air of doing nothing that need be noticed.

"Thank you, my dear," he said in an affectionate tone.

Magdalen carried another to her mother, with even more unobtrusiveness, as the latter's claim was less.

Gertrude Doubleday was a tall, large woman of sixty-eight, with solid features and small, light, attentive eyes. She was supposed to bear a likeness to George Eliot, and though she was aware that the latter's physiognomy was not her strong point, and had no misgiving about her own, she took a satisfaction in the resemblance and was gratified when a portrait on the wall drew attention to it. Magdalen resembled Gideon, but had a smoother face and less expression, indeed an odd lack of it. At thirty-eight she still had a look of youth, and gave her voice its sound. She was built on Gertrude's generous scale, and moved with a gentle heaviness that was her own. Her service to her family was seen as a life work, and the illusion could not be dispelled, as she herself held it. She and Gideon were easily fatigued, and needed little to fill their days. They accepted their own content and other people's surprise at it, and their mother's opinion that it had every ground. Gertrude's energy swept over them, and they saw it as they saw any other natural force. They were regarded as devoted to their mother, and shared or accepted the belief. Gertrude did not love her children less than other mothers, but she loved herself more. Personal crises marked her path, and she gained from them impetus and vigour that outlasted themselves. She was glad that her son was unmarried, as she liked his devotion and the credit of it. Her daughter's she valued less, or regarded as ranking lower, but her willingness to see her married did not mar her complacence in being the sole member of the family with full experience. Gertrude was capable of competing with her own flesh and blood. Her zest in her personal life faltered at nothing. With her son's contribution to her household, her income sufficed, and material care played no part in her lot. She said she had cause for thankfulness, and put into the feeling the same vigour as into more instinctive emotions.

"Are they nice children, Gideon?" said Magdalen.

"Yes, I should think they are; two boys and two girls."

"Isn't it three boys?"

"I believe it is, but the youngest boy learns with his aunt."

"His great-aunt, isn't it?"

"How much you know!" said Gideon, leaning back.

"Is it true that they are so badly dressed?" said Gertrude, with a touch of grim enjoyment.

"Yes, that is true, though I should not know if they were the opposite."

"Why should you not know what other people know?"

"Oh, just a little affectation, Mother."

"Why do you not affect things that add to you?"

"I think I thought it did add to me, Mother."

"Things that really add to us, cannot be assumed. We have to possess them."

"It is well to know that one kind of effort may be laid aside."

"People who see these children in church, say that their clothes have to be seen to be believed," said Gertrude, whose own power of credence had to function without this aid, as though she was an intensely religious woman, her religion consisted in unbelief.

"They are old and torn. At least they are old, and something tore while I was there."

"You would think they might at least be mended," said Magdalen.

"I think they are mended; indeed I did notice that."

"What kind of a house is it?" said Gertrude.

"Good to look at, less good to live in. Large and light and chill, and furnished with few and stately things."

"I expect we live in more comfort," said Gertrude, glancing round the room. "Is Mr. Lamb as cheeseparing and difficult as he is supposed to be?"

"Why did you not lay my foundation before I went? He came in himself. Mrs. Lamb had gone away, and he felt he should exchange a word with me."

"Well, naturally someone would come in on your first day. It would be only courteous."

"It was due to himself," said Gideon, in an idle tone.

"And a good thing too, if it led him to render what was due to someone else. I am all for the self-respect that results in regard for others."

75

"People have so much of all kinds of it. It would be nice to meet someone without it."

"I never think you have enough of it."

"Have the children got it?" said Magdalen, smiling.

"Children always have it, as I said, but these did not expect other people to have it for them."

"Well, how did Mr. Lamb strike you?" said Gertrude.

"As a man like myself. No, not like that. I expect he would say the same of me. No, I am sure he would not."

"He knew enough to come after you. I expect he has a pretty shrewd idea of what he is getting. You have your own name in the neighbourhood. And we have no reason to throw a veil over our private life. We are safe people; I think we can say that."

"I should like to see the children," said Magdalen.

"Well, you will soon have the opportunity," said her brother. "Their father wants us all to come to tea quite soon."

"Now are you being careful what you say?" said Gertrude, sitting up and using a half-excited, half-admonishing tone. "Are you clear what he said, and how he said it? And whom he asked, and for what day he asked them? Suppose we all went, and found that only one was expected?"

"They would hardly let us find it out, Mother," said Magdalen.

"Oh, I should know without their assistance. Trust a woman's instinct for that. There would not be much in their minds that I should not know."

"I hardly think a woman's instinct is as much to be recommended as is thought," said Gideon.

"Suppose, Mother," said Magdalen, in gentle, distinct tones, "that we ask Mr. Lamb and his cousin to tea here? And then leave the future to settle itself."

"Now I think that would be a very good plan. We have a home of our own after all," said Gertrude, speaking as if the circumstance were hardly usual. "And anyone can

76

come into it at any moment. I think I shall send a message through Gideon to Mr. Lamb quite soon. Or rather to his aunt, I suppose. That would be the correct thing."

"Yes, to his aunt, Mother," said Magdalen.

"I shall not see the aunt, unless she comes in to talk about the children, but I shall think nothing of her woman's instinct if she does not. But are we to ask all three?"

"Well, the difficulty would be to leave any one of them out," said Gertrude, in open estimation of the advantage of hospitality. "It would not do to take such a risk at the outset."

"Would you have anyone to meet them, Mother?" said Magdalen.

"No. Not the first time. No. Just their party and our own family group. I do not think we are at much of a disadvantage in our home. I do not think that sort of thing plays a great part in our lives. We are too much at ease fundamentally for that. And from what I can hear, the same thing can hardly be said of them. Mr. Lamb seems to ensure that."

"Why do you want to meet the man?" said Gideon, who did not know that his mother wanted to meet any man within twenty years of her own age, and was willing to meet any one outside this limit.

"I do not want to meet him," said Gertrude, who hardly knew it herself. "It is not my fault that he is the father of your pupils. I want to meet him in that capacity, of course. And I think it may be an advantage to you for him to see your home."

"He would hardly expect me to be actually homeless."

"It would be as well not to put it off too long, Mother," said Magdalen. "It is best to begin the acquaintance together from the first, and not to wait for Gideon to make progress on his own account."

"I can see people twice a week for years, and never know them any better," said her brother.

"And that is nothing to boast of," said Gertrude. "Well,

there is no reason for postponing it. No preparation is needed. We are not people who only make full use of our home, when guests are expected."

"Does that mean we are determined to expect guests?" said Gideon. "Something seems to mean it."

"Oh, you are in a contrary mood; we are not paying any attention. I am sure I am not afraid of the parents of your pupils; they have not proved an awe-inspiring company."

"This one is afraid of himself, and I am always afraid of people then. It shows there is something to be afraid of."

"Are the children afraid of him?" said Magdalen.

"They are nervous in his presence; they are not afraid he will do them any harm."

"Well, I should hope not," said Gertrude.

"I like the look of Mr. Lamb's cousin," said Magdalen. "I have always noticed his face in church."

"The short, round man who is so much with Mrs. Lamb?" said Gertrude, with her unsparing note. "He looks like a great, overgrown baby to me."

"If he looks like a baby, he must look like that sort of one," said Gideon.

"I rather like an ingenuous face on a man," said Magdalen. "Or do I mean a face with something ingenuous about it?"

"You mean you like Mortimer Lamb's face," said her mother, in a tone of respect and sympathy.

"I have given my attention to old Miss Lamb," said Gideon. "I do not miss my religious opportunities."

Gideon and Magdalen had no religious background, as there had been none available for them. Unbelief was to them a transmitted thing, and they were less loyal to it than their mother. Magdalen liked the ritual of church, and liked her brother's escort, and Gertrude saw nothing against the position of personally withholding her presence.

"Now do not adopt the line that we take no interest in a woman," she said. "That is far from being a failing of mine. And I agree that this woman commands attention.

Yes, it is a good face, a strong face, a face that is the better for its experience."

"I wonder if they think they are coming here as strangers," said Gideon.

"They do not know yet that they are coming here at all," said Gertrude, with a little laugh, by no means regarding the privilege as a matter of course.

The invitation was conveyed and accepted, the break being welcome in the time of Charlotte's absence, and some knowledge of the tutor's background not held to be amiss. The Lambs went through the day as usual, and the Double-days made a feint of doing so. When they met in the drawing-room to await the guests, this effort was at its height.

"I thought no changes were necessary," said Gideon, looking round the room.

"They are not prompted by actual necessity," said Gertrude, in a casual tone that held an exultant note.

"Except in so far as it is the mother of invention," said her son.

The tea-table presented a stiff and elaborate appearance, and Gertrude and Magdalen seemed to be equipped in conformity with it. The former moved about in a mechanical, absent manner, too conscious and expectant to attend to what was said.

"They are late, Mother," said Magdalen.

"Late, are they? Well, I dare say they will come at some time. If not to-day, then on some future occasion," said Gertrude, as though having no personal preference on the point.

"Here they are, Mother!"

Gertrude walked to her desk and took up a pen, and was engaged in examining it when the guests entered. She laid it down at once and advanced to meet them, glancing at her son for his aid. When he made the introductions her manner changed, and she led Emilia to a seat with an air of fulfilling her foremost obligation. Magdalen gave each

79

guest a gentle hand and word, and concerned herself with arrangements for their ease.

Gertrude took a chair and unconsciously arranged her dress, and then crushed it carelessly between the chair and the tea-table. The men began to talk, and Magdalen sat with an air of being about to join, while she watched for the moment to rise and hand the tea.

"Is that a relation of yours on the wall, Mrs. Doubleday?" said Horace. "I seem to know the face."

"It is no relation. It is a portrait of George Eliot," said Gertrude, covering a conscious expression by pouring out tea. "Or rather a reproduction of her most famous portrait."

"That explains its being familiar. But is there not a likeness in it to you?"

"Yes, people say there is," said Gertrude, handing a cup with a passing glance at the portrait. "Or they would probably say a likeness in me to it."

"The likeness is marked," said Mortimer, looking from the sleeves in the portrait to those of his hostess, in recognition that the likeness extended to these.

"Yes, it is marked," said Gertrude, in a quiet manner.

"You can even see it yourself, can you not, Mother?" said Magdalen, in a distinct tone.

"Yes, I can see it myself."

"Do we have the portrait on the wall, that the likeness may be estimated?" said Gideon.

"You know quite well that it is there entirely by chance," said Gertrude.

"I hardly think the likeness is a credit to us."

"I dare say you do not," said Gertrude quietly. "George Eliot was a plain woman."

"But I suppose there must be things in common underneath, Mother, to give rise to the superficial likeness," said Magdalen, her tone suggesting that this was a customary speech.

"I do not know how far the face is a mirror of the soul within," said Gertrude, in a light tone.

"You said you could see the likeness yourself," said Emilia. "You mean that when you look in a glass, you are reminded of the portrait?"

"I often think I am catching a glimpse of it, when I am brushing my hair or otherwise engaged at a mirror. And I have to remind myself that I am merely myself."

"It must be a proud thing to remind oneself that one is not a great person," said Mortimer. "I expect it shows that one is. The thing we remind ourselves of, are never true."

"What kind of things do you mean?" said Gertrude.

"Well, that other people are as important as we are, and that we shall be old ourselves one day."

"I am old now; I do not have to remind myself of that," said Gertrude, with a little laugh. "And I have never thought other people less important than I am."

"You are certainly great," said Mortimer.

"No, indeed I am not," said Gertrude, shaking her head in support of the disclaimer.

"The likeness has never made you inclined to follow in the steps of the original?" said Horace.

"I could not follow in her steps. That question is settled for me."

"Do you take a great interest in your little nieces and nephews, Mr. Lamb?" said Magdalen to Mortimer.

"Well, they make one side of my life."

"They are fortunate to have a bachelor uncle," said Gertrude, who generally interposed when Magdalen was talking to a man.

"If I had been able to afford to marry, I might have been a more distant figure."

"Now that is not what anyone said."

"I thought everyone said it. I make the mistake of thinking that people are talking about me."

"You make no mistake there," said Gertrude, in her natural downright manner. "What do people talk about but each other? If you think you can be seen at church every Sunday, and never excite a comment, you are wrong."

"But I do not think it. I have just said so. And I am glad I am not wrong."

Magdalen gave a laugh.

"It is a treat to her to hear talk of the kind she likes," said Gertrude, in an explanatory tone.

"You are not often in church, I think, Mrs. Doubleday?" said Horace.

"I am never there," said Gertrude, simply. "I think a public profession should represent something behind. I have not been able to go for many years." She glanced at the portrait, as though finding a further bond.

"Your son and daughter are sometimes there, I believe?"

"Yes, they go at times."

"You believe in liberty of thought and action?" said Mortimer.

"I hope so," said Gertrude gravely. "I would grant that to everyone. And in the case of my own children the obligation is doubly binding."

There was a pause.

"How long are you to be father and mother both?" said Gertrude to Horace in a gentle tone.

"I fear for some months. It can hardly be less. My aunt is a great support to me."

"I have heard other compliments paid in that direction," said Gertrude, looking at Emilia. "My son was quite impressed by the grounding of the little people. It must have meant effort and patience."

"It has given zest to my later years," said Emilia, "and I have avoided the mistake of clinging to office too long."

"Why are people so proud of not claiming to be young, when they are old?" said Gideon to Mortimer.

"They are proud of being strong enough to face it. And I think your mother and my aunt are the only people who do so."

"That is what they think themselves," said Gideon.

Magdalen rose, smiling and shaking her head, and

moved between the men, to separate them and recall them to their duties.

"I think that those who train the young, are the makers of history," said Gertrude, looking round. "They reach out into the future more than any other class. The work may not stand high in the eyes of the world, but I am proud that my son has chosen it."

"I think you are rather unfair to the world, Mother," said Magdalen. "Teaching is highly respected work."

"It will be a strange Christmas for you," said Gertrude to Horace, not attending to her daughter.

"It will indeed. That is the word. It will be utterly unfamiliar."

"And that is the wrong thing for that season. A familiar sadness might have a place, does have a place, as we know. But not the quality of strangeness."

"We must simply do our best with it."

"I suppose I cannot do anything towards making it—not better for you, but easier?" said Gertrude, even more gently, making a movement to lay her hand on his, but not completing it. "Sometimes the entirely unfamiliar is easier than the unfamiliar on the old background. It would be a great pleasure, a great privilege for me and mine, if it could be so."

"It is offering too much," said Horace.

"It is," said Gideon, half to himself.

"It is offering very little, offering almost nothing," said Gertrude, her tone rising as she felt the first step was behind.

"It is asking something for ourselves," said Magdalen.

"And if strangers may ask it, we should like to have it," said Gideon, feeling he should support his mother. "Not that I know what it is."

"It is anything it may prove to be," said Gertrude. "Anything that involves the use of our home, or our hospitality, if we must use such a word, or ourselves. The last is indeed at your service."

"Perhaps we may ask for yourselves at the midday Christmas meal, that means so much to the young," said Emilia, feeling that some response was due. "That would solve many of our problems."

"You would not find the new background of this house better? Or rather more to your purpose?"

"We could not advance upon you, a company of eight."

"And why could you not?" said Gertrude, on an almost sweet note. "Our accommodation must be small, compared with yours; that is as it must be. But that sort of thing is elastic. Where there is a will, there is a way."

"I hardly see it," said Gideon. "A table is not elastic."

"Indeed it is," said his mother. "A second table can be added. We are not short of furniture. And children do not know or care if chairs match."

"No, we are not short of that," said Gideon, looking round in a dreamy manner.

"Our own table is small, as we use it," said Horace. "But we are used to adapting it; we can put in another leaf."

"That is real elasticity," said Gideon. "We will not offer the spurious for the genuine."

"No, we will accept the genuine," said his mother, in a quiet tone.

"It is very kind of you," said Emilia.

"Yes, it is kind," said Gertrude, in the same tone, "when we hoped to be in an even happier place. But we will be content to do our part in the most acceptable way."

"I fear we should go," said Horace. "We must not leave the ship any longer with no one at the helm."

"I feel for you so much," said Gertrude, retaining his hand. "It is a great burden on you, a great demand. I can realise it, if anyone can; I have carried my own burdens."

"It is something to have friends who try to share them," said Horace.

"He used the word, 'friends', as easily and naturally as you please," said Gertrude, returning to her children. "It seems that he intends us to act that part. Well, they are interesting people, an addition to our life. I think they saw we meant to be of help to them."

"They have done harder things," said Gideon.

"Do you think we insisted on it, Mother?" said Magdalen.

"Oh, I don't think I took too much on myself, in suggesting that we should help them over a difficult place. What would happen to any of us, if people were afraid to do that?"

"Nothing," said Gideon, "and now something is going to."

"Oh, I think they meant what they said. They do not strike me as people who would resort to the common kind of subterfuge. I think they are sure enough of themselves to avoid that. I feel we may take their words as their own, and that they would prefer us to do so."

"Which of them did you like the best, Mother?" said Magdalen.

"I think perhaps Mr. Lamb. He strikes me as a man who might easily be misjudged. Indeed even at my distance I misjudged him. There is something deep and almost tragic in his face; I can see that he has lived. I think he felt that I did not miss him."

"I think I liked Mr. Mortimer better."

"Well, his is an easier note, a lighter appeal. He has lived less, whether or no he has lived less long. Perhaps that is a natural preference."

"And how about old Miss Lamb?" said Gideon.

"Now I will not have this way of disposing of people as old, just because they have passed their prime. There are many years to come for her, many things yet for her to do. What she has done for those children is a proof of that. And I find it a good face, a deep character. It confirms the impression I had gained. About Mr. Lamb I feel that I judged less soundly. I was too ready to judge by hearsay, to take the accepted view. I think he saw that I was prepared to form my own."

"I wonder what else he saw," said Gideon.

"Now you make a mock of everything and defeat your own object. People who jest always, jest not at all. Magdalen and I can be serious or not, as occasion calls. It comes to this: a woman's words have a meaning."

"I wonder what they are saying of us," said Magdalen.

"I should not be afraid to hear it," said Gertrude, standing straight and aloof, as though to confront the situation. "I think it would be sincere and said in a spirit of friendship, and no one should be afraid of that."

"What a very unusual view!" said her son.

"Now I do not believe in this theory that friends speak evil of each other. If they do so, they are not friends. It is neither my experience nor my practice. No, my friends are safe as far as I am concerned. When they have become my friends, that is. When I do not know people, it is different."

"So it was," said Gideon.

"I don't think I was mistaken about Mortimer Lamb, Mother," said Magdalen. "I think the opinion I had formed of him, was a true one. I should call it almost a youthful charm."

"Yes. Yes, I know what you mean. In some people the surface does not harden. It is a class to which I make no claim to belong myself; there is little sign about me of what I once was. And in Mr. Lamb too there are few traces of youth. It is a matter in which the cousins are not alike. Less so than many of us."

"I have been accused of having such a young face and voice," said Magdalen, in a tone that did not refute the charge.

"Well, that is a point that you and Mortimer Lamb have in common," said Gertrude, in an almost obliging manner.

"Were they going to walk home?" said Gideon.

"Yes," said his mother. "Yes. They came in a carriage and dismissed it. They would just act simply. Possibly the horses had done enough for the day. They may only have one pair. They would not disguise it."

The Lambs were doing as their hostess guessed, and for the reasons she gave.

"So for the first time in our lives we have guests on Christmas Day," said Mortimer.

"Charlotte is away from us for the first time," said Horace.

"We do seem to need an excuse," said his cousin.

"If we do, we have a good one," said Emilia, "and it is taking three people to fill her place."

"We could not break up a family on Christmas Day," said Horace. "It was a case of all or none."

"They were prepared to have eight of us," said his aunt.

"Prepared in every sense," said Mortimer. "I wonder you managed to save us."

"I did so in the only possible way."

"I rather like the tutor," said Mortimer. "But I cannot respect him; he does not dare to be himself. He maintains a false front before his mother."

"I should say the last person before whom it is necessary to do so," said Horace.

"Now that is nice of you, my dear boy, the word of a friend."

"We need not make fun of them," said Horace, coldly. "We are a family ourselves."

"So we are, and we are to have three guests on Christmas Day. That ought to teach us not to make fun of anyone."

"You seem to think there is something odd about it."

"It seems to me so odd that I can hardly credit it. It makes us seem like any other household."

"And are we not like any other?"

"Don't you really know, my dear boy? Mrs. Doubleday did not. The tutor does not tell her things. I have no respect for her either; she has not won her son's confidence."

"We shall have to tell the servants about the guests," said Emilia.

"Must we do that?" said Mortimer. "I thought that servants always knew everything without being told."

"When we tell them, we often find they know."

"Well, of course they know then; that is taking too much credit."

"So you walked home, ma'am," said Bullivant. "The carriage did not wait."

"The frost was too much for the horses," said Horace.

Bullivant glanced at Emilia, as though in that case it might have been too much for the lady.

"We must consider dumb animals," said Horace, in a tone of rejoinder, "and these horses are valuable beasts."

A twitch crossed Bullivant's lips at this statement of the case.

"I think too much compensation is made to animals for being dumb," said Mortimer. "After all, it is not our fault. Neither is it that we are articulate; we can be too much penalised."

"Don't you think you should sometimes be penalised for that?" said Emilia.

"They cannot make their feelings known," said Horace.

"But they always are known," said his cousin; "people seem to pride themselves on knowing them. More credit is due to Emilia, who could have made hers known, and did not. Bullivant, we are to have guests to luncheon on Christmas Day."

"Yes, sir," said Bullivant, in a confirmatory tone. "Will it be all three?"

"There will be two ladies and one gentleman," said Horace.

"Yes, sir; another leaf in the table, but not the best silver."

"Not the silver we use every day," said Horace.

"Oh, no, sir," said Bullivant.

"Is the best silver any good to us?" said Mortimer.

"It is always in reserve, sir, in case of its being indicated."

"Will you tell Cook about the Christmas luncheon?" said Emilia.

"I will mention it, ma'am, in case of need," said Bullivant, as he withdrew.

"You see they do know things without being told," said Mortimer. "I do not think dumbness would matter to them. So perhaps it does not matter to animals; it is best not to worry about it."

Horace followed his aunt upstairs, and Bullivant found himself again in the hall. He had his own relaxations, and one of them was a word with Mortimer.

"I hope you will excuse our having guests at Christmas, Bullivant."

"That is hardly the part I play in the matter, sir."

"I hope Cook will not mind?"

"Service is Mrs. Selden's watchword, sir."

"Or George?" said Mortimer.

Bullivant raised his brows in an honest waiving of the question of George's preferences.

"Do you know anything about Mrs. Doubleday's family?"

"No, sir. His being in the house as tutor constituted my first awareness of him."

"The children seem to like him."

"The right man in the place, probably, sir."

"Would you expect a tutor to have a mother and a sister?"

"Well, hardly perhaps, sir, as concerns this family."

"Mr. Doubleday has both."

"Well, it is a thing that might be, sir."

"I think he is afraid of his mother."

"Well, sir, that might be said of many of us."

"Were you afraid of yours?"

"I would never open my mouth against her, sir."

"Do you feel that she can hear you?"

"There are things beyond us, sir."

"I suppose she is dead?"

"You are right that she has passed on, sir."

"Do you expect to be reunited?"

"Well, sir, I would not be definite, united perhaps being

hardly the word in the first place. But anything derogatory applies only to myself."

"Do you wish you had been a better son?"

"Well, there are things in all our hearts, sir. Not that I ever forgot that she was a woman. It was only that I was confronted with her being other things."

"Will you think of it on your deathbed?"

"That will be rather late in the day, sir."

"It might be thought to be the right moment."

"Well, in that case, sir, it may be put into my mind. But I shall not go to seek it. Making my peace at the last moment is hardly in my line. And my mother would have condemned it. That was her tendency, sir. Indeed the whole thing was that her standard was too high. In one sense I could not have had a 'better' mother." Bullivant ended with a smile and turned towards the kitchen.

"All three, Mrs. Selden, according to your surmise."

"Taking the whole of what was available, as though less could have been offered!" said Cook. "It would be thought they would be in advance of that. Not that I should have held the current opinion. Well, Miriam, does staring teach you anything? In which case you must be attaining a standard by now."

"Why shouldn't three come?" said Miriam, unable to break the thread of her interest.

"Because mere acquaintance do not visit as a family, as you should know."

"Well, perhaps hardly as yet, Mrs. Selden," said Bullivant.

"Asking our family would lead to theirs being substituted," said George, on an equal note. "That would be the course of affairs."

"As is transparent to anyone," said Cook. "But I wonder the master rose to it."

"It was due to him, Mrs. Selden," said Bullivant, with a note of remonstrance, "and it is between the ladies that the word would have passed."

"Eleven at luncheon on Christmas Day," said George, "and the day supposed to be a holiday!"

"You had better impart your view of it to the master," said Bullivant. "He may not have acquaintance himself with it."

"And would probably modify his course accordingly," said Cook. "And that is not the essence of the day, with any upbringing."

There was silence, while Bullivant hummed a sacred air, in sympathy with the atmosphere.

"I hope you will acquit yourself with credit, George, and support me with ease and unobtrusiveness. It is this insistence of yours that is our obstacle. It will be practice for you against a real occasion."

"I fear those times are past," said Cook. "We have let them escape us, and regaining a point is what presents the difficulty."

"I should like to have seen them," said Miriam.

"Well, who can say? Things may come from small beginnings. The first shall be last, and the last first," said Bullivant, still in the mood induced by Cook, but scarcely considering her in his adjustment.

"Well, well, these things may hardly be literal," she said.

"It is the future state that is actually referred to, I believe, Mrs. Selden," said Bullivant, elucidating matters but hardly improving them.

"I wonder what the mistress would say to this use of her absence?"

"I think the purpose was to compensate somewhat for it, Mrs. Selden. And Christmas has always had its secular side."

"I ask nothing further than to be in my seat on that night," said Cook, not feeling that her place in chapel required to be further defined.

"I do not observe the formality of any attendance," said Bullivant.

"Well, it is possible to commune anywhere."

"You have understanding, Mrs. Selden, beyond the common range."

"Well, I do not obtrude my own practice, as intolerance is not what it should give rise to. All have the right to judge."

"Do you frequent any place of worship, Miriam?" said Bullivant.

"I go to the orphanage service, and they have asked me there on Christmas night."

"And you, George? Will you repair to the scenes of your early days?"

"No, I never go near them. I am welcome in private homes."

"I have little bias myself towards institutions," said Cook. "Not that Miriam is not correct to go to hers."

"Nor would it demean George to go and do likewise," said Bullivant, still on a Scriptural note.

"That is other people's view," said George, "and our own is best, when it comes to what is for ourselves."

"I have nowhere else to go," said Miriam. "I have never seen the inside of a home."

"Now is that really a fact?" said Bullivant.

"It may be," said Cook. "She has only been out of the orphanage for a few months."

"Well, well, it was a home to you, Miriam," said Bullivant.

"It was where I lived," said Miriam, in an uncertain tone.

"There are people there who care for you?" said Bullivant, on a melodious note.

"Well, they want my welfare. They say they had me from six months," said Miriam, as if taking their word for this.

"And do you have a nice assemblage on Christmas Day?"

"We have hymns and tea," said Miriam, using an

incidental tone, as Cook would have stinted her of neither of these.

"Talking of homes, this house is not much of one," said George, "anyhow to the children of it."

Bullivant and Cook exchanged a glance.

"The gentry follow their own ways more than others do," said Bullivant. "The higher they are, the more is that the case."

"They have less call to conform," said Cook. "It is not a matter the inexperienced would be conversant with."

"I wonder what the tutor thinks of it," said George.

Bullivant and Cook had expressed this wonder, and saw the unfitness of George's doing the same.

"He has been in houses," said Cook. "His calling would lead him into them."

"And they would not all be like this one," said George, persistent in assuming knowledge along this line.

"He would not follow, Mrs. Selden," said Bullivant. "There is no criterion for him."

"Isn't it better to be high up?" said Miriam.

"It is not always better for the people themselves," said Bullivant. "From royalty downwards that is the trend."

"We are a good way down from royalty," said George.

"Well, there are intervening steps," said Cook. "But those who are further down still, can hardly estimate the matter. It is for them to do their duty at their point of the scale. And I am not aware that the voicing of opinion is included in it. And there is not much duty being done at the moment, that I can perceive."

Miriam and George accepted their dismissal, and Bullivant looked at Cook.

"It is natural that the young should be at a loss, Mrs. Selden. It is a precarious matter to explain."

"And that being so, better not attempted. A false move would have its widening circles."

"We are further downhill since the mistress went. I wonder how it augurs for Christmas Day."

"A certain degree of conformity is observed with guests."

"But will it be with these, Mrs. Selden? Will the master feel it is due? And when people are not quite on our level, it adds to the—the inconvenience."

"The discomfiture," said Cook.

"I can suffer much in walking round the table," said Bullivant, bowing his acceptance of the word. "And with George seeing things with such simplicity, and Miss Emilia and Mr. Mortimer giving no sign! They are not straightforward circumstances."

"And the complexity recoils upon itself."

"You have language, Mrs. Selden, beyond what would be looked for."

"I was always one for expression. More than one has said to me that they would be glad of my power in the line. 'Thought falls short, Miss Selden, if there is not the where-withal to clothe it,' were the words of one."

"It is not only George that it is beyond," said Bullivant. "But it being outside his scope, there is no need for him to express his criticism."

"It makes no contribution," said Cook.

"It does not, Mrs. Selden," said Bullivant, rising and settling his coat, to be at ease for the coming encounter. "His duty and his simple respect will suffice. Opinions, and opinions of an adverse nature, are not required. We did not look for this result of ignoring his origin. It is not the expected outcome."

CHAPTER IV

"CHRISTMAS DAY AT last! It only comes once a year," said Nurse at the door of the girls' room, giving what recommendation of the day occurred to her.

The sisters sat up and looked at the foot of their beds, where stockings had previously hung.

"It will come three hundred and sixty-five times, for all the difference now," said Tamasin.

"Jasper asked if we could still have stockings," said Sarah, looking at the ceiling. "Aunt Emilia said that Father had forbidden it, but I don't think Jasper was quite sure. I don't think Marcus was either." She made no mention of anyone further, and Tamasin looked at her in sympathy.

"We still have meals and presents. It is something that we do not grow too old to eat."

Avery ran into the room with a filled stocking in his hands, and emptied the contents, already examined and replaced, on to Sarah's bed.

"I still have a stocking, but it is no one but me."

His sisters did not damp his elation, such moments in his life being too few to be grudged. The elder boys entered and stood to watch the display, Jasper's eyes taking on a look of interest and purpose.

"Don't let him touch them," said Avery to Sarah. "I don't want them made into other things. I like them what they are meant to be."

"If I promise not to touch them," said his brother, "will you give me a sweet?"

"After dinner," said Avery after a pause, preferring to keep things intact to the last moment, and then looking round with a beneficent air. "I will give you all one."

"You boys are too big to be in your sisters' room," said Nurse.

"Then they are too big to have us there," said Marcus, who disliked differentiation on the ground of sex.

"Well, go and dress in your own. No porridge this morning unless you want it."

This advantage brought the five to the breakfast table, and porridge was refused for the sake of the exercise of will.

"Not a very nice breakfast for Christmas morning," said Avery.

"Well, think of your luncheon," said Nurse.

"Must we go to church?" said Jasper, recalled to the time that intervened.

"Yes, of course, on Christmas Day."

"Christmas Day is as bad as the other Sundays," said Avery.

"It is not a Sunday," said Sarah.

"It sometimes is," said Jasper. "It was one three years ago."

Avery looked at him, but did not pursue a line of so much effort.

"Why do we go to church, if it isn't Sunday?" he said.

"It is the most important day in the year," said Nurse, whose religious instruction would hardly have served the uninitiated.

"Shall we come out before the sermon?" said Jasper.

"No, not on Christmas Day. And you are growing too old to do that."

"Let us keep our early privileges," said Tamasin. "No new ones seem to arise for us."

"A stocking was one of the old ones, wasn't it?" said Avery, in a sympathetic tone.

"Now a happy Christmas to you all," said Horace. "And a present for each of you from Mother, Aunt Emilia, Cousin Mortimer and me. We have come ourselves to bring them."

This was felt to be an almost excessive observance of the

day, and the children kept their eyes from elders thus affected by it.

"That is four presents each," said Avery.

"How many altogether?" said Horace, holding up his hand to check a general response. "No, let Avery say."

"How many?" said Avery, looking round.

"Four presents each for five people," said Sarah.

"Five times four," muttered Marcus.

"Or four times five," said Jasper.

Avery looked from one to the other in nervous doubt.

"Five times one are five, five times two are ten, five times three are fifteen, five times four are twenty."

"That is right," said Horace. "But it was a roundabout way of doing it."

"It is right," said Avery, looking round.

"Now whose present will you open first?" said Horace.

"I have opened all mine," said Jasper.

"You should have waited for the others. Why should you act by yourself?"

"Jasper was excited," said Avery, in condonation of his brother.

"Master Avery must never use his knife, unless someone is with him," said Nurse.

"I never will," said Avery, earnestly. "Sarah and I will always open ours together."

"I expect you will use the desks all your lives," said Horace. "Anyhow, you should do so."

"Five desks, and all black and all the same," said Avery, with the complacence of one whose years might have condemned him to a difference, and to a colour with more appeal for youth. "Always we will use them."

"And Mr. Mortimer has given you paper and envelopes to put into them," said Nurse, hardly visualising any further use for these.

"Have I?" said Mortimer, looking at the gifts that had been bought for him as a complement to Emilia's. "Yes, so I have. Well, God bless you, my dears."

"Now, how about the books?" said Horace.

"Thank you, Father," said Avery, feeling this step was in the right direction. "I will read it until I can say some, and then Sarah will read it to me."

"That is what he likes," said Marcus.

"Well, there might be worse ways," said Horace.

"Other ways are worse," said Avery, looking round. "Now everything is fair, isn't it?"

"Everything happens to be equal," said his father. "But fair is not the word. It would have been fair for you to have nothing. No one is obliged to give a present to anyone."

"They are at Christmas."

"No, they do it out of kindness and to celebrate the Day. And it would have been fair for some of you to have better things than others."

"No, that would not be fair."

"Yes, but it would. People can do as they like about giving presents."

"Yes, but they *were* fair," said Avery. "Even you were, weren't you? We have a nice book each."

"It is quite beyond him," said Horace, looking at Mortimer. "Children will think they are entitled to things."

"Well, I found they were. The matter had to be attended to."

"I always question this way of mixing up pleasure with serious things."

"Well, pleasure would be best, unadulterated. But everything has its alloy."

"Now this half-crown is mine," said Horace to his children, "and I am not obliged to give it to anyone. But if I gave it to one of you, the rest would not think it unfair, because no one has a claim on it."

"On someone's birthday it would not be unfair," said Avery.

"You others see what I mean, don't you? Now I will give the half-crown to you all, sixpence each."

"That is quite fair," said Avery.

"Hush," said Sarah.

"You can take your Christmas collection out of it, and keep the rest. What you give at church is your own affair. Now how will you do it?"

"I shall give a halfpenny," said Jasper, lightly, keeping his eyes from his elders.

"I will give a dear little farthing," said Avery.

"There, you see, you are doing different things," said Horace, maintaining a neutral front towards this estimate of the claims of charity. "Avery is not giving as much as Jasper, but he can do what he likes with what is his."

"I am giving as much."

"No, a farthing is less than a halfpenny."

"Suppose you all give a penny," said Nurse, with a view both to moral discipline and to the effect in the plate at church.

"Yes, then we shall all have fivepence," said Avery, and hesitated to add that this would be fair.

"Now we start for church in a quarter of an hour," said Horace, in a tone so different as to come with a shock, and to throw doubt on any theory that religion went through life. "Presents and pleasures out of our minds. It will be the time to think of other things. You had better sit quiet for a while, to get into the proper spirit."

"I had a stocking," whispered Avery to his aunt, as though this degree of secular interest were allowable between them.

"You are all quite clear about the meaning of the Day?" said Horace, looking searchingly at his children and speaking with a sound of reproach.

"Yes, Father," said the four eldest, in convinced and convincing tones, fearful of incurring an exposition of their faith, in which grounds of reproach were indeed involved.

"How long is it before we start?" said Avery, when his elders had gone, beginning to sort his possessions.

"About fifteen minutes," said Nurse.

"Fifteen minutes left; no, fourteen; no, thirteen," said Avery, regarding the minutes as passing at this rate.

"You are thinking of seconds," said Sarah.

Her brother gave her an arrested look, and stood with an air of having made an advance.

Horace was standing in the hall with his cousin and aunt, visualising the situation of waiting for his children, and alert for the moment when a minute's delay should give rise to it.

"Heads up, prayer-books in hands, boys on the outside of the girls! Jasper and Sarah, Marcus and Tamasin, Avery and Nurse, Cousin Mortimer and Aunt Emilia and me."

"Father puts himself last," said Avery.

"We might be the couples going into the ark," said Tamasin.

"A Scriptural scene befits the Day," said Marcus. "And we look old-fashioned enough to act the part."

Sarah was silent, not finding it a matter for jest.

"The children look rather a scarecrow tribe," said Horace.

"They gave up having better coats, because they were worn so seldom," said Emilia, in a tone that held no comment. "They were just outgrown."

"Well, they can come out before the sermon. Then people will not notice them."

"Is that the right means to the end?" said Mortimer.

Horace felt a doubt of this, as the graduated row of figures emerged into the aisle. He held himself stiffly until the unimpeachable form of Nurse brought up the rear. Nurse did not grow out of her clothes, and so had new ones at intervals, a working of cause and effect that Sarah saw as inconsistent. She kept her eyes fixed on the children, to mark the necessity of their being watched over as important beings.

"Well, we are safely out of sight," said Tamasin, "but people have had their glimpse of us."

"People say that children should be seen and not heard,"

said Marcus. "Father did not act on the principle to-day."

"I am not sure he did not," said Sarah.

"But it is better to come out," said Avery, "especially at Christmas. The sermon would be sad, and it is not the fault of anyone who lives now."

"You are thinking of Easter," said Marcus. "Don't you ever listen to any of it?"

Avery looked at him and did not speak. He would have tried to listen to the sermon, but hardly regarded the rest of the service as designed for the purpose.

"Will there be crackers at dinner?"

"I am sure there will," said Nurse. "I know your aunt has ordered them."

"I will ask if you and I can take ours upstairs," said Sarah. "Father may let us do that, as it seems like saving them. And then we can give the part that explodes to Jasper."

"I mind crackers and fireworks more and more," said Avery in a grave tone. "Even next Christmas I shall mind them. When I am a man, I will stop them."

"Then you will always be a baby," said Jasper.

"No, I shall be a man who can stop things. I shall forbid it."

"Where is your Bible, Master Jasper?" said Nurse.

"It is in rags, so I keep it in my pocket. I did not want one for Christmas instead of a real book," said Jasper, who was not without his own views on literary matters. "Father has not noticed it yet."

"He hardly dares to look at us," said Tamasin.

"Well, we don't much like to look at him," said Avery.

"Nurse is at a loss," said Tamasin. "She often finds herself that."

"I should not like to be a nurse," said Jasper.

"No, you are not kind enough, are you?" said Avery.

The families of Lamb and Doubleday assembled in the hall, and Horace surveyed his children, as if anticipating no inconvenience from them.

"It is a good thing our coats are the worst of our garments," said Tamasin to Marcus. "We could hardly go out before luncheon, as we can before the sermon."

"So these are our little men and maids," said Gertrude, "and one a very little man indeed."

"The four eldest have only a year between them, Mother!" said Magdalen, in a tone of making an announcement.

"I am afraid we swell your numbers very much," said Gertrude to Emilia, as if she expected the fear to be dispelled.

"We are enjoying our full table," said Emilia, finding it best to deal with it in another way.

"And we have to feel all the time how much the person whose place we are taking, would be preferred to us," said Magdalen.

"We feel guilty of presumption in attempting to take the place at all," said her mother.

Emilia smiled at the protestations of uneasiness at her board.

"Mother did not take three chairs," said Marcus.

"Neither did she," said Gertrude, kindly. "There is no question of filling a place; we are using the wrong words."

Horace smiled at his guests, as it was his custom to smile in public over the utterances of his children, that indeed gave him at such moments all the amusement he derived from them.

"They are certainly not a family of chatterboxes," said Gertrude.

"They are not used to joining their elders at table," said Horace.

"We have never done it before," said Jasper.

"Well, only with the elders of your family."

"Oh, yes, with those."

Horace joined in the laughter that followed, welcoming the impression produced of family ease.

"We do not count at all," he said to Gertrude.

"It means that you count in the right way."

"Now shall we be premature over the crackers?" said Horace, taking one from the table. "The eldest and youngest men of the family will take the lead."

Avery drew back and looked at Sarah.

"May Avery and I take our crackers upstairs and open them later?"

"No, of course not," said her father. "The crackers are here for us all to enjoy together, not for people to take away by themselves. Now, Avery, a pull and a bang to wake you up! We do not want sleepy-heads on Christmas Day."

The words seemed to throw a light on something that required it. Gideon felt that a question had been answered, and Mortimer knew that it had.

Avery put his force, enhanced by his feelings, into the pull, lost his hold and caused his father to fall back against his chair. The latter regained the cracker and tapped it on his son's shoulder, before thrusting it again towards his hand.

"Hold it tight and pull it hard," said Jasper, looking as if his own fingers were ready for the work.

"Give it a quick pull, and it will go off easily," said Sarah, in a quiet tone.

Avery did so; Horace was not prepared for the jerk; and this time it was Avery who fell backwards.

"Come, sit up and try again," said Horace, ignoring his son's knocked head and filling eyes, and sitting with hand outstretched and tapping feet. "The others are waiting for their turn; we must not think we are the only people at the table. Anyone would think you had never seen a cracker before."

"He has not seen one for a year," said Emilia. "He has had no chance of getting used to them."

"Well, he is having the chance now," said Horace, in a light tone.

"Mother, the little one is crying," said Magdalen, in a

lowered voice, as if not sure if public comment were in place.

Gertrude smiled and made no reply, conveying the impression that it was not.

"Crying for that! Well, what a boy! I should rather say, what a baby!" said Horace, not looking at his son. "Come along, you other boys, and show him how to do it. A cracker in each hand, Jasper; a cracker in each hand, Marcus. That is the way."

The boys gave themselves to the moment, while Avery looked on, awed by their hardihood, almost troubled by the expenditure of crackers, and following the contents of these with his eyes, as they were discarded.

"Now do you want to pull one, before they are gone?" said Horace, finding that his method was hardly based on supplies.

"May I have the things that come out of them, for my share?"

"Very well; snap them up," said Horace, in some sympathy with this thrift, sweeping some of the things together with his hand. "Now the rest are for the girls. Our baby does not want one."

Avery, at ease in this situation, collected the property and put it aside. He was concerned with the things that had value for him, and his father's opinion was not among them.

"Now it is time for you all to run upstairs," said Horace. "We shall be leaving the table soon. Bullivant and George want to get to their own dinner. They are having it after ours." He used a manner of simply and naturally revealing the working of the house.

"So that they can have what is left?" said Avery, in a sympathetic tone. "And there is a lot, isn't there?"

"Of course not," said his father. "They will have their own Christmas dinner, just as you have yours. You are not the only people to have a little extra done for you at Christmas."

"No, everyone does," said Avery, with appreciation. "And it isn't a little, is it? It is a lot."

Gertrude turned to Horace as the door closed.

"It must be a hard task to steer the course between indulgence and firmness, that is to say, between inclination and duty. I know the temptation to make the easy choice."

"The question is whether the good of the moment is the real good," said Horace. "To do one's best is often thankless work."

"No," said Gertrude, in a quiet, firm tone, "the bread cast upon the waters will return after many days. I have had my share of the dear burden of the young." She rested her eyes on her own children.

"The time will pass and restore their mother, but some of the problems will remain. In a way they go with me."

"Yes. Yes. No problem lifts, that is our own."

"The children did not say good-bye to us," said Magdalen to Mortimer.

"They are not versed in manners and customs."

"They must miss their mother very much."

"Yes, and no one can help them there."

"I think, from the way they look at you, that they find you a person apart."

"That is a good description of me. I have no proper place."

"I did not say that."

"Well, you hardly could."

"I did not think it either."

"It was nice of you to shut your eyes to it. It is a tiresome habit to look things in the face."

Magdalen laughed, and Gertrude at once gave a smile in her direction. Gideon intimated that it was time to leave, and she rose at once, bowing to his knowledge of the house.

"Did you enjoy your talk with Miss Lamb?" she said, as they went home. "I should think she is an interesting companion."

"So does she."

"I should have said she was the last person to talk for effect."

"So she is; she attends to the matter."

"You do not deserve to know unusual people, if you find fault with their very unusualness."

"I wonder what the children are doing now," said Magdalen. "Do not you, Gideon?"

"I never picture my pupils' life behind the scenes."

"I wonder you can resist it with this family."

"I am sometimes surprised at myself, but a rule is a rule."

"I think their uncle seems very interested in them."

"That is another point you have in common, a love of children," said Gertrude.

"Somehow one feels glad that they have his eye over them, Mother. I do not know what gives rise to the feeling, but it is there."

"It would not need much pursuing," said Gideon, "but they must go by themselves into their dim, deep world."

The children had done as Gideon said, and found Nurse awaiting them.

"I hope nothing has happened?" she said with a searching look.

"Nothing of an untoward nature," said Tamasin, "if that is what you mean."

"A little trouble over Avery's crackers, nothing that mattered," said Sarah.

"I did not pull any," said Avery, in a reassuring manner.

"Well, you can read your new books while I am at my dinner. I shall only be gone an hour."

"I don't want to read," said Jasper.

"Why not? There is always something you can learn. It is not only lesson books that teach you."

"That is Jasper's own feeling," said Tamasin.

"I will give them all a sweet," said Avery, running to his box with an air of solving all problems. "I will give them one each out of my box, because it is Christmas."

He opened the box and regarded the contents, picked out the smallest sweet and gave it to Tamasin, took the next in size and ran to Marcus, and did the same with the next two sweets and Jasper and Sarah. The last was of a superior kind, and his eyes lingered on it, as it left his hand. They did not question his right to do as he would with his own. They thanked him and ate the sweets, Jasper putting his whole into his mouth, and earning from his brother a look of hurt surprise. The latter then selected two sweets for himself, placed some other objects upon the box and came forward to join the rest.

"Shall I give you a box to keep your toys in?" said Jasper.

"Yes," said Avery, on a dubious note.

"My box that I have been making out of the proper kind of wood?"

"Suppose you lend it to me?" said Avery, feeling that this would impose a lighter obligation, and looking at the collection that undoubtedly required a home.

"What will you give me for it?" said Jasper, passing over the suggestion.

Avery considered with the undisturbed look of one who had not expected his first idea to succeed.

"You may read my book."

"But you may read mine. So that does not count."

"I will read them both to you," said Avery, who was more addicted to the printed word than his brother.

"No, Marcus reads to me in bed. That is not giving me anything."

"I will give you *another* sweet."

"Will you give me your cardboard box of sweets for my lasting box of wood? Then when the sweets are gone, you will have the box for your own for ever."

Avery considered at his ease.

"But the box will be my own? You won't use it or want me to lend it to you?"

"No, I have begun another one. But this is the best."

"Will it always be best, even when the other is done?"

"Yes, it is made out of harder wood."

Avery paused for another moment, pushed his box towards his brother and withdrew it, and then giving it a final thrust, examined the wooden box to see if it confirmed his impression, set it down with a satisfied air and began to arrange his possessions. Jasper addressed himself to the sweets, and Avery thrust the other two sweets into his hand, and turned an undivided mind to his toys, talking to himself as he disposed them, and sometimes talking to them.

"Don't gobble the sweets," said Sarah to her brother. "They are half gone, and you gave your box for them."

"I don't mind. I can make another box. I don't like the box as well as making it," said Jasper, surveying the sweets in concern that desire should so soon fail.

Avery left his toys and ran up to his sister.

"I gave my box of sweets to Jasper. And those two I had in my hand, I gave them to him too," he said, his tone becoming light as he turned away. "For his wooden box to keep my things in, and he likes making the box best."

"Well, you must not be sorry. You have done it of your own will."

"I shall have the box for always. And other people eat the sweets. Even Jasper lets them. But I gave one to each of you, didn't I?" Avery glanced at the sweets in consideration of his own claim, but saw the matter in some light of his own and returned to his possessions.

Nurse entered the room and sent her eyes about it.

"Why don't you read your new book, Master Jasper?"

"I will lend it to the others, if they like. And Marcus is reading it."

"Why does he not read his own book first?"

"Because it is abridged," said Marcus, not looking up. "I like a whole book, not part of one."

"The whole book might not be suitable for you," said Nurse, seeking to render the position acceptable.

"I will change, if you like," said Jasper. "Our names are not written in them. An abridged book is only a shorter one, and the book looks quite long."

"I don't know that the master meant you to change."

"He would not mind," said Avery, in a preoccupied manner. "It does not make them cost any more."

"Perhaps Miss Sarah will read one of her *Tales from Shakespeare* to you all," said Nurse, regarding Sarah as the proprietor of these.

The others gathered round their sister, Tamasin closing her book and Marcus inserting his finger in his place. Sarah read as they liked and approved, giving an impression of the print without superfluous or discomfiting emphasis. They drank in the words, as if they had no other means of access to them, Nurse listening with equal interest and as an accustomed member of the audience. Avery held a leaden soldier in his hand, and kept it turned to the reader, now and then adjusting it with an air that could only be described as maternal.

"Now here is the tea," said Nurse. "You must come to the table at once. The master does not like you to be careless because it is Christmas Day."

Avery selected some toys and put them at his place, guarding them from view with his hand.

"Two scones each," said Jasper.

"I only want one," said Avery, in rapid parenthesis, breaking off a piece to offer to his leaden charge.

"Come, don't play, Master Avery," said Nurse, in a tone too automatic to suggest an admonition.

"I hear a footstep on the stairs," said Tamasin. "I felt that a visit was due to us."

"Father only means to come and see us," said Avery, looking at Nurse for support.

"Well, Christmas Day has come and gone," said Horace. "I hope it has been a good one."

It was a pity that his words were not put as a question, as no one replied.

"Has it come up to your expectations? You must know your own opinion."

"Yes, Father," said Jasper.

"I had a stocking," said Avery.

"I know you had, and the others had got beyond them. So that was right for you all."

There was a pause.

"You did not want them, did you?"

There was still silence.

"You did want them!" said Horace, his voice breaking under its load of incredulity.

"Tamasin is only ten," said Marcus, "and Jasper and Sarah had them when they were eleven and twelve."

"And very unsuitable it was; that is why I put a stop to it. You did not want to be made ridiculous. Or did you want to be?"

"Children do have stockings."

"You did want to be!" said Horace. "Here is a boy in his twelfth year, who has had good Christmas presents, a suitable Christmas Day, and already has a tutor, who is out of conceit with things, because he has not had a stocking filled with toys! Well, I should not have believed it; I hardly can believe it."

"It is funny, isn't it?" said Avery, in an uncertain tone.

"You two eldest did not want stockings, did you?"

There was another pause.

"You did want them!" said Horace, investing his tone with a quaver of shrillness.

"We had got used to them, Father," said Sarah.

"But so you had to your cradle and your alphabet. You did not want to keep on with those. Or I suppose you did want to. What a very unusual thing! Would you have liked to have stockings all your lives?"

"No, but until we were older."

"Then we know what to do next year. Stop the presents,

stop the luncheon downstairs, stop all the reasonable things, and give you a stocking filled with gewgaws. Well, it will be easier and cheaper."

"We had the stockings as well as the other things," said Marcus.

"Oh, that is what it is. You have been deprived of something! That is what eats into your souls. Something has been taken from you. Well, I hope the tutor will put something into your heads beyond this mere acquisitiveness. It is not a pleasant thing. And you had been told that you were to give up stockings this year."

"Aunt Emilia might have given them to them," said Avery.

"Well, I am glad I prevented it. I am glad I did not yield to the unspoken pressure. So that was what was in the air; I felt there was something. Well, here is a matter, Nurse. Here have I been subjected to a volley of shafts, because the Christmas stockings have been discontinued!" Horace spoke with a tremor of laughter, as though he could not suppress it. "Christmas stockings for boys and girls of this age! What are we to do about it?"

Nurse offered no suggestion.

"Now," said Horace, changing his tone, "we will go downstairs and I will read to you the story of Christmas, the true story that underlies all we have been doing to-day, all the good things that have surrounded us. And then you will come back and be quiet until you go to bed."

"Will it be sad?" whispered Avery to Sarah, as they went to the stairs.

"No, it is only about the baby being born."

Avery turned and made a rapid selection from his stores, and returned his hand to his sister's.

"Now we will sit round the fire," said Horace. "No, not so near that we are thinking of our own comfort instead of more important things. What are those toys, Avery?"

"They are listening," said Avery, turning them to face his father.

Horace raised no objection to the addition to his audience, indeed looked faintly gratified by it.

"Which Gospel do you prefer?" he said, in a tone that assumed his children's knowledge.

"Saint Matthew's," said Marcus.

"You all feel the same?"

"Yes, Father," said four voices, while Avery looked at their owners in wondering respect.

"Now we have had our pleasure, and we must not yield to the temptation to forget what is underneath. We must give our minds to the real meaning of the Day. What are you laughing at, Tamasin? Now I require to be answered."

Tamasin and Marcus strove with their mirth.

"Well, have your laugh and get it over," said Horace, in a tone of carrying forbearance to its extreme limit.

His children were instantly grave.

"Laugh and get it over," said Horace, giving them a nod of some vehemence.

They could have done anything more easily.

"Well, if the amusement was just affectation, we will have our reading and put this exhibition behind. It is your welfare I am thinking of. I am not doing this for my own sake."

Horace glanced at his son and daughter, and as a result rose and closed his book and walked from the room.

Marcus and Tamasin were still shaken; Jasper displayed no interest; Sarah's face was inscrutable; and Avery showed his understanding by giving little, deliberate laughs from time to time.

"Why do they really laugh so much?" he said to Sarah.

This put an end to the emotion, and its victims faced each other and the future.

"Will Father read again?" said Avery. "You and I and Jasper didn't laugh."

"I don't know. I would not in his place," said Sarah.

Avery gave her a long look.

"It is not always Father's fault, is it?" he said, in his tentative manner.

"We had better go upstairs. We are not supposed to sit in the dining-room."

"Marcus and Tamasin mustn't, must they?" said Avery, shocked by the idea of delinquents in such an environment.

"Father kept saying how much better he liked ordinary things than religious ones," said Marcus.

"Well, they must be serious, of course," said Sarah. "No one can help that."

"They are sad, aren't they?" said Avery. "But we have to talk about them sometimes."

"That is really what Father said."

"You are on Father's side when you ought to be," said Avery, half to himself.

"Well, did you have a nice reading?" said Nurse.

"We did not have one," said Jasper.

"Marcus and I laughed," said Tamasin.

"As much as that?" said Nurse.

"Yes, as much," said Avery, in a grave manner.

"We can't expect to sleep, free of a cloud, on Christmas night," said Tamasin.

"It is the night when we should all do so," said Nurse.

"It is a good night, isn't it?" said Avery, looking at his possessions as if they confirmed this view.

"Would you like me to read to you?" said Nurse.

"The Christmas story might be counted to us for righteousness," said Tamasin.

"No, the master was reading you that," said Nurse, as though matters were not so easily mended. "What about another of Miss Sarah's *Tales*, if she will let us have one?"

"The same one, the same one," said Avery, on a clamorous note.

"Does anyone mind hearing it again?"

"No," said Marcus and Tamasin, feeling it was not for them to mind such a thing at the moment.

"No," said Jasper, who would never have minded it.

"No," said Sarah, who was minding other things.

"Well, what is the book?" said another voice, as Horace stood before them.

"*Lamb's Tales from Shakespeare*, sir, the book you gave to Miss Sarah," said Nurse, in a tone that betrayed no diplomacy.

"So you can listen to a story," said Horace.

"We like to hear something that we don't know," said Marcus.

"Well, of course you know the actual foundation of the Christian faith."

"Sarah and I were listening, Father," said Jasper.

Avery looked uncertain if his own state of attention warranted the claim.

"Nurse could read it to us now," he said.

"No, Nurse was not reading it," said Horace.

"Then Father could read it," said Avery, not turning his eyes on anyone.

"Do you want me to?" said Horace.

"Yes, please, Father," said Jasper, his voice seeming to be designed to lead the rest.

"Yes, please, Father," said Tamasin and Marcus.

"Are you an exception, Sarah?"

"No, Father."

Nurse was ready with a Bible at Horace's hand, and sat down with her own hands empty of book or work. Avery kept his playthings hidden in his chair, as if their participation could hardly be open on this occasion.

Horace did not look to see if gravity attended his words, as the matter was not in doubt.

CHAPTER V

"Good morning, Miss Buchanan," said Gertrude.

Miss Buchanan looked over her counter in silence, as it was not her habit to indulge in avoidable speech.

"Is it not a relief to have this milder weather?"

Miss Buchanan was not obliged to say, and therefore did not do so.

"Do you find it increases your custom? Or does that maintain an average?"

Miss Buchanan raised her eyes, as though seeing no reason why the question should be asked or answered. Conversation as a matter of form did not play a part in her life. If it had done so, it would have played a considerable one, and she saw nothing to be gained by it. She made an effort to gain what she needed, notably her bread.

She was a large, pale, ponderous woman of fifty-eight, with heavy hands and feet, a full, square face, indefinite features and small, pale, quick eyes. She had thick, tight plaits of hair, clothes that were not regarded even by herself, and an openly forbidding expression. She kept a general shop that deserved the name, as it provided the necessities of civilised life and many of its superfluities. It moreover exhibited a notice to the effect that letters could be addressed and called for there.

On this secondary traffic Miss Buchanan turned an equivocal eye, that did not add to the ease, already not complete, of those who availed themselves of it. Among these was Gertrude Doubleday, who had established in her home so complete an openness in correspondence, that she had herself to seek some method of eluding it. She had no guilty secrets and no dark side to her life, merely some relatives whose lack of advantages precluded the further one of her open recognition.

It can seldom be said that there is a key to a human personality, but there was one to Miss Buchanan's. She had spent her youth at a time when education was available, but could be avoided, and her parents had preferred her immediate service to her ultimate gain. The result was that she could not read. Her provision of facilities for those who could, might have suggested some breath of sympathy, had not her attitude to life gainsaid it. She lived in fear that the truth might emerge, and conducted all transactions with wariness and distance. She preferred a single life to a husband who knew her secret, and solitude to friends who might suspect it. She would have repulsed customers if her living had not depended on them. People showed her letters, drew her attention to newspapers, and generally obtruded their dependence on the art and its mastery. She might have acquired it, but it had assumed insuperable proportions. No one saw her as a tragic figure, or knew she was a successful one. She carried her head above her tragedy, and her secret was her own.

She relied on the postman for the names on the letters, on the ground that she found handwriting difficult, a position that involved no breach of truth. She was enabled by practice to memorise these at the moment. She kept no accounts and had everything paid for on the spot, and possessed moreover a facility in figures, that had developed with use. She would have been a good subject for the education she had missed. She was never seen with a book, as she judged too soundly to resort to this cover for the truth, and was often seen with needlework, both usual circumstances in the village. Some of her work appeared in the window, and no one knew what happened to the rest, but no one wished to know.

Gertrude glanced about for some usable commodity, as it was her custom to represent her real mission as a secondary one.

"Have you any rice, Miss Buchanan?"

"No letters for you," said the latter, searching on her shelves.

"But the right kind of rice, I hope. The kind that goes with curry, not the sort that makes the puddings."

Miss Buchanan changed the receptacles without a break in her movements, and made up the package without enquiry for further needs, as there was no other purpose to be served.

"It is a showery day," said Gertrude.

Miss Buchanan handed the parcel.

"Don't you want me to pay for the rice?" said Gertrude with a smile.

Miss Buchanan extended her hand.

"I am sorry I have not any less," said Gertrude, proffering a coin.

Miss Buchanan broached her cash-box and handed the change.

"I envy you your quickness at figures. It is a gift I should like to have myself."

Miss Buchanan cast her eyes over Gertrude's face, not finding it unnatural that a gift should be useful to both.

"A poor thing for a gift for anyone," she said, in sudden, deep tones.

"Oh, I do not know. Some little talents are not so common, and are of great use. If you use the word, 'little', that is. It was your idea that the gift was a small one."

Miss Buchanan did not pursue the topic, indeed found that all topics led in one direction, that of books.

"I will wait for a minute, until those clouds have passed."

Miss Buchanan was silent.

"If I may, that is."

"Yes."

"Here is the postman," said Gertrude, turning to the door and taking in a letter.

"You should not take in the letters. People would not have them sent here, if they wanted to be open about them," said Miss Buchanan, in instant and almost harsh reproof, and meeting Gertrude's eyes as she ended.

"The postman put it into my hand," said Gertrude quietly. "You should ask him to give the letters direct to you."

"You would not like it yourself."

"Oh, I should not mind," said Gertrude, with a little laugh, glancing at the envelope. "And it is mine. So no harm is done."

"You should not look at the envelopes; the letter might not have been for you."

"But it is. So all is well. And in future we must both take more care. And do you not think you are a little too downright in your methods—and even in your manners—over the letters? After all, you chose to deal with them."

Miss Buchanan glanced at the envelope, as if to confirm Gertrude's statement concerning it.

"I suppose your own letters are brought here with the others?" said Gertrude, in a casual, conversible tone, wishing to gloss over the awkwardness. "Do you have many letters from friends in other parts?"

"No," said Miss Buchanan, who had none, indeed could not have the friends, in case they should send the letters.

"There is some writing paper in that corner. Will you tell me the kind?"

Miss Buchanan handed a packet, and Gertrude put up her glasses.

"You did not use your glasses to read the address on the letter."

"Oh, one's own name is so familiar," said Gertrude, glancing at Miss Buchanan over the glasses, and then keeping them lowered to scan the shelves. "No, not that kind. The kind that is marked: 'Second quality.' That means the poorest, but I do not want it good. I have my own stamped paper for writing to my friends. No, do not open the boxes; the description is outside."

Miss Buchanan laid several boxes before Gertrude, with

a faint movement of her shoulders, as though pandering to familiar exactions.

"Yes, that kind, please. Why do you not put each kind with its own envelopes? You only have to look at the labels, and it would save you trouble."

Miss Buchanan replaced the boxes as they were, in a manner that suggested that she knew her methods.

"And now for the lightning calculation," said Gertrude, handing her coin with a smile.

Miss Buchanan returned the change without a movement of her face, accustomed to the interchange and comment beyond the point of response.

"Would you like me to lend you a book called *The Science of Numbers*? It is a popular book, put simply for the ordinary reader. I think it might interest you."

A hunted look crossed Miss Buchanan's face.

"I have no time to read."

"Not a little at a time? When you are alone at night."

"If I were able to read, I should not have to be alone," said Miss Buchanan, so nearly with her lips that her breath was quickened.

"Oh, those little bits at a time!" she said.

"You mean you like to read a whole book at once?"

"No, I do not mean that."

"Perhaps you would prefer some lighter books? Or perhaps you do not care for reading? I dare say the newspaper takes most of your spare time."

Miss Buchanan naturally did not take a paper, and the task of accounting for this took some of her time and much of her patience.

"Oh, papers! They put anything into people's heads."

"You like to sift what you read?" said Gertrude. "I am sure I know the books you would like. I shall bring some, and hear what you think of them. I know you will be honest."

Miss Buchanan, unable to support this statement, made a gesture of sudden recollection and disappeared behind the shop.

Gertrude stood in the doorway with the letter in her hand, and her face raised to the sky. Her daughter was coming to meet her, and now came into sight, and she stepped outside the shop with her eyes still lifted.

"The clouds have passed; I think we can venture homewards."

"They were never heavy, Mother. And why do you come so far to get these things? The other shop is nearer, and has pleasanter people in it."

"It might well do that. Poor Miss Buchanan does not suggest such a word. But I like to give a little custom to her. She has her living to earn."

"They say she repulses any advance, so that nothing can be done for her."

"Well, she did not repulse mine to-day," said Gertrude, in a light tone. "She actually asked me to stay and wait for the shower. That is why I waited. I was not really afraid. One hesitates to repudiate kindness that goes so against the grain. Will you just run back, my dear, and put this letter into her box? I took it from the postman by mistake; I was quite flustered by the access of cordiality. I do not like to go myself, as I ought not to have touched it. But it does not matter, as I could not see the name. By the next time we meet she will have forgotten it. She is not very systematic with the letters; I have noticed her odd ways."

Magdalen took the letter and retraced her steps; gave it an automatic glance and slackened her pace; glanced at it again and went on, swinging her hand, as though hardly aware that she held it. At the shop she paused to look in the window, putting the letter into the gauntlet of her glove, and then turned as if in recollection, and went back to her mother.

Gertrude was tracing a pattern on the ground with her umbrella, and looked up with a smile.

"So you managed without entering the lion's den. And the lioness did not spring out upon you?"

"No, she was safe in her lair."

"Poor thing! She spends too much time in it. I wish we could do something for her. She is a person who gives me a feeling that she needs some kind of help."

"We can do nothing but give her our custom."

"Yes, well, I have always done that. It does seem to me that a single woman, supporting herself, has a right to expect as much as that from her neighbours, even if she is not placed quite at their door. It is not so much trouble to take a little walk."

"Why does she put up that notice about letters?"

"Well, I suppose some people have no address, or have their reasons for not using it. And it makes a little extra profit."

"The notice says the letters may be called for. That looks as if the people who expect them, live in the place. I suppose they are private letters."

"I should say they are, definitely and deliberately private," said Gertrude, with her little laugh. "I do not know if this was one of them. She should have taken it in herself, if it was. Perhaps it was one of her own, though it is somehow a new idea that Miss Buchanan has letters."

"Miss Buchanan conducting a correspondence!" said Magdalen with a smile, aware of a flight of fancy, though not of its extent.

"She has not much time, with the work of her house and shop. But I have offered to lend her some books. It might be truer to say I insisted on it."

"Will it be much good? People say she never even takes a paper."

"They share such things between them. She might not have one to herself."

"I cannot picture Miss Buchanan taking her turn, and getting through a paper in an allotted time," said Magdalen, still protected by her imagination.

"Well, come along, my child. You are inclined to take your time, and your brother will be in for luncheon. Do not linger in your room before you come down. Women must not keep men waiting."

Magdalen did not do these things. She came down almost at once, with her clothes untouched and a smouldering look in her eyes, that recalled occasions of her childhood. Her mother assigned it to some emotional disturbance over her own words, and took pains to be fond and flattering to her, but without result.

"I have no more work to-day; I can begin to live," said Gideon.

"If you put your heart into your work, you would live the whole time," said Gertrude.

"The course would be fatal to me. Already I see my life as a series of narrow escapes."

"People cannot make an effort from morning till night, Mother," said Magdalen.

"That would be my definition of a day's work. Mr. Lamb and I agreed that the failing of our energy should be the sign that our work was done."

"Some people's work would never begin, on that principle," said Gideon. "What a crude line for your talk to take! And what a brutal conclusion! I did not know Lamb was as ruthless as a woman."

"We cannot broach any subject without your bringing in Mr. Lamb, Mother," said Magdalen. "We never say a word without your quoting him. People will be talking about it."

"Then they can talk. I can be a natural, open person and an interested friend, without concerning myself with them."

"Carelessness of opinion is not a virtue."

"Isn't it?" said Gideon. "It seems that it must be; it sounds such a very noble thing."

"Well, it may be one of my qualities, virtue or not," said Gertrude. "I am sure I do not know if it is."

"It is a very dubious quality," said Magdalen. "Other people become involved. I think you forget that."

"There is something that you forget, my dear, and that is yourself."

"Are you really unconscious of what you are doing, Mother? You are getting more and more involved with Mr. Lamb, and his cousin is driven back on himself, and has nothing to do but think of Mrs. Lamb and write to her, and generally hasten the day of the overthrow of everything. And when the children are fatherless or motherless, as the case may be, we shall have to face the truth that it is upon your head. Or anyhow other people will face it."

"They can do so; I care not what they do," said Gertrude, with a snap of her fingers. "I am my own mistress. I am indifferent to their kindly offices."

"Let us leave other people out of it," said Gideon. "It is not their business, and it seems they do not realise it."

"Mother is blind to the result of following her instincts. She blunders forward without a glance to the right or left."

"I might say the same to you," said Gertrude. "Indeed I must say it. Homes have been broken up for less cause than this. It is not my concern or my fault that Mortimer Lamb and his cousin's wife are what they are to each other. If they are anything; I do not know; I do not pry into other people's lives; I recognise that they are their own."

"It is a pity you have not a little more insight into them. You stumble across them as if they did not exist. You think of nothing but the impression you are making on the man of the moment. Nothing but your own little success counts. It looms so large that you are blind and deaf to other claims."

"To your own claims, you mean; that is what is generally meant by that. You have not had your own success, and another woman's is not the right remedy. My poor child, that is not the truth? What are you trying to say? Say it to your mother, but do not wrap it up in ugly little speeches that have no meaning."

"I want to say nothing but what I have said. It is playing with fire, Mother. To work on the feelings of a married man, and accept any result. Tragic things may come of it; tragic things are coming." Magdalen stumbled into her mother's arms and hid her face on her shoulder.

"Well, what a light to shed on my daily path!" said Gertrude, looking over her daughter's head to smile at her son. "It may be stony-hearted of me, but I had not bestowed much thought on Horace Lamb's affections, though he has certainly gone some way towards winning mine. He is a pathetic figure to my mind. I should say it is he, who is thrown back upon himself, not his cousin. That something has come between them is not our fault. So run away for a while and come back to us quite yourself. We shall not begin luncheon without you; the man must wait for a woman this time."

Magdalen vanished, and Gertrude smiled and sighed as she took up her needlework.

"What is this that has come upon us?" said Gideon.

"It is upon Magdalen that it has come, and with a force in proportion to its coming late. I hope it has also come upon Mortimer Lamb, or there are breakers ahead."

"Have not some of the breakers spent themselves? It is fortunate that all my engagements do not lead to this. It might mean a premature retirement."

Gertrude was not in need of this kind of help.

"Poor child! It is a transparent case," she said, with a compassion that was not without its zest. "It is fortunate that she has not bottled it all up within herself. There is not much risk of that in our family. And as long as it gets the light and air, there is no great danger. Things only ferment and fester in the dark. I knew it would all come out to her mother. But I had to exercise some patience first. It was a minute before I realised what it all meant. She relied on her mother's intuition. Well, she had every right to do that; I am only sorry it failed for a moment."

"She suddenly sees and knows so much. She does not seem the same person."

"Her perception is sharpened by her feeling," said

Gertrude, shaking out her work. "There is not much that a person in her state does not see, especially a woman. Does not feel, rather; it is a matter of the heart rather than the head. But it soon passes to the head; it translates itself into knowledge."

"We must not betray her to anyone."

"Now do you really think that warning is necessary for her mother? Who is the natural person to guard her from prying eyes? Do you think I would let them touch her? Am I a bachelor brother like some other excellent people? I think my Magdalen is fortunate. She has all the deeper feeling about her, and the easier as well, to fill in the gaps. Yes, the brother's feeling will do its work."

"My feelings are not easy; they go deep like everything about me."

"Now there is the spice of jealousy! There is the feeling of the male, when another usurps his place. We are all showing the natural reaction. Yes, we are true to type."

"So Magdalen likes Mortimer Lamb better than us?"

"She does at the moment; we must just accept it. It may pass off; it may take the vanishing course. Here she comes, the poor, dear child! Now careful is the word; discretion is the better part." Gertrude put a finger on her lips, with the touch of excitement still about her.

Magdalen edged into the room and seemed to thread her way across it, though there were no obstacles in her path. She came to the table and paused without looking at her mother. The latter took off her glasses and came to supply the plates, while her daughter waited to hand them.

"Gideon; yourself, dear child," she said with a smile. "My Magdalen is herself again, thinking of what she can do for other people."

Magdalen slipped to her seat, as though this side of her personality might be elusive.

"Yes, there is no doubt that something has come between the Lamb cousins," said Gertrude, in a manner of resuming the subject to avert a permanent avoidance of it.

"I doubt if the elder knows the nature of the barrier; he is a man to whom integrity would be so much the matter of course."

"There has been no equality between them," said Magdalen, her tone suggesting that there was turmoil beneath her calm. "Mortimer has spent his life in a difficult place. And Charlotte's giving him a woman's natural sympathy would lay the basis of feeling."

"That is how it began, I dare say, my wise little woman. But a feeling does not stand still, you know. It moves in one direction or the other, and there is little doubt of the direction in which this has moved. In Mortimer's place I would have had a profession by hook or by crook."

"Money was not forthcoming," said Gideon. "It would have had to be by crook."

Magdalen gave an emotional laugh.

"Well, the brother comes to the rescue," said Gertrude, rising. "I will leave the feeling that has stood a lifetime, to do its work. After all, that came first."

"It does not preclude another," said her son. "I could be glad to see another added to it."

"I always think that is an odd kind of gladness," said Gertrude, standing with an impartial, open air. "I never quite believe in it, or in the feeling that allows it. One of them cannot be the real thing. A really strong feeling does preclude others. It must. It does."

"I believe Mrs. Lamb is to return soon," said Gideon.

"In about six weeks," said Magdalen.

"How do you know?" said her mother

"Oh, I have no idea. I suppose I heard it somewhere."

"You have not been meeting Mortimer Lamb without my knowledge?"

"How could I meet him? How could I meet anyone without my family's watching me from before and behind?"

"You would be poorly off without your family, my child. It is the only thing that is your safeguard at the moment."

"Everyone wants to cast off his family sometimes," said Gideon.

"Now I do not," said his mother, with the same open air. "I simply want to share everything with them. I should never keep anything or anyone in my own life apart from them. It may be unusual; that I cannot say."

"I should think it is unique," said her son.

"Well, I have heard the word applied to myself. Whether rightly or wrongly, I am not the person to judge."

Magdalen gave another laugh.

"Sharing so often amounts to sharing other people's things."

"Well, it is difficult not to want to share those," said Gideon.

"It would only make them the more one's own," said Gertrude. "I should feel it gave me more of them, not less."

"Well, that is a good reason for sharing," said her son.

"Yes, that is the way to look at things, and talk of them, and deal with them," said Gertrude, still standing before her children. "A share for everyone, an open yielding of them to everyone's eyes. Then nothing can ferment or decay underneath. It will remain whole and sweet, secure in the natural safeguard of the light of day. Is not that so, my Magdalen?"

Magdalen went rapidly and almost furtively from the room.

"Has she any real feeling for Mortimer Lamb?" said Gertrude.

"My dear Mother, we can see she has. And why should she not? He seems a pleasant person. And I dare say his cousin would do something for him."

"It is his cousin's wife who holds the purse-strings, and she is prepared to yield him everything, herself included, as far as I can pursue the truth."

"Do you really think there is a break-up coming there?"

"I do," said his mother, in a deliberate tone. "I cannot shut my eyes to it."

"Then no wonder Magdalen is upset; she could not have more reason. Is Horace Lamb prepared?"

"He has no inkling of it as yet. He is not prepared. His bark is approaching the rocks and carrying him along unawares. Of course he is not a happy man, not satisfied in his lot. But he must feel the shock; there must be the rough moment of the crash and the turn, before the calm."

"Poor Magdalen!" said Gideon.

"She will throw it off and be herself again. She has enough in her life to satisfy her."

"She does not find it enough. She is no longer satisfied."

"What has been, will be again. We know who had her heart, and will have it."

"She had given it to no one else, but she has done so now."

"It may not mean so much; she is of an emotional nature."

"Emotions are not less strong, because people are prone to them."

"She has a very good brother," said Gertrude, as if this were hardly to be expected. "It will be enough for her again."

"Her emotions took the only outlet. They have found another. Things can never be the same."

"No. No. Not the same. That will not be the word. There will be the difference. She will be an awakened person. She has not been that, my Magdalen. She will have more to give."

"Not to us. People do not give away their feeling, to have it left. You have said that yourself. You are not consistent."

"I dare say not; I hardly try to be. There is so much truth on all the different sides of things."

"You will have to be patient with her."

"I can be patient. You need not fear for her mother. And

so you need not fear for her. Indeed I think I have been patient already. And now I have an errand of my own. When Magdalen comes back, just be yourself with her."

"Unfortunately that is all I can be."

Gertrude spent some time in her room, and came downstairs in her outdoor clothes, and Magdalen came smoothly from the back of the hall and joined her.

"So you are going to walk with me, my dear?"

"We are going to the same house. So we cannot very well walk apart. We hardly have any choice."

Gertrude was taken aback both by words and tone, and walked on, now and then uttering a commonplace. They reached their destination without having mentioned it.

The door was opened by Bullivant.

"Is Mr. Lamb at home?"

"He is recovering from a chill, ma'am, and is resting this afternoon."

"Will you say that an old friend wishes to see him?"

Bullivant almost looked a question.

"Yes, I know I do not come under that head," said Gertrude, smiling. "Well, I will stand on my own claim. Ask if he will see me."

Bullivant returned with a face that might have been a mask, and was one, if a mask is a cover for what is behind, and Gertrude, as she preceded him into Horace's room, glanced back as though at some threat, and almost saw the mask withdrawn.

"Got in and welcome, Mrs. Selden! It makes one wonder what the mistress's word would be."

"If she were able to voice it, I think we can guess her comment. My own outlook is similar. I have no leaning to the spurious. A thing must ring true for me, whether it be word or person. Never pose as being what you are not, Miriam, and can never be."

"It can be seen what I am."

"Well, be satisfied with it. A good, useful girl is enough, without her picturing herself as more than can be genuine.

It would be a counterfeit, which is an odd thing to aspire to."

Miriam was silent.

"And if there is an element of living for others in your lot, be thankful for it, as I have been, as something that is for your highest welfare."

"I think ordinary welfare would be enough," said Miriam, not without a gleam in her eye.

"And what have you to complain of?"

"Nothing," said Miriam, with sincerity and haste.

Gertrude had gone up to Horace and taken his hand, while her daughter followed with a suggestion of walking on tiptoe.

"Now you get back to your sofa," she said, putting her hands on his shoulders. "You got up from it, as we came in. Don't think that I did not see; don't think such things escape me. You will be back on it before we exchange a word. We heard you were not yourself, but I hope that a friend is welcome and may help you to become so."

"I have been shut away from life. It is time the interlude ended; it is the easier part."

"Yes, it is life that is difficult."

Horace smiled at Magdalen and motioned her to a seat, unable to follow her mother in blindness to her presence, and Gertrude moved, as if unconsciously, for her to pass.

"Friends can always help each other," she said, not resuming her position, indeed hardly aware of having left it.

"I do without help. It does not come into my life. I am supposed to be above it, to give it, to do anything but need it."

"And your position calls for so much. Father and mother both. Protector, counsellor, ruler, if it must be. It is a heavy course to steer alone."

"It was thought I was going to be ill, and I seem to need help, not for the illness, but for having escaped it. I feel the danger of recovery; I could have been ill more safely."

"We have all felt the security of illness," said Gertrude, "except those like my Magdalen there, who have never left the first haven. For none of us is the chief danger there. It lies, as you say, outside. But in your case it threatens yourself, and not as you seem to think, others through you."

The talk was maintained by Gertrude and Horace, heard by Magdalen, and at length interrupted by Emilia.

"Now an end must always come. We have a grateful invalid, and must hope for obedient friends."

Gertrude rose at once and went to the door, with hardly a glance at Horace, no glance at her daughter, and just a pressure of Emilia's hand as she passed.

"Obedience to a higher authority is indeed one of the duties of life—of our duties to life. I know it. I have had to impose my own will."

She left the house, seeming in some way exalted, and Magdalen followed with short, hurried steps, as though in an effort to keep up with her. She wore a more settled expression, and her mother resumed their normal footing.

"So Mortimer Lamb was not there to-day."

"Well, we did not ask for him. It was Mr. Lamb whom you wanted to see."

"Well, I think our visit did him good. It seemed to be what he needed. It is easy to prescribe solitude, when the right companionship is the real need. Monotony is not a good medicine."

"When his wife returns, there will be more life in the house. It will be itself again."

"And a queer self that seems to be, from what one can gather. A self that carries the material for explosion within it. Well, we can only wait. It will soon come."

"You sound as if you wanted it to do so."

"I see no advantage in delay, if it is the destined thing."

"Well, we will hope it is not."

"What good will that do? People talk as if their hopes will influence the future."

"And also as though their prophecies will. And the

hope in this case seems to me a more generous thing."

"The breaking up of an unhappy home is no cause for tears," said Gertrude, gently. "It is a good and healthy change, and the sooner it comes, the better."

"There cannot be a sadder thing than children deprived of their mother."

"No," said Gertrude. "No. I am at one with you there. The children and mother must not be parted. Things must not be arranged like that."

"Well, I do not suppose you want the children."

"No, I have children of my own," said Gertrude, turning and taking her daughter's face in her hand. "And I would not change them, even though one is a mischievous person, who does not understand her mother."

Horace and his aunt were left alone.

"I hope you are not exhausted," said Emilia. "Nothing is so tiring as two people talking at once."

"That did not happen," said her nephew. "I do not know why the daughter came."

"In the hope of seeing Mortimer. But I did not send him in. I do not push those things in one direction or another."

"That is a new idea to me."

"So I thought. To me it is getting familiar."

"Does Mortimer know?"

"He can hardly be blind to it."

"He cannot be thinking of it."

"No, I suppose he could not support a wife."

"I have never thought of his wishing to do so."

"No," said Emilia. "When someone has not the means of support, we think that giving him that meets all his need."

"I cannot imagine my life without him. He would have to remain in the place."

"You could impose your own conditions," said Emilia.

She gave her nephew what he needed, picked up a letter and put it at his hand, and left him to recover.

When she returned she found another difference. He was pacing the room in a manner that was new in him, and hardly seemed to see or hear. She supposed he was startled by the threat of losing Mortimer, and encouraged his going to bed as a means of escape into solitude.

CHAPTER VI

"Now I am not expected," said Charlotte. "I am guilty of the folly of an unexpected return. You are doing what I do not approve, and I must expect you to be doing it. And you have not done any of the things you meant to do before we met again. You put them off to the last moment, which is always the best, as it holds so much. And what is the good of fulfilling a person's wishes, when she is not there to feel them? And I have come to seem a stranger to you. When people are out of sight, they are out of mind. Minds by themselves seem to be so little good."

"You are back in the minds now," said Emilia, looking at the children. "And we have often had our work to keep you out. They have done their part."

"And none of the children has grown out of recognition. Indeed none of them has grown at all. They are smaller for their age than I thought. Even Jasper has not advanced any further into the awkward stage. And Mortimer does not look an older and more ordinary man, or at any rate not more ordinary. And Emilia is not just a thought frailer; she is just the same; she has never been frail. And although Horace has been ill, he has not that look of having just escaped death. And after all, we have all escaped it; I suppose he has really escaped it the least."

"You have escaped it, haven't you?" said Avery, clinging to her hand. "You might have been drowned in the sea."

"There ought to be something between death and a safe homecoming," said Charlotte. "Neither of those enhances people's importance. Returning is what everyone does, and disappearance cannot really add to anyone. You will soon be saying that it seems I have never been away, and that tells its tale."

"Father did not tell us you might not come back," said Avery.

"There was no need, my little son," said Horace. "I was sure that Mother would come back, and I was right."

"Were you sure?" said Avery to Sarah.

"Yes, as sure as it was possible to be."

"And Bullivant does not look a day older," said Charlotte. "And he is moving about amongst us just as he was on the day I left. Of course it is the most likely thing, but I feel rather surprised and grateful! And I think George does look a day older, indeed quite a number of days. It is all a great success."

"And the right kind for a short time," said Emilia, while Bullivant's glance at George showed him hardly concerned with a difference that had no result.

"Things do take so long," said Charlotte. "The only real change I see, is that everything seems to be better."

She looked about her home and saw she had struck the root of the difference. Things were better, the food, the fires, the lights, the children's clothes, these last indeed being those she remembered as their best.

"Did you expect me? Had any rumour reached you? Did you know the boat had arrived?"

"We knew nothing," said Mortimer, speaking for the first time. "We had heard nothing. It is a complete surprise."

At the sound of his voice Charlotte caught another change. She knew why she had thought him looking older. He seemed to be apart from Horace and the children, who were strangely at one and at peace. His welcome was more uncertain than she had expected, as the children's was more childish and less deep. A relapse into childishness was what had made her think them smaller. The voice of her eldest son, addressing her youngest, broke her thought.

> "'Fie, fee, fo, fum,
> I smell the blood of an Englishman.
> If he be living or if he be dead,
> I'll grind his bones to make my bread.'"

Avery fled across the room and into his father's chair, and Horace put his arm about him.

"You will have tea with us to-day, because Mother has come home. There is no need to devour each other. Bread and butter is better to eat than little boy."

Avery fell into mirth and maintained it until it had an artificial sound, with the evident purpose of pleasing his father.

"You are not very tidy for tea in the drawing-room," said Emilia.

"We look better than we did in our old, small clothes," said Jasper.

"So you are not smaller than you were, but larger," said Charlotte.

"It was the clothes that were small," said Avery. "And they did get smaller. Clothes can shrink."

"They hardly deserved the name," said Tamasin, "if clothes are coverings."

"I don't suppose people looked at us in them," said Marcus.

"It may be proper to suppose they did not," said Sarah, "but it was not the truth."

"They look at us less in these," said Tamasin. "They seemed to prefer the sight that was less suitable for them."

"It is people's disadvantages that people think about," said Sarah, "even children's."

"What a pack of little cynics!" said Horace.

"We can stay for the sermon now," said Avery, looking at his mother. "That is one thing that is not as nice as before."

"You and Nurse can come out, if you like," said his father.

"Mother and I can go out," said Avery.

"No, Mother will stay with me. It must be with Nurse or no one."

"Then it can be with Nurse," said Avery, in a comfortable tone.

"We are getting more like other children," said Marcus. "But I think we know more about things than they do. It seems that the less people have, the more they get to know."

"Well, a little childishness will not come amiss," said Horace.

"Not now, will it?" said Avery. "Not even for Sarah."

"Not for any of you," said his father.

Charlotte heard her husband and children, and felt she did not know where to turn her eyes. She checked an impulse to glance at Mortimer, felt that he controlled a similar impulse, glanced at Emilia and saw the same thing.

"Why are you inclined to find fault with us, now that Father doesn't do it?" said Marcus to his aunt.

"Is that the case? Well, someone must exercise a wholesome check."

"Why should it be wholesome?"

"Well, if there is reason to find fault, it probably is."

"But Mother won't do it," said Avery, leaning against Charlotte.

"We must not expect things before their time," said Horace.

"It was a sorry business when they were expected," said Marcus, half to himself.

"Aunt Emilia should have found fault with me," said Horace, keeping his eyes from his wife. "I was left to do it for myself."

"And people don't often do that," said Avery.

"Mother will be glad," said Jasper. "She won't always have to be against you."

"Mother and I want the same thing in our hearts."

"I expect you will sometimes forget to be different," said Marcus.

"No doubt I shall, but you will be patient with me. And I may not forget so often. I am as glad of the difference as you can be. I suffered from my own mistakes. It was not only you who had to pay a price. I see the whole now."

"Does being ill make people see things?" said Marcus.

"I should have thought they would have to be very ill for that," said Jasper.

Horace smiled to himself.

"Are you cold, Sarah?" he said.

"No, not yet, thank you, Father. I am only taking precautions."

"Prevention is better than cure," said Tamasin.

"I will make up the fire," said Jasper, running forward. "I would have made a pile, if I had known Mother would be here."

Horace watched him with an easy but unseeing expression. Emilia glanced at Charlotte, and Bullivant did the same.

"I will carry Mother's cup to the fire," said Avery.

"I smell the blood of an Englishman," said Jasper, advancing towards him.

Avery turned to escape, tripped over a rug, and fell with the cup shattered about him.

"Poor Mother's refreshment is deferred," said Tamasin.

Avery gave a loud laugh that quavered into tears.

"He is not hurt, is he?" said Horace.

"He would not cry if he were not," said Marcus.

"I meant really hurt."

"Well, I don't suppose he is injured."

"No, he is not hurt, Father," said Sarah.

Avery looked at a cut on his hand, as if he could hardly support this view.

"I will bind it up for you," said Jasper.

"Jasper does smell the blood of an Englishman now," said Tamasin.

"No!" said Avery, in strong repudiation of the idea.

"One of you bring me some tea," said Sarah, sitting down by her mother.

"Why don't you get it for yourself?" said Marcus.

"You can wait on your elder sister. I have done a good deal of looking after you."

"You have not done much lately; you are not as nice as you used to be."

"She used to be too nice," said Avery.

"Perhaps I did," said Sarah, looking at Charlotte. "It is not true that it makes people happier to think of other people before themselves."

"That is too unnatural to be wholesome," said Tamasin, "but none of the rest of us is prone to the error."

"We must see that Sarah does not fall into it too much," said Horace.

"It is best to be just nice enough," suggested Avery.

"Out of the mouths of babes," said Horace, smiling at his wife.

"Have you all done your work for Mr. Doubleday?" said Emilia.

"Procrastination is the thief of time," said Jasper, in a careful tone.

"It has stolen it in this case," said Tamasin. "It is too late to do it now."

"Well, Mother does not return every day," said Horace.

"Unhappily the tutor does," said Tamasin. "It is getting difficult to find excuses for him."

"Well, you are provided on this occasion," said her father.

"With whom did you learn the most?" said Charlotte. "The tutor or Aunt Emilia?"

"Aunt Emilia," said Marcus.

"I am not sure," said Sarah.

"I am," said Tamasin. "I learned more from Aunt Emilia."

"Sarah learns more from Mr. Doubleday than we do," said Marcus. "But Jasper does not seem to learn at all."

"And he is the one who made the tutor necessary," said Horace, in a rueful manner.

"Well, he cannot always depend on his family," said Charlotte. "He must find his level. The plan will serve its purpose."

"Mr. Doubleday has found the level, and thinks it a low one," said Tamasin.

"What does he think of yours?" said Horace.

"Better, but not too well."

"And Sarah's?"

"Better still," said Tamasin, taking a seat in front of her father and lifting her eyes to his.

"Why do you always sit where Father can see you?" said Marcus.

"I hope she always will," said Horace.

"Even in the other times she used to," said Avery.

"I like to think of that," said Horace. "Now I shall not be able to read to you to-night. My excuse is the same as yours to the tutor. Mother does not return every day."

"Sarah will read to us," said Avery, "and that is the best. Things are always best, that are once the best, aren't they?"

"That is quite fair," said Horace.

"You wish you had always been like you are now, don't you?" said Marcus, looking at his father.

"Yes, I do, but it is never too late to mend. And I hope I have not found it so."

"In a way I should have thought it always was. Are people often so different from what they seem?"

"I may have been an extreme case. I fear you have much to forget."

"Do people ever forget things that have gone on for a long time?"

"Then much to forgive," said Horace.

"It seems all the nicer now, because of its not being nice before," said Avery, with his note of suggestion.

"My little kind son!" said Horace.

Emilia rose and left the room, as though to put a check on the talk, and Marcus looked after her uncertainly.

"May I come to the first part of the reading?" said Horace.

"Sarah can read to a grown-up man," said Avery, putting his hand in his sister's and then transferring it to Horace's.

"So it is safe to leave us together, Charlotte," said Mortimer, at once. "That means one thing. We are to make the most of the chance."

"What is it? Is Horace going to die? Or has he just escaped death? I did not know he had been as ill as this. Is this the self we are to accept? Are we to forget the past, in your case fifty-four years of it? I must hear the tale; I must hear it from human lips."

"The change is before your eyes. I need not describe it. It came after the illness, but may not result from that. Horace suddenly became the father that you see. What is behind it we cannot know or guess. He hardly speaks a word to me. He is as different as he is to the children, but in the opposite way."

"What has he come to know? That is the question; that is the solution, the climax. I think he must know the whole. Horace does not guess. If he did, he would have guessed long ago."

"We cannot take the children from him, now that he is bound to them by every natural tie. Kindness and sympathy soon win children's hearts. It is an easy way."

"They soon win anyone's. The way may not be so easy, but it is the best. It almost wins mine, as I watch it. It recalls the hopes of my youth. But for Horace to take it, and take it openly! I believe it when it is before my eyes."

"It will often be there," said Mortimer. "As often as the children are, and that is much oftener than it used to be. They are becoming the meaning of his life, and he the centre of theirs."

"He will never give them up," said Charlotte, as if the words broke from her.

"That is what it means, Charlotte. And you will not give

them up either. You are a mother before you are anything else, and you were a wife first of all. What can you give to me, to make it all worth while?"

"I should have nothing to give you," said Charlotte, breaking into tears. "Anxiety for the children, remorse at leaving them, fear lest Horace should fall back into his old ways, or go too far with the new. It would be little indeed. I could not offer it."

"I would take it, if you did. But I know you will not, and so do you. The home has become a happy one, and our hopes were based on its unhappiness. Horace saw that our future was founded upon the sand."

"What else has he seen? And when did he see it?"

"He must see it all. He must have come on some proof. How, I do not know. When, I do not know exactly. I have no clue. No letters came to the house. Indeed no letter has come from you for weeks. I was dependent on Horace for news of you."

"You should have had a letter when he had his last. I sent it to Miss Buchanan's. It must be there unless it has gone astray. You had better ask at some time, in case it falls into the wrong hands. It is enough that Horace should know our hearts. And now we dare not look forward."

"And Horace dares. I do not know if you know it, Charlotte, but Horace is a very brave man. He has shown great courage in the last weeks. He made the change suddenly and fully, and before every eye. He walks up to the cannon's mouth with every minute. Indeed he spends his life in front of it. He will walk up to it now, as personified in you."

"I can personify it," said Charlotte, clenching her hands.

Horace entered the room with Emilia, as though bringing a witness to the coming scene.

"Charlotte," he said, looking his wife in the eyes, "I have not spoken to you of the thing that is between us. It may be that I shall not speak of it."

"I shall speak of it to you," said Charlotte on the instant.

"We will not have a great and unnatural silence. Mortimer and I could not suffer the things in this house; we were at the end of our power to suffer. We could let helpless children suffer no longer, after seeing them do so all their lives. We thought of the way of escape for us all, and we were going to take it. It would have been the right way, and the only right one. But I have come home to find this difference, this difference that there might always have been. If you had been like this always, Horace! If you had lived this life from the first! This is proof that you could have done so, that you could have made the hard path easy. It does not show the past years in a better light. But for the moment our case is gone. Whether it may return or not, is another thing, but for the moment it is gone. The future is in your hands, and you have the power to hold it. But the past is my tragedy and your fault. You must not be a martyr. You put me to a longer martyrdom."

"The past will not return," said Horace. "I know that my road is a rough one, but the knowledge will help me to follow it."

"You know you are making the effort late? You have those years to live down. The children have those years in their memories, their spoiled childhood in their hearts. Any lapse must come as something added to these. You have Marcus to deal with as well as Avery. Avery has been protected; things have been softened for him; he does not stand outside the truth. The others cannot help their position. You must just accept it. They will be hard on your mistakes. That is your legacy from your own past."

"You speak well, Charlotte."

"It is the result of my not having spoken before. I have not always been silent in my heart."

"Why did you observe this silence? What was the reason of it? Why did you not speak of the sufferings? They might have been eased. It would have been fairer to you and to me."

"I spoke many times in the first years, and found the

uselessness of speech. You know that, Horace; your memory is not so poor. You were not the man you are at the moment, the man you have suddenly become. It is an utter and sudden change. And it shows what you might have been. It points the way to the past that might have been ours, and will never be. It does not only do one thing."

"I did not know you were a hard woman, Charlotte."

"You know that seeing her children suffer day by day will make any woman hard. You are not without ordinary knowledge. You are not so much a person apart. If you did not know such things, you would not have done as you have done. And you know the truth that lies behind us. You crushed the spring of childhood, bound it with constraint and fear, forced it to deception and visited the wrong you caused. You burdened and wrung a mother's heart. You did it month after month and year after year. You knew you were doing it. You know now what you did. Your present course proves your knowledge. I may speak well. I have often heard these words echoing in my heart, and wondered you did not hear them. I am saying them now, not to accuse you or spoil your efforts, but to vindicate the innocent. Mortimer and I did right, not wrong, as you did always wrong and never right. And now it is clear between us, and need not be said again."

"Do you not expect me to have things to say on my side?"

"No. I know you have nothing to say. And you also know it."

"What do you expect from me, Mortimer?" said Horace, as though he did not hear his wife.

"I expect nothing, my dear boy. I have got out of the way of looking for a word or a glance."

"We will put that note aside. It comes to seem a strange one. I have to say the one thing, that I know the truth. And I want no word from you. I can see you have none to say."

"It does seem to fit in," said Mortimer.

"You will not do as you have done. You will not live

under my roof and eat my bread, and seek to undermine my life. You will cease to be a base man and a false friend. You have done ill by me; I am not going to say more; I have done ill myself. But my sin has been more helpless, and I have suffered and made amends. And I am not the only one who will start again. You will lead another life, or there is nothing more between you and me. Whose bread will you eat, if it is not mine?"

"Charlotte's. I must eat someone's. I have none of my own."

"Will Charlotte give up her children for you?"

"That is what it is. I knew the meaning of it. The children are to be bound to you."

"That is the meaning, Mortimer, though it is not the only one. I have seen for some time that I took the wrong part in my family life. But I could not bring myself to alter it. This has brought me to it, shown me the way I must take; forced me to it, if you like."

"It seems to have done a good deal for you. You may come to be grateful."

"You have not asked anything from me, but you have always taken it, and it came to your meaning to take my all. For me there has been a reward in changing my life; for you there will be less reward. But you will do it, as I have done it. You will not remain under my roof, a menace to those it shelters. There are two things that you may do. You may marry and remain on the place, and I will afford you a roof and a competence. Or you may leave it, and I will still see that you can live. You may not remain here unmarried. You need not ask the reason. Is there anything more to say?"

"I hardly think so, my dear boy. I do not think there can be anything left. There can hardly be so much."

"So you admit the truth of my words?"

"Have I done that? Then I clearly have nothing to say."

"You have been a good friend to me, Mortimer, or rather you have been a dear one. But you have cut the ground from under our feet. Now that we both begin again, in remorse for the past, in amended lives, we cannot do it together. In future we go forward apart."

"Just as our mutual influence would be so good. We seem only to have had the worst of each other. And how am I to go forward?"

"You can help yourself, and there are others who will help you. I will do my best for you, though you have not done yours for me."

"Well, I must leave it to you and the others. You are in a beautiful place. I do not wonder you talk about it. It must be wonderful to have power, and use it with moderation and cruelty. We can so seldom be admired and self-indulgent at the same time."

"If you marry, you may remain here. And there is some-one who would fill the place. You know that Magdalen Doubleday would take it. Could you ask anything better?"

"You know I did ask it; you did not pretend not to know. It is my asking something better that has led to this."

"She would make you a good wife, Mortimer. And she is the most blameless creature. I am sure she has never hurt a fly."

"Well, that is nice of her. Most of us do begin by hurting flies. Not that she would be blameless, if she did it."

"She would give you all she has. Her heart is in her eyes when she looks at you."

"How did you know? You were the person who did not see it. My heart is in my mouth when you talk of it. Perhaps it does sound as if we might have something in common. But not the most fundamental things."

"Why do you not take to her?"

"Well, I think you have given the reasons. We seem to see her with the same eyes."

"You have not so much to give."

"Have I not, my dear boy? It is for you to decide. Giving has not formed a part of my experience. I have learned to accept, which is in itself a gift."

"Well, take what she has to give, in that spirit."

"But I do not think she has anything to give. I do not think tutors' sisters have."

"Do you not count herself?"

"I try not to," said Mortimer.

"I said I would see that you could live."

"Why do you not leave me to die, instead of planning a living death?"

"You could not be left to your plans for yourself. And you do not want to die any more than I do."

"Well, perhaps just a little more than that."

"The love of life is strong in us all. You would know that, if you had ever faced death."

"Why do you talk about my facing death, when you have said you would see that I could live?"

"There is that cottage by the mill."

"So there is, and that must be somebody's fault, though one does not like to be hard on people. Do you mean it would do for someone to face death in? It would certainly be damp."

"It is really a little house."

"So it is. Really a little one. Of course that is what a cottage would be."

"You cannot ask much, Mortimer."

"I wish my name were not Mortimer; it has such a reproachful sound. I can ask a little more than that, though of course I am surprised at myself."

"No other man would in your place."

"Is that really so? I have not known men. I have not even known you."

"I feel that about you, Mortimer," said Horace, sadly.

"Then we are equal; so perhaps this talk may cease. It is a little awkward for me; I think you have allowed it to be so. And I am not the man you think. When I meant to take Charlotte from you, I thought it would be better for her. And I still think it would. And when I meant to take the children, I thought it would be better for them, though now

147

I see that perhaps it would not. If you are going to be a perfect father, of course it would not. They themselves would be against it, and they would not always have been that, Horace; this time your name can carry the reproach. It depends on how far you can maintain your course. It was a good one for you to take. If Charlotte has to choose between the children and me, we can foresee her choice. But how did you discover the truth about her and me?"

"You have no right to ask that question."

"Have I not? I really did not know that. I thought you would want to tell me."

"Well, you will think of what I have said."

"No, I shall not; my thoughts will shy away from it. It will lie at the bottom of my mind in those depths that we dare not disturb. We all have those hidden, untouchable places, though I do not think I have had them before. It shows they can be started at any age."

"Bullivant will soon be wanting this room. The daily routine has to go on."

"That is known to seem so strange; it is supposed to seem that it should stop. But it might seem stranger if it did; that is a thing we shall never know. How many more meals shall I eat in my old home?"

"Not many more," said Horace.

"I somehow do not think things will taste the same in the house by the mill. Have you thought about my appetite there? Or am I really going there to face death?"

"To face life, to face a better future. And you are not to face them alone."

"And troubles are lighter when they are shared. It seems that they ought not to be; it does not sound a kind view of life. So I shall be one of those people who marry to escape solitude. And I would rather marry for some congenial thing. I shall not find escaping solitude that."

"Magdalen will marry you for love. You will be more fortunate than she will."

"Shall I? I thought it would be the other way round. But

I am learning to distrust myself. I suppose you will come to see me?"

"It will be best for us not to meet too often."

"Oh, not too often, just the right number of times. You will always be welcome in the little house by the mill, Horace. And you will try to think the best of me. I have always tried to think it of you, even when the best was not very good. When I saw you becoming perfect, I did notice a difference. I feel we are saying a farewell, and perhaps I am saying one to the old Horace. And of course there is one thing I must ask."

"Things will not be hard for Charlotte."

"My request is granted before it is uttered. I do not think that has happened to me before. My requests are not always granted even after they are uttered. And uttering has a way of not making them sound their best. It does not seem to suit requests. I would rather not utter a request for a better house than the one by the mill; I would rather it was granted before it was uttered."

"I can do no more for you, Mortimer. The truth is the kindest thing."

"Is that so? I wonder what would be the unkindest. It is the same old Horace after all. I ought to feel a sneaking gladness about that, but I am not quite sure."

"I wish I could talk of the same old Mortimer."

"You may be entitled to the last word, but I call that taking advantage of it. And how can you talk of me as the same, when you have arranged for circumstances to crush me?"

"I thought you were more of a man, Mortimer."

"You always thought better of me than I deserved."

"I fear that is the truth."

"You really do take advantage, but perhaps it is. Most people thought I was hardly a man at all. And now I am going to be a husband. It does not seem to fit."

"What was your plan for yourself?"

"Do I really give you all these opportunities? I wonder if

Magdalen will like your consistently making the worst of me."

"This is the last time you must talk about her like this. You must get a grasp of your position and hers. You must make her a good and loyal husband."

"Shall I really be that? My self-respect is quite restored, and so is your respect for me. And I could not have borne to forfeit your respect, Horace."

"That is the saddest part of it all for me."

"It is not for me. I never believe that material troubles are not the worst."

"I have said you will not have those."

"Shall I not have the house by the mill and just enough to live on? Have you only been threatening me, Horace?"

"You know you cannot remain in this house. And you know you did not intend to remain. You forget that your plans are known to me."

"I hardly forget that. This interview must have some foundation. But I cannot think how you came to know. I suppose you are going to tell me."

"It is better not," said Horace.

"It would surely be better for you to have the relief and triumph, and for me to have my curiosity satisfied. I cannot think how you can resist it."

"To think of Charlotte the object of whispering tongues and prying eyes! You were to do her no good, Mortimer."

"Why must you imagine such things? You do not know how open and above-board we were going to be."

"No, I do not know that."

"Dear, dear, what an opportunity! How I should have admired you, if you had not taken it! I do rather admire you, Horace. I believe you have behaved like a man through this interview. I cannot help wishing you had behaved like a woman, and had your little triumph and let everything out. It is no wonder we like the society of women, when they cannot keep anything to themselves. It is really very nice to share everything. But you have not done badly in your narrow, masculine way."

"Neither have you, Mortimer," said Horace, with a half-smile. "You kept me walking on thin ground. There was but a frail crust between my feet and the whirlpool beneath. What did you feel when you saw me walking on it?"

"I felt I was on thin ground myself. And I was right; it has given way."

"Well, there is no bitterness between us. There is none on my side, only disappointment and sorrow."

"There is disappointment on mine too. I could hardly pretend there was not. And I do not understand your not feeling bitterness. It adds to my discomfiture. Perhaps it is meant to do that. So it may be bitterness after all."

"Well, there can be none on yours."

"I thought it was the party in the wrong, that always felt it. But I am glad it is not. That sort of subtlety makes me ill at ease."

"Did you know of Magdalen's feeling for you?"

"Yes, and I was too kind and flattered to repulse it. So perhaps my foundations are laid. Did you know of the mother's feeling for you?"

"I recognised her interest and friendship, and I have been grateful for them."

"We shall see her reaction to the romance between Magdalen and me. That will clear the situation, and I think it needs it."

"They are coming to see us to-morrow afternoon. You will be able to use your opportunities."

"Perhaps Magdalen is coming to give them to me. It would be like her generous self. I must begin to talk about her in the right way."

"You should be grateful for any human feeling. It is not an easy thing to win."

"I should have thought it was. You and I have both won it lately, and I saw you winning the children's. Perhaps we are winning personalities."

"It really seems the best solution, Mortimer."

"I will try to bear it for your sake, Horace. It seems that I owe you some amends. I will make a lifelong atonement."

The guests were betimes on the following day, and Gertrude walked straight up to her host.

"Now we are here at an unconventionally early hour, but I am not going to apologise for it. I cannot think that putting off seeing our friends has so much to recommend it. So I am here before the accepted moment in an unrepentant spirit."

"We are glad to see you at any moment," said Emilia. "And my nephew's wife is at home to welcome you, and will soon be here. You have heard of her sudden return."

"I expect almost as soon as you knew of it yourselves," said Magdalen, smiling. "In a village all news travels apace."

"You look wearied by the effort of taking up the old round," said Gertrude to Horace, almost while her daughter spoke.

"I have had things to trouble me, but I am more myself than I have been. I see my way."

"Come and sit by me and talk to Mr. Lamb," said Gertrude to her daughter, who was accepting a chair from Mortimer. "That is the seat Miss Lamb was going to take."

"No, I will join in the talk with you and my nephew," said Emilia.

"You must hardly know what to do with the uprising of the past," said Gertrude to Horace, not looking at his aunt.

"He is going to meet it," said the latter. "We shall soon be in our old groove."

"A groove is a thing we should avoid, if we can. I have always done my best to do so."

"I think I only mean our settled routine."

"Change is the salt of life to all of us," said Gertrude, in a grave, clear tone. "Our happiness and our mental health depend on it, and so our duty to others. We should not be afraid even of great change."

"It sounds an alarming thing," said Emilia, "and it suggests more than would be possible in a family."

"All things are possible," said Gertrude, gently. "And changes in a family are often the most to be desired; the most salutary, the most health-giving, the most for the welfare of many bodies and minds."

"Such changes are indeed difficult," said Horace.

"Difficult? Yes. But how often are things the more worth while for that! We are all pilgrims with obstacles in our path. We must not be afraid to surmount them."

"We need not make or imagine them," said Emilia.

"There is truly no need to do that. They are there, whether it is our will or not. But there is the more satisfaction in overcoming them. Nothing is more bracing, nothing is more worth while."

"We seem to be disagreeing," said Emilia with a smile, "and I am not quite sure about what."

"We are not very used to each other's company," said Gertrude gently. "I do not suggest that two are company and three none, but I am going to ask that daughter of mine to yield up her place. She took it as your eyes were on it; I saw it happen."

"No, we will not disturb her. I am happy here."

"But I think you would be happier elsewhere," said Gertrude, bending towards her and slightly dropping her voice.

"No, I should be less at home; this is my accustomed place."

"Things are not always the more congenial for that. It does not do to assume it. You were going to talk to your other nephew, and he is the one who is deserted. Magdalen, come and sit by your mother. You wrested Miss Lamb's seat from under her very eyes."

"No, I do not think I did that, Mother," said Magdalen, making no movement.

"Magdalen and I ought to be together," said Mortimer. "I feel we are the changelings in our families, and should make a pair."

"Pairs are made in heaven, surely," said Gertrude, in an easy tone that was belied by the change in her eyes.

"Perhaps that is what I am trying to say."

"Well, you did not succeed."

"Then I will try again. This pair was made in heaven. Is that plain?"

"I do not think Magdalen is the changeling in her family, if by that you mean the odd and separate one. I think I hold the unenviable place. The two young people are absorbed in each other, and I am the one who moves in a separate sphere, impartial and aloof. I think I am the one at disposal, if new pairs are to be made."

"But they are not. This pair has always existed, if we had known."

"Things are not much good, if we do not know about them."

"But we know all the better now. We can make up for lost time. And I want to hear what Magdalen thinks of the house by the mill."

"That very little house?" said Gertrude. "A cottage, really."

"Yes, that one. It is not a cottage. My cousin knows about it. And be it never so humble, there is no place like home. And I see that both those things would be true of it."

"I think it is a very nice little house," said Magdalen.

"Well, I do not," said her mother. "I think it is a damp, murky, little place. I should be very sorry for anyone I cared about to be domiciled in it. Indeed I would not consent."

"You and my cousin think so differently," said Mortimer. "So there are obstacles in our path. But we must not be afraid to surmount them. I was glad to hear you say that."

"Obstacles! I was not thinking of damp and mud and

mist, and general river murkiness, when I used the word. A loss of health is too much of an obstacle. I do not think we want that in our path; I do not think we will have it."

"People have always lived in the house, Mother," said Magdalen. "It was occupied until quite lately."

"And what kind of people were they?"

"I think the better kind of working people."

"Well, there you are," said Gertrude. "They would not be used to the same standard of health and comfort. That may not be as it should be, but so it is. I hope it may not always be so, but as long as it is, we must reckon with it. And what was the people's reason for leaving? Answer me that?"

"My cousin must answer it," said Mortimer. "Horace, we are talking of the little house by the mill. "Why did the people who used to live there, leave it?"

"I am not sure. I think they wanted a different situation."

"There you are!" said Gertrude, rising. "That is enough for me. I do not wish to hear any more about it. And I should think they did want a different one. I would not consent to anyone who belonged to me, living there and breathing that damp air, and trying to think there was no place like home, when that was the place involved. I quite agree about the probable uniqueness of it."

She went to the door, upright and firm of tread, forgetting to take leave of her hosts in the turmoil of her feelings. Emilia intercepted her and offered her hand.

"This is a hurried visit. At the next one my nephew's wife will be with us, and you will see us as we are."

"I am looking forward to your knowing me with my life complete," said Horace. "You have helped me over my widowed time, and must not desert us now that the old days return."

"I somehow can't see the old days," said Gertrude, coming to a pause and speaking with a smile and a frown. "Something seems to have eluded me somehow. Unless the interregnum had its own atmosphere, and I took it for the real one. I hardly think I shall feel at home in the old conditions, that are for me the new ones. I think I belong to the passing time that carried me with it, and will have its own memories. Come, Magdalen; if I am to be reconciled to your living in that cottage by the mill, instead of your own comfortable home, you have your work before you."

Magdalen followed, willing to be relieved of emotion for the moment, and they walked for some distance before her mother spoke.

"I wonder if the Lambs will ever settle into a definite scheme of life. They do not seem to know what they want. And when they do, they only half want it."

"I think that things were in the balance, Mother, and now have settled themselves on the right side. We ought to be glad the dangers are past."

"And we are, when it means that we get what we want for ourselves," said Gertrude, turning and putting her hand under her daughter's chin. "But we must not be too sure of anything in that household. I have never met such a baffling atmosphere."

"I am taking nothing that belongs to anyone else."

"Neither are you, my dear one. You have a right to your happiness, and now we will give ourselves up to thinking about it. Your happiness will make your mother's," said Gertrude, transferring her zest from her own life to her daughter's, not without a certain relief in her own undisturbed future. "The cottage by the mill does not appeal to a mother's eye, but the joy of keeping you in the place will reconcile me to it, if anything can. So my Magdalen will be Mrs. Mortimer Lamb, but she will always be the little Magdalen to her mother."

"It will not alter the damp, Mother," said Magdalen with a smile.

"No, and we must see what can be done to counteract it. We must look to the stoves and the chimneys, or rather I must do so. I wonder that Horace Lamb cannot afford his cousin a better house. He finds him useful on the place. And he should feel grateful to you for attracting him away from his wife. I fear he is a man whose eyes are turned solely on his own life."

"You will have two sons, Mother," said Magdalen, in a soft tone.

"That had not escaped me; I was conscious of my own enrichment. My Magdalen is doing much for herself and other people, and it is not like her to do one without the other."

"I shall be glad when the next days are over for Mortimer. He will have to bring home to his family his changed view of his future. He will not flinch from the ordeal, but it will have to be faced."

"I think Miss Lamb may be depended on to give him fair support," said Gertrude. "My impression of her from the first was of a person of singular integrity. She is the one who lives up to my first conception of her. It is extraordinary how often my first flash of insight proves to be the true one."

Emilia's first service to Mortimer was to contrive for him to be left alone; her second might have been to acquaint Bullivant with his solitude, if she had felt any doubt of the latter's awareness of it. He entered to clear the tea with a face so blank, that it suggested the want of any suitable expression.

"Are we to talk of things, Bullivant?" said Mortimer.

"Well, it would prevent a ban on them, sir."

"Does it all embarrass you?"

"Well, sir, it has not the ease of the accustomed."

"My life is settled for me, and I have accepted it. Do you think we have acquired a taste for despotic dealing?"

"Well, it has comprised our experience, sir; we might as well say we had acquired a taste for life itself."

"Have you ever thought of marrying, Bullivant? There is nothing between you and Cook?"

"Nothing beyond respect and long association, sir. We

accept the conditions of our calling. A home within a home has always its perilous aspect."

"She hardly looks a motherly woman."

"And is not, sir, if you will not mistake my meaning, as I did not mistake yours."

"Are you going to congratulate me?"

"May I add my congratulations to the remainder, sir?"

"Were you very surprised?"

"Well, it was unexpected, sir."

"Can you imagine me in the house by the mill?"

"It requires an exercise of the mind, sir."

"Mrs. Doubleday says it will be damp."

"We may look to her to reconcile herself to it, sir."

"And shall I do the same?"

"I cannot say I can picture it, sir."

"The master does not want me to come here too often."

"He does not know himself, sir, or else I do not know him, which is not the case."

"Bullivant, do you know the whole?"

"I know what may become a servant and friend of the family, sir. Who comes to know more, is none."

"Have you lost your respect for me?"

"To know all is to forgive all, sir."

Bullivant began to collect the tea-things, and looked at some scattered objects left about the room with an equivocal eye. He stepped rather high over the traces of Avery's accident, advanced to gather up some toys from the hearth, as though covering an appreciable distance, and carried the tray to the kitchen with lips compressed.

"It cannot go on, Mrs. Selden. It will defeat itself."

"It gets more pronounced, does it? I wonder how the mistress was struck by it."

"The mistress's face remained an enigma," said Bullivant, not thinking to say the same of himself. "George, is it for you to take this tray, or for me to retain it?"

"The mean is not called golden without foundation," said Cook. "But it may have been the master's cross that his nature was not forthcoming, and he may have gone the further length in casting it off."

"I thought a cross was supposed to be carried," said George.

"George, if you have nothing better to do than to blaspheme——" said Bullivant, pointing to the scullery.

George bore the tray in this direction.

"You shall not be exposed to levity, while I can prevent it, Mrs. Selden. Such talk remains what it is. As often, I must follow George."

"So, George, is this to be the last of the things we have to contend with? It is going further and faring worse than had entered the heart of any of us. I suggest that you withdraw, and come to an understanding with yourself, and with what it is not for me to name. I am but a man, when all is said and done."

Bullivant sighed with the heaviness of one who met superhuman demands from mortal resources, and watched George follow his suggestion, or anyhow the first part of it.

"I trust Miriam, that you can separate the grain from the chaff in George's conversation."

"Well, I know the difference."

"We cannot always exercise our choice in associates."

"No," said Miriam, who would not in this case have spent so much time with Cook.

"Evil communications corrupt good manners."

"George is not evil," said Miriam, in an uncertain manner, feeling that this was not yet the case.

"No, only ignorant and overweening in his ideas. It is strange how pride arises in the last and least. It would be thought that George would be content with his position, taking into account his starting-point."

"Yes," said Miriam, in full agreement.

"And what is the subject of the conversation?" said Cook, who had seen George pass the kitchen, and inferred that Bullivant had succeeded to his place.

"I was expressing the hope, Mrs. Selden, that Miriam

could separate the grain from the chaff in George's conversation," said Bullivant, feeling that his words would bear quotation, and doing them this justice. "Evil communications corrupt good manners."

"Well, I hope she will not admit too much chaff into her own. And communications are not the chief part of her obligations at any time, though anyone present at an encounter between her and George might not come to that conclusion."

"We must look to the time, Mrs. Selden, when George must hear of Mr. Mortimer's engagement," said Bullivant, as they returned to the kitchen.

"We will impose silence on the matter," said Cook, with some sharpness. "It will come to our concerning ourselves with the boy as a chronic obligation. The subject is not to be discussed, and there is an end of it."

"But will it come to his thinking the more?"

"I should not say so. Thinking does not form so much of our occupation at any time, and it would hardly make up so much of the whole that constitutes George."

CHAPTER VII

"Rice and a nutmeg, please, Miss Buchanan, and a letter if there is one."

Miss Buchanan put a nutmeg on the counter.

"You need not always buy rice," she said, pausing with her hand on the receptacle, and her eyes on Gertrude's face.

"Not buy rice, when I have a family that eats it! It is easy to see you are not a family woman."

Miss Buchanan's eyes rested on Magdalen, as the representative of the household in question.

"I did not know you had letters sent here, Mother."

"Well, now you do know. You are getting old enough to be admitted to your mother's little secrets," said Gertrude, tapping her glove against her daughter's cheek. "There are some things I do not want the servants to see. You will understand that, when you have a house of your own. Does Miss Buchanan know how soon that is to be?"

"Yes," said the latter.

"Then news travels especially fast to you, because we do not yet know the exact date ourselves."

"The house is ready and waiting."

"I know nothing about the house, except that it arouses my maternal misgiving on the score of damp."

"It is not to have anything done to it."

"Now you are a satisfying person to meet! No one else has been able to tell us so much about our own future. And as it is of great interest to us, we are most glad of the light upon it. I wish you could tell me that the house was to be replaced by another. That is what I should like to hear."

Miss Buchanan was silent.

"Put the nutmeg into your pocket, my dear, and take this rice that Miss Buchanan grudges to you. She does not know much about satisfying young appetites, in spite of her fund of information."

Miss Buchanan did not need to speak, as her eyes said plainly that Magdalen's age put her beyond such allusion.

"I hope it will not be long before you have the custom of another household," said Gertrude.

Miss Buchanan did not respond.

"Though you give me the impression that you do not care whether you do business or not."

Miss Buchanan agreed that the balance was even, as she disliked to do business, and depended on it for her bread; and therefore allowed her silence to indicate consent.

"Mother, here is Mortimer!" said Magdalen.

"So it is," said Gertrude, glancing behind her and continuing to talk with more consciousness. "So we are all engaged on domestic errands together, before the time when we are naturally privy to each other's. But if we can do anything for masculine inexperience in the meantime, we will gladly anticipate our duties."

Miss Buchanan stood with an expectant air, waiting for the first customers to go, and leave the last to his errand.

"I came to ask about a letter," said Mortimer, who was too distraught by his own troubles to maintain a secrecy that had lost its meaning; "one that should have come here, and seems not to have done so."

"We also came about a letter," said Gertrude, in an open, natural tone, that seemed designed to put him at his ease. "It is convenient at times to have letters reserved for our own eyes."

"Yes, if they reach them, but this one of mine has failed to do so. I want to know if Miss Buchanan can throw any light upon it."

Gertrude stepped forward a pace and lifted her eyes to Miss Buchanan.

"Mr. Mortimer's letter?" she said, as though in easy reference to a member of her intimate circle. "It should have come here and has not done so; he is a little uneasy about it." She smiled and dropped her voice as she took Miss Buchanan into her confidence.

"When should it have come here?"

"In the first week in February," said Mortimer. "It came from overseas and should have been delivered then. Another letter, that was posted at the same time, and addressed to the house, was delivered."

"Only one letter came here in that week," said Miss Buchanan.

"Are you quite sure?" said Gertrude.

Miss Buchanan did not speak.

"I know you are an entirely reliable witness."

"Then why did you ask the question?" said Miss Buchanan with her eyes.

"Was the letter addressed to me?" said Mortimer.

"It was for Mrs. Doubleday, since you know each other's business."

"Well, we have reached a stage when that is natural," said Gertrude.

Miss Buchanan's silence said that she would not depend on such an outcome.

"Well, there is clearly no clue to the matter," said Magdalen.

"Now, I wonder if I can throw any light on it," said Gertrude, in a retrospective, open manner, willing to emerge into useful prominence. "I picked up a letter by mistake in that week. I have so few letters sent here, that I remember the approximate dates. Indeed I actually took it from the postman, and Miss Buchanan scolded me about it. I was expecting a foreign letter and did not use my glasses. And when I realised it was not for me—something about the envelope was unfamiliar—I sent my daughter back with it. And she brought it back to the shop and left it. I remember quite clearly. Do not you, Magdalen?"

"I think I remember something about it, Mother."

"No letter came back here," said Miss Buchanan.

"I remember it quite well," said Gertrude. "I do not

know the address on the letter. Naturally I did not examine it. When I realised it was not for me, both it and I were protected by the instinct to avoid other people's private affairs. And Magdalen naturally did not examine it either. So we cannot bear witness to its nature or address. But we are sure of what happened."

"The letter did not come back here," said Miss Buchanan.

"Yes, indeed it did, if you will forgive me. It came back in my daughter's hands and was put into the box."

"There is no box."

"Then it was put on the counter. I remember the episode accurately. I waited for my daughter at the bend of the road. I have a very strong memory."

Miss Buchanan might have made the same claim, but always felt that her memory was involved with her secret.

"Did you see your daughter bring the letter back to the shop?"

"Well, I was not actually watching. I was waiting at some distance. In fact I was drawing patterns on the road with my umbrella, a habit I have when I am unoccupied. I remember the occasion as well as that. But I know she did bring it back. I saw her go and waited for her."

"Then it is she who has made the mistake."

"But what mistake can there have been? Think, Magdalen, my dear. Did you put the letter on the counter? What actually did you do with it? Was Miss Buchanan in the shop when you returned?"

"I am sure I did not make any mistake, Mother. No, Miss Buchanan was not in the shop."

"Well, you and Mortimer must thresh it out between you," said Gertrude, using Mortimer's name with a conscious note, as she directed her voice to Miss Buchanan's ears. "I did not fail in any part of my duty. When I found myself in possession of something not my own, I at once took steps to restore it, and no one can do more than that. If this scatter-brained girl has made any blunder, it is not to be laid to my door, and she is the last person to want her responsibilities to devolve on her mother."

Miss Buchanan's eyes again rested on Magdalen.

"Well, as long as the letter is not at large," said Mortimer, supposing that Magdalen had had some accident with it, and been reluctant to reveal it to Gertrude. "That is the essence of the matter."

"Yes, that is the whole thing," said Magdalen.

Mortimer moved to her side.

"You will tell me at some time what happened to it," he said in a low tone; "or we shall begin by having secrets from each other. And it will be better to begin by having this little secret to ourselves."

Magdalen gave him a faint smile, and Gertrude glanced at them and looked away, recognising their position and its privileges.

"Did you deface it and feel it must be destroyed? Why did you not tell me?" said Mortimer, reflecting that Magdalen would have welcomed a chance of a private confession, and following the train of thought. "Oh, did you know who wrote the letter?"

"How could I know that?"

"You might have known Charlotte's writing. It has appeared about the village, and it is an unmistakable hand. And of course there would have been the postmark. So you did not follow your mother's example and avoid looking at it?"

"I could not help seeing it. My sight is not like hers."

"And you thought it better that I should not have it?"

"Well, it could have done you no good."

"I knew that some couples read each other's letters, but I did not know it was only each other's, and not their own. And we had not become a couple then, though perhaps you knew we were one at heart. I think we should read our own letters in future, or it will not be much good for people to write them. I feel they do mean them to be read. I will read this one when you give it to me, and I may keep it as a memento of the past. It will prove that it is dead and gone. It would not need a memento, if it were not."

"I cannot give it to you."

"So you acted for my good and destroyed it. But it did not work out in that way. I had to ask Charlotte what was in it, and that was the way to arouse the old feelings."

"At any rate there is no deception between us."

"But that is what there has been. And I am wondering how much more there is. Is the letter really destroyed?"

"You must trust me," said Magdalen.

"But that is what I cannot do. At any time you might act for my good. When people do that, it kills something precious between them. If you will give me the letter, it will bind us closer, and I think we do need the bond."

"It is just possible that I might do that, but I can make no promise."

"Tell me what you did with it. We cannot base our future on evasion, or not on as much as this. The worse the truth is, the more I shall respect you for telling it. And I do not respect falsehood. I am a simple man and think it wrong to tell a lie."

"What did you think of your own wrong-doing?"

"I suppose I am delighted with that little flash of spirit. Well, I thought badly of it. I am full of compunction and remorse."

"It ought to make you judge other people more lightly."

"It makes me see how bad wrong-doing is, and how unworthy people are when they indulge in it."

At this moment the postman came to the door and stood, proffering an envelope.

"No!" said Gertrude, standing aside and shaking her head. "I am not going to have anything to do with it. No letter that comes to this door passes through my hands. I have had my lesson and do not want another."

Miss Buchanan extended a hand across the counter, and held the envelope before the postman's eyes. He glanced at the onlookers, uncertain whether to reveal the name, and she tapped the letter on his shoulder in disposal of his scruples.

"They know each other's affairs, and just now there is no one else."

"Mrs. Doubleday," said the postman, and Miss Buchanan gave the letter to Gertrude.

"What is the postmark?" said the latter; "I have not my reading glasses. I will read the letter at home, but I should like to have some clue."

Miss Buchanan returned the letter to the postman, but he shook his head and went his way, having no more time for unofficial business.

"Do you have trouble with your eyes, Miss Buchanan?" said Mortimer.

"No, but I find handwriting difficult."

"The postmark is stamped in printed characters. I suppose your sight is too long for a close range. Can you tell the time by the church clock? I want to correct an uncertain watch."

"I never look at things at that distance," said Miss Buchanan, not breaking her rule. "I have enough to attend to close at hand."

"There is a jewel loose," said Mortimer, examining the works of the watch, "and it has fallen on the counter in the dust. It will be worse than the needle in the haystack. Thank you, Miss Buchanan; you must have eyes like a lynx. There is nothing amiss with your sight."

Miss Buchanan turned to the shelves to cover a smile, unused to this approach to a compliment, interchanged some packets and turned back again. Mortimer saw that her goods were placed in separate groups, according to their kind, so that the shelves had an odd and broken aspect.

"You are in a lonely situation here, Miss Buchanan. Would you like the loan of some books?"

"Oh, no," said Gertrude. "Indeed she would not. You are not first in the field there. I was before you and was repulsed with ignominy. Books for Miss Buchanan! She would rather waste her time in any other way. And yet I cannot help a feeling that she has a natural bent towards them."

"I have not much time after the work of the day, and there is needlework for my spare hours."

"Is that piece in the window yours?" said Mortimer. "It is very fine work. Your eyes must be good indeed."

"We had better be going, Mother," said Magdalen. "Miss Buchanan does not want us here all day."

"I should like to get to the bottom of this mystery of the letter," said Gertrude. "I do not like to go away, with the problem behind me, unsolved. I am not happy in the feeling that we are somehow responsible. Cannot you think what you did with the letter, you unsatisfactory child?"

"I did nothing unusual with it, Mother. Though I cannot say exactly what it was."

"Then we have no choice but to leave the matter. But it goes against the grain. Other people's letters! The most sacred of sacred things! Good-morning, Miss Buchanan."

Miss Buchanan made no reply.

"Good-bye, Miss Buchanan," said Mortimer.

"Good-bye," said Miss Buchanan.

"Now we part here," said Gertrude, turning to shake hands with Mortimer. "We have an errand along this lane. I hope you bear us no malice over the letter. Our consciences are clear."

"Perhaps I may walk with you. I have a lonely hour before me."

"Now we never force duties of this kind on other people. It is a dull, little, charitable concern, and we are prepared to steer our own way through it."

"I shall not interfere with it. I have never had anything to do with charity. I have only taken it. But I do not want to return to the reunited family, and see my aunt rejoicing in others' joy. It is enough for her, as she does rejoice in it, but I only rejoice in my own joy."

"And very natural and healthy at the moment. What else could be expected of you? Well, you can both wait here while I pursue my lawful and charitable occasions. I will not be longer than I must. It is simply that I have a promise to keep, and see no question about it. But I dare say you will not find the time too long."

"I shall have to waste some of our precious minutes," said Mortimer, at once. "I am sorry to harp on the same matter, especially as it is the one awkward thing between us. But I do want to understand about it, so that our life can be based on mutual confidence. I know you will help me to make it mutual. You saw my name on the letter and felt you must know what was in it. But wasn't it rather soon for us to observe the customs of married life?"

"We could hardly begin too soon."

"So you acted on principle. I might have known you would do that. I judged you by myself and thought you yielded to temptation, or rather that you resisted it without success. I have so often resisted temptation, and always without success. When people resist it with success, I always wonder how we know they have had any."

"I suppose I met it and yielded to it."

"Well, you will give me the letter. After all, it is mine and not yours. I have not endowed you with all my worldly goods yet. And the letter is all my worldly goods; everything else belongs to Horace."

"It is not in my possession."

"And you will not tell me what you did with it. So there is not to be truth between us. Our hearts are not open to each other."

"I want them to be," said Magdalen, almost with tears.

"But you refuse my first request, when no other can hold quite the same place."

"I wish I need not refuse it."

"I feel I must know what became of that letter. And I want to hear it from your lips, so that I can say they have never withheld anything from me."

"I dropped it on the ground, that is, on the floor of a room."

"By accident?"

Magdalen was silent.

"You dropped it on purpose; you dropped it for someone to see it. You would have destroyed it, if you had wanted to be rid of it. Your mother? Your brother? My aunt, to warn her of the truth? But I think she had always known it. It was only Horace who did not know. The person most concerned in a thing is always the last to know of it. No one can mention it before him. You dropped it for Horace to see it! And he saw it and read it, and laid his plans! And the plans have succeeded and so have yours. I understand it all now. I see how a marriage can be based on complete understanding, and why such a marriage is not always a success."

"What could I do?" said Magdalen.

"Well, perhaps it was your only course. Perhaps everything is really that. We just fulfil our natures. I wonder if this brought yours to complete fulfilment. I ought to say that I have never liked you so well. It is a sign of the meanness of my character that I cannot say it."

"We must both try to forget it."

"People never succeed in doing that. It is only a way of saying that it is a dangerous thing to remember."

"It would not have been right to break up your cousin's home."

"It was not right to read a private letter. I am afraid you and I do not do what is right. There seems to be that likeness between us. Perhaps there is almost too much resemblance. People who marry should be different. We should not have the attraction of opposites. It would not do to have too many things in common, especially when one of them is a tendency to evil. It does seem that only one of us should have that."

"I am sure we could be happy together."

"But we both have to amend our lives, and who could be

happy doing that? Certainly not two people doing it together. We should mark each other's failures. I think I have seen that tendency in us already. It would be the beginning of the end, and that is always worse than the end itself. A quick release is the merciful thing. We must let it all become a memory. We can hardly prevent its being as much as that. And neither of us will live in the house by the mill. The cloud is a dark one, but it has its silver lining."

"I do not think you ever wanted to marry me."

"You knew I did not. You knew I wanted to marry Charlotte. You had your own proof and took your own steps to prevent it. I cannot say you are the only woman in my life. So I see I have not enough to offer you."

"I should have found it better than nothing. I should have had yourself, and that is what I asked."

"I don't quite like to be as little as that. Of course I have a low opinion of myself, but I should hardly like such a one in my life-companion. It scarcely seems enough foundation for two lives."

"I have not a low opinion of you."

"Well, do you know, I have of you? And that is so unworthy of me, that I see I must withdraw from your life. How could I ask you to marry a man who did not respect you? I should not think a man has ever asked a woman that, or not a man worthy of the name. Of course I do not mean that I shall not always keep a corner of my heart, that will be Magdalen's corner. You did not think I meant that?"

"I do not know what you mean."

"If you really do not, I shall have to tell you. And I would so much rather not. I do not think the corner would ever be quite the same. So let us part while it is still safe and unblemished for us. After all, it is all we have."

"I suppose it is the only thing. There would always be another woman between us."

"That is why I was going to marry you. So that I could live in the same place and always have her between us. But something has shown me that it would have been a wrong course. It would have been fraught with danger. And my motto is always: 'Safety first'. But I will tell you something that I could breathe to no one else. She is not as much the meaning of my life as I thought. Separation has estranged us, or shown us the truth, or done some other shameful thing. I am so glad to have the word to breathe to you; I should not have liked to part without one. And now our parting is quite a success. I do not think my life has any meaning. And I find I do not want it to have any. I am one of those creatures who drag out a meaningless existence, and they are not so much to be pitied as people think."

"I do not think you are the man I thought."

"So it is beginning already, the cat-and-dog life that we should lead. I might have said you were exactly the woman I thought. I am glad we have not dragged each other down to that. Here is your mother coming from the cottage. I will not stay for her to witness my humiliation. I will accept my dismissal. God bless you, my dear girl."

Mortimer walked away as Gertrude came out, with the light of recent benevolence still in her eye.

"So our companion has gone," she said in a pleasant tone. "I am afraid I kept him waiting. No doubt he has claims on his time."

"He went just as you came out of the door. There is nothing between us, Mother."

"Nothing between you! Why, I thought you had made up your minds. No one could have thought anything else. Has there been any trouble?"

"We were mistaken, Mother. Both of us were. We were mistaken in ourselves and in each other. Neither is what the other thought. That is the best way of putting it."

"But how can you have found out so much about each other in this short time?" said Gertrude, who thought a lifetime the proper period for self-exposure. "It must be some misunderstanding. Do not stand on your dignity, my dear. It is men who must have things made easy for them, not women. Do not wreck your life for a moment's pique. You will have long enough to regret it."

"Mortimer is going away. And we may not meet again. I shall come back to you and Gideon. I know I have lived apart from you of late."

"But, my poor child, what a sudden and utter change! We only want your happiness. Would it be any good for me to see Mortimer, or for your brother to see him? I feel that you want to marry him."

"I shall never want to marry anyone else, and neither will he. He gave me his word for that. We shall always belong to each other, and that is the main thing."

Gertrude's eyes said that it was nothing at all, but her lips were silent.

"There is something between us, that can never be explained, and never be removed. We simply have to accept it, and it must always keep us apart. But each will be to the other something that no one else can be. And I have his last words to remember."

"And what were they, my dear?" said Gertrude, as she folded her arms about her daughter.

Magdalen buried her head on her mother's shoulder.

"'God bless you, my dear girl,'" she said.

Mortimer hastened along the road, anxious to increase his distance from those whom he thought of as his pursuers. He was admitted to the house by Bullivant, who seemed to lie in wait for some tidings that were tolerable to him.

"Bullivant, this may be the last time that you welcome me back to my old home. I must ask you to sort my clothes and pack those I shall need, and to forward my letters to the address that I shall give you, or that you will give me, when you have found it. You must find me a modest and suitable lodging not too far away. I am going forth into the wide, wide world."

"Yes, sir. So it is not to be the house by the mill. Perhaps I may say that I am glad."

"That has already become part of an unreal world."

"Perhaps it always was, sir, as far as you were concerned. So it is not to be Miss Doubleday either?"

"No. The unreal world was complete with wife and home, and all of it is unreal."

"Perhaps I may presume again to be glad, sir. Assuming that that is your own feeling."

"No, I think you may not, Bullivant. I am not marrying Miss Doubleday, because I am not worthy of her. There is nothing to be glad about in that."

"Worthy is the word for the family, sir, if I may assign one. And it is hardly one that would be applied to you. And the arrangement you are making is of a temporary character, and need not give rise to misgiving."

"It is for ever, Bullivant. You must remember that."

"I shall not be guilty of any lapse, sir."

"You do not ask me the reasons of my going."

"You can tell me, sir, if such is your inclination."

"Why should I wish to have secrets from you? I expect you are my only friend. People in a predicament always have only one. The master has banished me from his hearth and home."

"The first has hardly been our strong point, sir," said Bullivant, without raising his eyes, "or not until these latter days."

"But now its very austerity is dear to me."

"Well, sir, it reaches back into the past."

"The master is quite justified, Bullivant."

"I am not taking anything upon myself, sir."

"Bullivant, do you once more know all?"

"Well, sir, omniscience under any head is a large claim."

"I hope you do not discuss the matter."

"I should have hoped on my side, sir, that you knew me better. Whom have I to discuss it with, save only the women and George? And is either choice likely?"

"I know I can trust you."

"I can corroborate that, sir."

"Well, I am in your hands. I must go to-morrow."

"Yes, sir. Will it be early?"

"In the first half of the day."

"Yes, sir. The master will miss you. That is to say, he will reach the stage."

"He may find he does not love me less well, because I have wronged him. But he has the children."

"That situation remains precarious, sir. I have found myself wondering if the foundations will hold. I have asked myself the question more than once."

"And have not answered it yet?"

"Not to my satisfaction, sir."

"I suppose that is talked about among you all?"

"Well, sir, it is a matter open to the ear and eye. And being a permissible topic, Mrs. Selden and I have admitted it to the table."

"Bullivant, do you know Miss Buchanan?"

"The proprietress of the general shop, sir? I should be said to have her acquaintance."

"And do you not think she needs a friend?"

"I can hardly say, sir. Our intimacy has not progressed to that point. Intimacy indeed hardly being the word."

"Would you guess there was a secret in her life?"

"Well, no, sir; I know no harm of her."

"Can you keep a secret on her behalf?"

"It should go without saying, sir, where a woman is concerned. Whether it be on the line of sin or sorrow, my lips would be sealed."

"It is only sorrow," said Mortimer.

"I am glad of that, sir. That is to say, I recognise that the first is the sadder thing. Bereavement according to the common lot would hardly have passed her over. Into all lives some rain must fall."

"This is outside the common lot, as it stands to-day. Miss Buchanan cannot read."

"Indeed, sir? I had no suspicion of it. And I have not met anyone who had."

"I am glad to hear it. That is her lonely triumph."

"Indeed, those are the words, sir. It must have meant a great overcoming of circumstances. It is hard to see how certain difficulties have been circumvented."

"I do not suggest that you should teach her to read."

"Well, no, sir, that would constitute a delicate situation, and would involve a degree of approach and handling. It would be better to try and ameliorate her lot in other ways."

"And it would also involve betraying that you knew of her disability, and that must on no account happen."

"No, sir, it would render the objective of her life null and void."

"That is the matter in a word. But could you not ask her here, and give her a change of scene and companionship, and see that she keeps her secret?"

"It ought not to be beyond me, sir."

"I have told you the truth, in order that you may protect it. It should be safer for your knowing it. No doubt her solitary habits are due to a fear of betraying it."

"I should say the situation has its element of pathos, sir."

"You see it as I do. I suppose you can count on Cook's support?"

"I have never asked for it in vain, sir, in anything that does not come under a worldly head, as in this case may be safely claimed. Of course, Mrs. Selden has her bounds."

"Well, this should be within them, but she must not suspect the truth."

"We understand each other there, sir. It should not be beyond me to steer my craft, so to speak, clear of the rocks. A woman, and a woman with a difficulty, is safe with me, and the difficulty as well."

"You are kinder in your attitude to Miss Buchanan than to Miss Doubleday."

"Well, sir, the former's approach to us is not so near. Using 'us' in the family sense. And Miss Doubleday is in no need of my offices, being placed beyond them. Though hardly placed as I could have wished, in the circumstances that threatened us."

"On this last day of my old life I am thinking of another and not of myself."

"I had not failed to mark that, sir."

"And there is someone else whom I would recommend to your offices."

"I can hazard the guess, sir, and I will meet any need of his that comes within my scope. Indeed I might claim that my heart had said the same thing. And I might come to letting fall a word that the enjoinder came from you."

"That might do good to us both."

"And what better reason for doing it, sir?"

CHAPTER VIII

"THIS MAKES QUITE a little occasion for us, Miss Buchanan," said Bullivant. "I think you and Mrs. Selden are hardly acquainted. You have only had chance encounters."

"But should have others in future," said Cook. "It seems that neighbours should maintain the usual interchange. From each point of view that is the case."

"We thought we would have tea in the kitchen, according to our practice," said Bullivant. "To tell you the truth, we have followed that routine for some time. The servants' hall is fast becoming a name. Our scope is more contracted than in other days."

"Many things are more curtailed than formerly," said Cook. "But doubtless we are not the only ones. The gentry tend in that direction; there is the one movement for them. And many would say the kitchen was the homelier place."

There was a murmur, as all said it, with the exception of Miss Buchanan, who said nothing.

"Here are two of our younger members, Miss Buchanan," said Bullivant, indicating George and Miriam.

"They will swell our numbers at the table," said Cook; "after which we shall be left to our devices."

Cook and Bullivant would have preferred to entertain their guest by themselves, and had encouraged the housemaids to go out to tea. George and Miriam presented a different case, as they were entitled to tea, and had nowhere but the house to have it.

"Shall we take our seats?" said Cook.

Miss Buchanan moved to the table, in a compliance that brought some feeling of relief.

"Do you take your tea strong or the reverse, Miss Buchanan?"

"Neither one nor the other," said the guest, using her rather loud voice for the first time.

"That is my own preference," said Bullivant.

"My bias is also towards the mean," said Cook, with her eyes on the teapot. "I am not in favour of excess in any direction."

"How do the young people like it?" said Miss Buchanan, both her utterance and its nature coming as a surprise.

"I am conversant with their preferences," said Cook, with nothing in her tone to indicate that she would be influenced by these.

"Do you find yourself much occupied in these days, Miss Buchanan?" said Bullivant.

"The same people come from the same houses, and often for the same things. My situation is convenient to some and not to others."

"And must remain so, in the nature of things," said Cook.

"I believe we are not in the habit of depositing an order with you," said Bullivant, as this aspect of the position occurred to him.

"You place your order all at once with the grocer in the town," said Miss Buchanan, not disclaiming knowledge under the head.

"And the most comprehensive and direct course," said Cook. "But needs arise at intervals that we might ask Miss Buchanan to furnish."

"I could oblige on occasions," said the latter.

"Which preserve is your fancy?" said Cook, adjusting two jars with their labels towards the guest.

"Greengage and redcurrant," said Bullivant, reading them out in a ruminative tone, as though with a view to his own ultimate choice.

"Well, not gooseberry or plum at any rate," said

George, who was aware of Miss Buchanan, and therefore more than usually aware of himself.

She seemed not to hear, and Bullivant followed her example, and their indifference was atoned for by Cook by instant and prolonged scrutiny.

"Greengage," said Miss Buchanan, "unless the red-currant should happen to be jelly."

"That would have been my own leaning," said Cook, "but economy is a factor in every household."

"It is said to be in this one," said Miss Buchanan, unaware how far her hosts identified themselves with the family.

"It would be said, whether or no it was the case," said Cook. "And our family is not on the modern lines, where show is the object. It is rooted in the past, and has its customs like all of its kind."

"And saving is one of them," said George.

Bullivant indicated the redcurrant jam to George, with a view to reserving the other for the guest, and George broached the jar with an air of being condemned to food of accepted indifference.

"You have the jam for Miriam, George," said Bullivant, in a tone of making a statement in passing.

George handed the pot, with the spoon already in it, and nonchalantly waited for its return.

"We get all kinds of scraping here," he said, delving into it with the freedom appropriate to a valueless commodity.

"You do not appear to be observing any kind at the moment, George," said Bullivant.

Miss Buchanan gave a laugh.

"I do not suppose that jam played much part in an orphanage bill of fare," said Cook, "not to call the sur-roundings by another term."

"Workhouse is the name," said George; "I am not afraid of it. Jam was once a week, but then jam was the word."

There was a pause.

"I am glad you harbour so much appreciation of your early routine," said Cook. "I should hardly have thought it would be so highly congenial."

"I wonder you made any effort to leave it behind," said Bullivant. "So my assumption that you desire a helping hand in that direction, is erroneous."

"I prefer jam that is not all pips; that is all," said George, routing in the pot as though for some substance distinct from these.

"What do you think of the preserve, Miriam?" said Bullivant.

"I like it," said Miriam, with an involuntary sound indicative of the feeling.

"Well, you need not express your appreciation except in words," said Cook, who did not consider such rebuke unsuited to her assistant, and found her acquiescent in the matter, owing either to her training or her nature. It was probably the latter, as a similar upbringing had not had the same effect on George, whose response to correction had once been such as to result in blindness to any subsequent lapse.

"Do you make your own preserves, Miss Buchanan?" said Bullivant.

"I make what I use myself. I cannot eat factory stuff."

"You can only sell it," said Bullivant, with a smile.

"Well, there is a demand, or it would not be made."

"It saves people trouble," said Bullivant, in a condoning manner.

"Which is all that people think of nowadays," said Cook.

"There is a lot of labour-saving," said Miss Buchanan.

"And why not?" said George. "Surely there is no sense in labour for its own sake."

There was the silence of disapproval, as the absence of a love of toil in George was recognised and condemned.

"One kind of shirking leads to another," said Cook. "Until at last there is nothing else remaining."

"Shirking was not the word I used," said George.

"And are we to bear in mind your exact phraseology? Is that incumbent upon us?"

"If you alter words, you alter meanings."

"Have you any news from the village, Miss Buchanan?" said Bullivant, his attention naturally not held by George.

"None but what comes from this house, and that will hardly be news to you."

"We should like to hear it nevertheless. It may take on a different aspect in the mouths of others," said Cook, hardly reckoning with the truth of her words.

"Well, Mr. Mortimer is both engaged to Miss Doubleday and not engaged to her."

"The former will not be the case, either now or at any time," said Bullivant. "I had it from Mr. Mortimer's own lips, with regard to the rumours that were circulating."

"There must have been something in it," said George. "There must be some flame behind as much smoke as that."

"You may not yet know, George," said Bullivant, in a controlled tone, "that where a lady's feeling is concerned, the matter is regarded as non-existent, if it should happen not to be tending to a climax."

"The village does not know it either," said Miss Buchanan, with a faint smile.

"Oh, that is it, is it?" said George.

"George, your manner of expressing yourself and Mr. Mortimer's are so divergent, that one is tempted to deny you the common bond of manhood," said Bullivant, in open exasperation.

"It is natural that there should be a difference," said Miss Buchanan, not winning any gratitude from George.

"And what else does the village give voice to?" said Cook. "We may as well hear those things about ourselves that are not familiar to us."

"Well, there is an estrangement between Mr. Lamb and Mr. Mortimer, and the cause of it is not far to seek," said Miss Buchanan, glancing from George and Miriam to their elders, as though in some hope that words suited only to mature ears would be audible only to them.

The look exchanged by Cook and Bullivant suggested an absence of such hope.

"There is a great deal of gossip going about, that does not merit attention," said Bullivant.

"But gets it all the same," said George, "and happens to be based on the truth. The circumstance glossed over has been the main one in the family, if you ask me."

"And was anyone making the enquiry of you?" said Cook.

"You assume knowledge, George, that you do not possess, indeed cannot, as it is without basis," said Bullivant, with some agitation. "You may think it enhances your importance to ape the surrounding yokels, whereas the truth is that—that——"

"That it operates in the contrary direction," said Cook.

"And there are people here, George," said Bullivant, "before whom you and I should guard our speech."

"Miriam," said Cook, in an almost gentle tone, "will you go up to my room and bring me my reticule from the dressing-table?"

As Miriam withdrew, Bullivant looked gravely after her and then at George, and an occasion was recognised when silence was more eloquent than speech.

"You asked me to repeat the talk of the village," said Miss Buchanan, in a tone that said more than her words.

"An unpremeditated request, for which we are entirely responsible," said Cook, in a hearty manner.

"Miss Buchanan's conversation was sufficiently entertaining," said Bullivant, "without our urging her to—to——"

"To steps foreign to her," said Cook, taking a small, leather bag from Miriam, and putting it down without a glance.

"Will you have some toast?" said Miss Buchanan, in a tone of calm after storm, passing the toast rack to Miriam.

"It is not for me and George."

"I cannot manage hot things for all ages and positions," said Cook. "I should never take my eyes from the stove."

"There are still a few little privileges for us of riper years, Miss Buchanan," said Bullivant, making a suitable adjustment of the rack.

"A cook's connection must be with the stove," said George, his feelings passing the point where suppression was in question.

There was a silence.

"Will you do me the favour to repeat your words, George?" said Bullivant.

"You would not ask for them to be repeated, if you had not heard them."

"A strange sequence of cause and effect," said Cook.

"I will repeat my request, George," said Bullivant.

"Repeating seems to be in fashion."

"It will not be so, George. You will not find it so. I shall not resort to it further."

"It will be said that Miss Buchanan's connection is with her counter next," said Cook, willing for a companion in her situation.

"Well it would be correct," said George.

"George!" said Bullivant, pointing to the door, and George, to the relief of everyone, including himself, found himself passing through it.

"Would you wish to follow George, Miriam?" said Bullivant, implying that the company Miriam kept, was her own affair.

"No," said Miriam.

"I am glad to hear it," said Cook, "and hope it is true in every sense. Not that there is any need for Miriam to maintain an indefinite sojourn from her duties."

Miriam departed and there was a sense of tension relaxed.

"Well, we three old fogeys can settle down," said Bullivant. "Not that the term is suggestive of anyone present beyond myself."

"You are rather hasty in your use of expressions," said Cook.

"There was no cause of offence," said Miss Buchanan.

"May Mrs. Selden replenish your cup, Miss Buchanan?" said Bullivant, extending his hand.

"Had Miriam finished her tea?" said Miss Buchanan, as she yielded it.

"Well, if she had not, she had made some progress towards it," said Cook. "She was the only person who broached that preserve, with the exception of George, in a supercilious spirit. Not that that attitude always has the suggested result."

"George is something of an enigma," said Bullivant, with a sigh.

"And one that too much of our time and attention cannot go towards solving," said Cook.

"What an original cup!" said Miss Buchanan, observing too late that it bore an inscription.

"What is the motto on it?" said Cook.

Miss Buchanan leaned forward with her.

"Thirst after righteousness—I will give you drink— waters of affliction," murmured Bullivant, reading from one cup after another a Biblical legend in affinity with its function.

"They are among my private possessions," said Cook, "that are few enough in the life I have adopted."

"They were a present to Mrs. Selden on an occasion at her place of worship," said Bullivant.

"It was in the nature of an anniversary," said Cook, "and I was held to have conformed in the highest degree."

"You are surrounded by your own possessions, Miss Buchanan," said Bullivant.

"Yes, I could not settle down amongst other people's."

"It is a good thing that all are not rooted to earth by such considerations," said Cook. "I have had to place my treasure elsewhere, and have not found it beyond me."

"And the same could no doubt be said of Miss

Buchanan, in the event of requirement," said Bullivant.

"Will you take a glance at the paper, Miss Buchanan, while I clear the table?" said Cook. "I am entitled to Miriam's services, but cannot have them without the girl herself, and am electing to dispense with both. You might give us any items that strike your eye. I have not glanced down the columns."

Miss Buchanan extended a resolute hand, but found it intercepted by Bullivant.

"Miss Buchanan will talk to me in the intervening period, Mrs. Selden. I do not waste the time granted to us by a guest."

Miss Buchanan had a sense of moving unscathed through dangers, and wondered if she could depend on her immunity.

The door opened and George entered, crossed the room in a careless manner, took up the paper at a juncture that involved his appearing to wrest it from Bullivant and Miss Buchanan, sat down in an armchair and began to read.

"Am I right in recalling, George, that I intimated a wish for your withdrawal?" said Bullivant, with a tremble in his tone.

"I don't know. Are you?" said George, just raising his eyes.

"So you feel you have the right to take matters into your own hands?" said Cook.

"Are you going to deign a response to Mrs. Selden's query, George?" said Bullivant.

"Silence is consent. Of course I have the right," said George, who had returned with the object of vindicating it.

A silence followed, that could hardly be called consent, and was broken by Bullivant.

"So you are of such mature years, George, that you and I associate on a ground of equality."

George looked up and nodded, and Bullivant found himself glancing at Cook, but withdrew the glance as an unsuitable appeal to a frailer being.

The silence that followed seemed as if it could not be broken by human agency, and was indeed only broken by Bullivant after he had invoked superhuman aid.

"Are you aware, George, that you have not lifted your eyes from that paragraph since you took up the paper?"

George not only lifted his eyes, but lifted his hands and cast the paper to the ground, and then rose and rushed from the room, with his arms flung out behind him.

"Dear, dear, dear!" said Cook.

"Well, well, well!" said Bullivant.

"Come, come," said Miss Buchanan, suppressing an impulse to say the word a third time.

There was a pause, while Bullivant felt that his surprise at this response to his appeal was due to his little faith.

"Well, I do not suppose that George will be long in attaining the point of recovery," said Cook, in an easy tone.

"Not that signs of that stage are apparent as yet," said Bullivant with a smile that was equally easy.

"Does this often occur?" said Miss Buchanan.

"It is an isolated incident," said Cook.

"And completely foreign to George's nature," said Bullivant, with no intention of violating the truth.

"We all act inconsistently with our natures at times," said Cook.

"Or the natures themselves are inconsistent," said Miss Buchanan.

"A profound remark," said Bullivant.

"And one that explains why we sometimes surprise ourselves and others," said Cook.

"You are addicted to thinking things out, Miss Buchanan?" said Bullivant, reflecting that this must often be his guest's resource.

"I should say you are a great reader," said Cook, "and I am sure Mr. Bullivant would say the same."

"I should think it would be all or nothing with Miss Buchanan."

"Yes," said the latter, feeling that of two alternatives she might choose either.

"What led you to think of having letters sent to your shop?" said Cook, who had always been curious on this point.

"It is a way of eking things out. The shop is not too well placed for trade."

"I expect you receive some curious missives, if only you knew," said Bullivant.

"You must often feel inclined to tear off the covers and cast your eyes over them," said Cook.

"Miss Buchanan is a more suitable character for dealings of trust than that," said Bullivant.

"An impulse that must be resisted, of course," said Cook, as though completing her previous speech.

"Miss Buchanan's 'clientèle' is safe with her," said Bullivant.

Miss Buchanan gave a questioning frown.

"The word not familiar to you, Miss Buchanan?" said Bullivant, bending towards her and using his musical note.

"Clientèle! Clients," said Cook. "The people who avail themselves of your services."

"Oh, those who want to hide their letters," said Miss Buchanan, as though a more pedestrian term would have been in place.

"Or who receive any kind of attention from you. You may see it in the papers a dozen times a day."

Miss Buchanan's conception of the daily journal became a degree more clouded.

"I can chiefly imagine Miss Buchanan reading news and political items," said Bullivant.

Miss Buchanan's imagination had gone further, and shown her reading the paper from beginning to end.

"You are not at liberty to divulge the names of those who resort to your facilities?" said Cook.

"My 'clientèle'?" said Miss Buchanan, with a twitch of her lips. "No, I am not."

"The system is confidential," said Bullivant. "But I wonder that people do not sometimes encounter each other."

"They do, but they pretend they came to buy something at the shop. Indeed they generally pretend that, whenever they come."

"Perhaps that is why the two businesses are often combined," said Bullivant, with a smile. "Anyhow you are the right person in the place."

Miss Buchanan did not gainsay it, as she felt it was becoming established.

"Which is always a compliment in any position," said Cook.

"The letters are kept apart, I suppose, each one for its owner?" said Bullivant. "I dare say your friends help you to sort them, when you are otherwise engaged."

"No, they must not see the names. I do everything myself."

Bullivant was silent.

"What kind of appearance do the letters present?" said Cook. "Different from those destined for average recipients?"

"No, they are ordinary letters. They happen to be private; that is all."

"And they remain so with you," said Bullivant. "Not that the term, ordinary, would probably be correct, if the envelopes were transparent."

"It is a good thing they are not," said Miss Buchanan, with her hint of a smile.

"Sterling honesty is clearly the primary essential," said Cook.

"You must see all kinds of writings in the course of the year," said Bullivant.

"I am not good at reading handwriting. The postman reads out the names on the envelopes," said Miss Buchanan, who knew better than to disguise her system. "He has to see them in order to deliver the letters."

"It is print that attracts you?" said Bullivant, feeling the common impulse to venture on dangerous ground.

Miss Buchanan made no denial, indeed had no reason to do so.

"I hope your household is regaining its proper lines," she said, with an instinct to turn to other people's weaker side. "Of course it is no good to pretend that nothing is known."

"I think we felt it best to pretend just that, Miss Buchanan," said Bullivant, in a frank manner. "But there was an element of contrivance in it, as you imply. And it failed of success."

"As anything based on the disingenuous is bound to do," said Cook; "in the true sense, if not in the current one."

"But I think we may claim that our household is regaining its lines, as Miss Buchanan puts it," said Bullivant, "that indeed it has regained them, and that it never went so far off them as was thought."

"Ill news flies apace," said Cook. "And gains additions. Not that a house of this standing should fail of setting a standard. We have not felt on our level."

"You are very much at one with the family," said Miss Buchanan. "I do not quite put myself into your place."

"And would hardly wish to," said Bullivant, smiling. "You are of an independent cast of character."

"It is a life where the claims of self may not play quite their usual part," said Cook, "which is a circumstance more adapted to some than to others."

"And to Mrs. Selden more than to most," said Bullivant.

"Mr. Lamb is said to be a difficult character," said Miss Buchanan.

"You are like the Athenians of old," said Bullivant, "always hearing some new thing."

"It is usually the same thing over and over again."

"As I suppose may be said of this," said Cook. "And the master is not cast in the common mould; that could not be claimed."

"It is not claimed," said the guest. "But I hear there is much less saving and scraping in the household."

"The master has had his principles and has lived up to them, never exempting himself, which is to be respected; and has lately permitted some relaxation to himself and others."

"Which is also to be respected in him," said Bullivant. "What else have you heard of us, Miss Buchanan?"

The latter saw that its revelation would be unwelcome, and was too uncompromising to modify it. Her sense of her own disadvantages did not lead her to gloss over other people's.

"Nothing to our credit, I see," said Bullivant.

"It is things to people's discredit that become rife," said Cook. "As is in the nature of things. Gossip is gossip, and not understanding or charity."

At this moment Miriam entered the room and directed her eyes to the supper table.

"Shall I set the supper?"

"What do you think?" said Cook.

"It is set," said Miriam, regarding it.

"Then was there any point in your query?"

"I thought you meant me to do it."

"And have you not seen cause to revise that opinion?"

"I am in time to set it," said Miriam, disposing of possible criticism.

"It is Mrs. Selden who has revised her opinion and set it herself," said Bullivant.

George entered the room with his hands in his pockets, and a hum proceeding from his lips. Cook and Bullivant glanced at him and then at each other, and he sauntered to the window and stood looking out, with his hands lifting his trousers, and the hum swelling in volume. The manner of his entrance was designed to balance his exit, which perhaps did require some atonement.

"Well, I think you may draw the curtains, Miriam," said Cook. "There is not much for you and George to contemplate in the gathering dusk."

"We are taking our seats early to-night, Miss Buchanan," said Bullivant, "in order that Mrs. Selden may turn her attention to her dinner."

"It sounds as if I were in the habit of taking a private collation later," said Cook. "Whereas the truth comes under the opposite head, my appetite being variable."

George took his seat a minute later than the rest, and in a manner suggesting that it was only by chance that he took it at all. His detachment was opportune, as the first item of the meal did not involve himself and Miriam. Cook had had her doubts about adhering to her plan, but had taken the resolute course. George sat in an apparent trance, his fingers executing a crawl across the cloth, and his voice crooning its semi-conscious refrain.

"Now, George, we have had enough of that hymn," said Bullivant. "And we prefer Mrs. Selden's rendering of it."

George, startled to find that his song was not only religious but owed to Cook, broke it off and accepted the second dish, seeming hardly to know what he did, and indeed only half aware of it.

"It is an advantage you have over me, Miss Buchanan, that your evenings are your own," said Cook. "Mine is a calling that does not abate from dawn till dusk."

"I have cleaning after the shop is closed, and I have no one to help me as you have."

Cook glanced at Miriam, as at a hardly appreciable incident in her lot.

"And you have books to make up, and letters to attend to," said Bullivant, his eyes going over Miss Buchanan's face.

"My goods are paid for at the counter. Books are too much on a single woman. I know how things are going. I can hold a good deal in my head."

"You give me the impression, Miss Buchanan, that in the event of your being subject to some handicap, you would develop compensating faculties to a higher degree."

"Perhaps I should," said Miss Buchanan, who had her own proof of it.

"Handicap?" said Miriam.

"Disadvantage. Affliction," said Cook. "Such as blindness or deafness, as Mr. Bullivant has implied."

George had been casting about in his mind for some remark by which to reinstate himself.

"No one at this table has been married!" he said, as though suddenly struck by the position, and actually struck by the mild disadvantage of it.

"And no one in the house but the master and mistress," said Cook, "as Miss Emilia and Mr. Mortimer happen to set us the other example."

"I don't suppose that was their purpose in not marrying."

"And would their purpose, whatever it was, be made known to you?" said Cook, feeling that George's recovery, though opportune, was too complete.

"Some occupations call more than others for the state of celibacy," said Bullivant.

"It would be a good way of hiding that you could not get married, to choose one of them," said George.

"Why, George, have you already had your disappointments?"

"I did not choose my work," said George, as though this could not be said of everyone.

"Dear me, what does George know about marrying and giving in marriage?" said Cook.

"As much as anyone else here," said George.

"George thinks that experience is the only road to knowledge," said Bullivant, with a smile for this innocence.

"Whereas we are the heirs of all the ages," said Cook. "Not that that would have its application in every case."

"It would have been pleasant to be the heir of something besides," said Miss Buchanan.

"We cannot choose our walk in life," said Bullivant, "and there would be many fewer, if we could. And that would not make for the balance of things."

"I have never had any desire to alter my single state,"

said Cook, "and I should say that is the case with Miss Buchanan."

"People never say they want to change it," said George.

"Do you corroborate that, Miss Buchanan?" said Bullivant. "I refer, of course, to Mrs. Selden's suggestion."

"Yes, on the whole, things being as they are."

"You have no desire for help in any department of life?"

"Help is not the only thing you get in marriage," said Cook.

"No, but we will hope it is one of the things," said Bullivant.

"It would be counterbalanced by the remainder."

"Well, not in every case, Mrs. Selden. A man would take certain things off a woman."

"And put other things on, and more than would redress the balance."

"Is it your intention to marry, Miriam?" said Bullivant.

"Well, there would have to be another point of view to that," said Cook, struck by this aspect of the matter only in Miriam's case.

"No, I would rather be alone. It is best to have things to oneself."

"Not a very lofty reason for remaining single," said Bullivant.

"It is the orphanage routine," said Cook. "Things would be communal beyond the natural point."

"Has a similar experience had the same effect on you, George?" said Bullivant.

"No, I don't think it has," said George, in a deliberate tone. "It seems to have been more the result of your own experience."

Cook opened her mouth so quickly that her words had no time to take a form. Miriam looked at George in doubt of his meaning. Miss Buchanan gave a laugh before she knew it, and determined her own fate.

Bullivant took up a printed list from the table and held it before her eyes.

"Which of these would be your choice, Miss Buchanan, in the event of your admitting a partner to your life, and holding a celebration?"

Miss Buchanan looked at the list with easy interest.

"I should not say that Miss Buchanan takes much interest in wines," said Cook. "It is merely my own impression, but it may emerge as correct."

"No, no wines for me," said Miss Buchanan, shaking her head and waving away the list. "I am a lifelong teetotaller. No putting of temptation in my path."

She relaxed with a sense of having had a narrow escape, and Bullivant did the same with a similar feeling.

"I have never committed myself by a pledge," said Cook, "but the principle has my respect. Indeed I follow it, except on occasions."

"I see no reason for forgoing a good thing, because some people abuse it," said Bullivant.

"Which is also a view to meet with toleration," said Cook.

"This party does not seem a very affable one, judging by the dining-room standard," said George.

"Now how have you had the opportunity of judging, George?" said Bullivant, in a reasoned manner, warned against losing command of himself. "Your part has been to second my efforts in the background, and observation in the direct line does not come into it."

"Oh, I have eyes and ears," said George, not reflecting that this would have been a small matter, if he had not also had a tongue.

"And to continue, George," said Bullivant, with the stronger impulse to do this, that he had a sense of general attention, "if you would disabuse your mind of curiosity and unsuitable interests, your advance in promptness and exactitude might hardly be estimated. Not to speak of the items of ease and finish."

"It is only a servant's life in the end," said George.

"The qualifications do sound rather much for the reward," said Miss Buchanan.

"What is the point of putting oneself out to advance in it?"

"And in what other sphere would you have the opportunity to advance?" said Cook. "Are your facilities so widespread?"

"There must be other lives. All the world is not a servant."

"Pardon me, George," said Bullivant, on his most melodious note, "all the world is. There is no one, from the first to the last, who does not serve in some way the stratum above himself. Even the Queen is the servant of the State."

"But not at the sink," said George.

"She would be the last person to see that work as more lowering than hers."

"How do you come by your familiarity with the Queen? What facilities have you had for it?" said George, who was making his own advance in his present sphere.

"The knowledge is open to all," said Cook, "who have the mind to receive it."

"Her work is the farthest away from soiling her hands. Mine happens to be the nearest. And I would rather have hers."

"And what ground have you for estimating your capacities as on that level?"

"Oh, I dare say it is all done for her," said George.

"If that is your view of work, George, and its place in the scheme of things," said Bullivant, in a careful tone, "I should not say there is much prospect of your exemption from your present obligations."

"I agree that the hope is of the slenderest," said Cook.

"You both seem to like to have things done for you by other people."

"We have reached the stage when we are entitled to depute the lowest part of our work."

"Lowest! There is your word. It is as high as any other, isn't it? As high as the Queen's. I knew what you really thought."

"You are not going the way to leave it behind, George," said Bullivant, shaking his head.

"Putting your heart into it means that you stay sunk in it up to the end."

"Sunk is not the word to be applied," said Cook, "except to those who merit it by their own downward course."

"What is your feeling towards your work, Miss Buchanan?" said Bullivant.

"Well, I do not compare it with the Queen's."

"Perhaps George would like to serve in a shop," said Miriam.

"Well, what is your response to that suggestion, George?" said Cook.

"In a way it might be better. But it would mean a small country shop and petty dealings."

There was a pause.

"Perhaps you would like to be Prime Minister at the outset," said Cook.

"Well, we should all like it."

"Now I do not think that I should," said Bullivant, looking into space, and using a voice in accordance with this breadth of vision. "I should simply feel that I was on a different point of the general system of things."

"Which would be the matter in a nutshell," said Miss Buchanan.

"Would you like to work in a shop, Miriam?" said Cook.

"No, I don't think I should," said Miriam, looking round the kitchen. "It would be less like a home."

"And how do you know what that is like?" said George.

"Some people can use their imaginations, though others cannot," said Cook, with a feeling of being trapped into paying Miriam a compliment.

"So you are content with your calling, Miss Buchanan?" said Bullivant. "Though no doubt we all have our own little obstacles in the way of success."

"I fail to see what obstacles there are in Miss Buchanan's

path," said Cook, "and if any existed, they have been overcome."

"I wonder what would be the most difficult obstacle in a life of trade," said Bullivant, in a ruminative manner.

"An indifferent state of health," said Cook. "A score on which I should be debarred from adopting it."

"What does Miss Buchanan feel about it?"

"Well, she has a right to summarise the matter."

Miss Buchanan did not exercise the right, though not doubting that it was hers.

"Perhaps some little personal disability," said Bullivant. "Something that would go through our dealings and isolate our position from other people's, though no one might be aware of it."

"Such as a hasty temper," said Cook, "though 'uncertain' might be a more comprehending word, as it tends to be a matter of the nerves."

"Why, I think people would know of that, Mrs. Selden, and I am sure it is not a quality of Miss Buchanan's," said Bullivant, betraying that he had imagined the other disadvantage as embodied in the guest.

"What sort of drawback had you in mind?" said the latter.

"Oh, some little thing like having no memory, or not being able to add or subtract, or something like that."

"Such things as Miss Buchanan would find it hard to imagine, as you have struck on her strongest points," said Cook. "She would feel she might as well not be able to read or write."

"You have chanced on my strong suit, Mr. Bullivant," said Miss Buchanan, not able to add that Cook had done the same.

"I often wish I could go back to school for a period," said Cook, "and make good some of my deficiencies."

"Do you feel the same about your schooldays, Miss Buchanan? Were they the happiest days in your life?" said Bullivant, perhaps feeling that phantom days would be free from care.

198

"What are your feelings on the matter, George?" said Cook.

Bullivant raised his hand and spoke in a low, rapid tone.

"No bringing in of George, if you please, Mrs. Selden. It is only the precursor of trouble, and in this case would bring up his past, that has been dealt with to exhaustion. Miriam, do you feel any desire to return to school?"

"Well, learning does not seem to teach people much."

"It certainly left you ignorant of most things," said Cook. "And it is not much in itself, as far as I can gather."

"I suppose she learned what was necessary," said Bullivant.

"It depends on what meaning you attach to the term. She cannot do much more than read and write."

Miss Buchanan's eyes rested on Miriam, as on the embodiment of natural ambitions fulfilled.

"How much do you read and write, Miriam?" said Bullivant.

"I read a book sometimes, and I can make the lists for Cook."

"I am careful to ensure that she does not lose what she knows, but, if anything, adds to it," said Cook.

"What more can any of us do than she does?" said George.

"Has it been encumbent on us to show you the limit of our capacities?" said Cook. "In which case I have not been aware of it."

"It was not a question to come from you, George, to the assembled company," said Bullivant.

"As may be said of many of George's utterances to-night," said Cook. "He has not enhanced the occasion. And I think the remaining questions he has to put, may be put elsewhere."

George and Miriam rose, and Miss Buchanan followed their example.

"It is time for me to go home."

"The moment has come very quickly," said Cook. "But

I hope it may often be repeated, together with those that precede it."

"It cannot be deferred, Miss Buchanan?" said Bullivant, in a tone that suggested a bow.

"No, it is time I was at home. I have work to do before I go to bed."

"Now I wish you had someone to lift things off you a little," said Bullivant, as he helped her into her coat.

"That would mean giving as well as taking, and all lives have their weaker side," said Miss Buchanan, with no suggestion that this was not true of those just revealed.

"Well, so your proposition was not exactly accepted," said Cook, as Bullivant returned from the door.

The latter looked his question.

"Your offer to relieve Miss Buchanan and attend upon her needs, was not taken up with alacrity."

"I am at a loss for your meaning."

"You know what I mean."

"Pardon me, Mrs. Selden, I do not."

"You had not made previous mention of your intention to change your state, or rather of your disposition to do so."

"I had not. For circumstances did not call for it."

"The call is at the moment, I suppose. Your decision is of a sudden character."

"You read too much into accepted formality, Mrs. Selden. I might be tempted to accuse you of ignorance of the ways of the world. There are ways in which a man may serve a woman, that do not imply an access of interest."

Bullivant retrieved Cook's scarf and placed it on her shoulders, and she felt a natural uncertainty how far to appreciate the attention.

"Men have found themselves committed before now," she said.

"Miss Buchanan is not of a character to build upon nothing. You do an injustice to a lonely woman, who has had much to contend with."

"I fail to see why loneliness is a commendable characteristic. It might be more of one to be of an interested nature, and willing for normal intercourse."

"Other people's problems are not known to us."

"Hers are known to you in some way, it seems to transpire."

"We are all at times the recipients of confidences."

"You have not been made the repository of Miss Buchanan's, unless I have been much mistaken," said Cook, betraying that she had no real anxiety upon Bullivant's relation with his guest. "That is not an interchange that would take place."

"You are correct in the surmise, as I have been at pains to imply. I was not referring to her own communications. There are other channels."

"So someone has been gossiping about her. You would be better advised not to lend your ear."

"Gossip is not the word," said Bullivant. "There are some whose very names refute the term, and the proof of it is that my lips are sealed."

"They might be sealed more closely. People can be betrayers of confidences as well as recipients."

"I hope that does not apply to me. I hope there has not been anything unguarded in my words to betray my trust. I do not disguise that one was reposed in me."

"The knowledge that something is being concealed, constitutes a step towards knowing its nature."

"You have not been led to suspicion? I may not have been wary enough in my course. I may have admitted an element of rashness. I do not deny it, if it is the truth. It is not my habit to practise concealment, as it is not my nature. If we harbour the same thing in our minds, let it remain there; let it not pass our lips."

"There could hardly be another piece of knowledge of that calibre. And the passing of the lips leads to a lesser risk of brooding and betrayal. The question, is which of us is to give voice to it."

"Mrs. Selden, I see that the initiative should be mine.

But somehow the words do not take a form. And has the truth actually passed from my mind to yours? That is what has not emerged."

"Well, the veneer wore thin to anyone who could form conclusions. But I was the only one of your hearers to whom that would apply," said Cook, ending with a note of comfort.

"Mrs. Selden, I approach the matter in all respect, both for womanhood and the particular woman involved. It is indeed misfortune rather than fault; all honour is due to her for her overcoming of it. And now the words sound trivial, in spite of the deserved tribute. The daily solace of our leisure hours is denied to Miss Buchanan. In short, she is not able to read."

"'In short' was hardly the term perhaps," said Cook, with a smile.

"I could not approach the matter harshly or abruptly, Mrs. Selden. There was one way of making the revelation for me, and in that way it was made. And I fear that to you revelation was not the term."

Cook was silent for a space.

"But what was the object of your tactics with the wine list? And your allusions to handicaps and obstacles?"

"Mrs. Selden, I do not defend myself. It was an impulse of the moment, not to be condoned."

"Why did you want to occasion discomfiture to a lonely woman, who has had much to contend with?" said Cook, with a light in her eye, as she used Bullivant's words.

"I think this disposes of your theory that I am guilty of excessive interest in her."

"There are other points to which the term, guilty, can be applied."

"I cannot explain it to myself. It was skating on thin ice, which is a regrettable human impulse. The vein of impishness in me has been my bane."

"I also have a confession to make," said Cook, in a rapid, expressionless tone. "I could not sleep with it lying on me like a weight. The truth did not transpire in the way I led you to infer. I saw there was something, and felt the instinct to pursue it, and implied that I knew it, to lead you to its betrayal. If truth is better than falsehood, there it is. I am not denying that there are things that are better still."

Bullivant did not deny it either.

"Mrs. Selden, I should not have thought it of you."

"There has been a good deal that I should not have thought of *you*, to-night."

"This should help us to see that George must have his failings."

"Yes, if assistance on that point is needed."

"It must lower our opinion of ourselves."

"It will do that rather than heighten our view of George. We have met a good deal of human nature to-night, and have made our own contribution. The vein of impishness may be present in all three of us," said Cook, her expression suggesting that it was at work at the moment in herself.

"The secret will be safe with you, Mrs. Selden?"

"More so that with you, I presume, considering that you had no more to gain by imperilling it. I should not take such a step without ultimate object."

"Well, I hope the occasion served its purpose," said Bullivant, leaving a matter that could not be helped by words. "It made a break in a routine that has not too many. Bright spots are few in some lives, and therefore should not be tampered with, as I freely admit."

"And George and Miriam were here to enhance the occasion," said Cook, drily. "Not that Miss Buchanan appeared to think it the worse for them."

"I am becoming tired of the problems that George presents," said Bullivant, with a frown. "He has no idea that preoccupation with his affairs can have its bounds."

"And any attempt at correction recoils upon ourselves. The solution can only be some climax that will bring things home. I am the last to be an ill-wisher to youth, but George will only be saved by a catastrophe induced by himself. There can be no other turning point."

"No doubt you have your eye on Miriam, in so far as she has to be with him."

"If I made a habit of taking it off, it would not be feasible for her to be here at all. Which would be one way of solving the problem."

Cook drifted into devout song, and Bullivant's subdued support of it suggested a sense of proved unworthiness to join in sacred observance. Such a feeling did not operate in Cook, who sang as though the act itself were something of an atonement. Bullivant had also to keep his ear open for a possible bell. No bell fell on it, but its alertness was not wasted.

"They don't seem to think they have much to sing about," said George's voice. "And they are more right than usual. Servants they are; servants they sound; and servants they remain, in spite of all their satisfaction."

"A servant I am, and a servant I remain, George," said Bullivant, in a low, melodious voice, addressing the idea of George, and the walls of the kitchen, and glancing to see if Cook were also of the audience. "So it is; so it has been; so it will be; and I am satisfied."

CHAPTER IX

"FATHER HAS NOT opened his letter," said Avery. "I will open it for him."

"No, it is not your letter. You must leave it alone," said Horace.

Avery looked into his face and glanced at Sarah.

"Letters are private things," she said.

"But it does not matter if Avery opens them," said Marcus, "as he cannot read writing."

"It is time that he could," said his father.

"But then he could not permit himself to do so," said Tamasin. "What good would it do him?"

"He will have letters of his own in time."

"Sarah will always read them to me," said Avery.

"It is time you grew out of that," said Horace.

"It took Jasper some time to grow into it," said Tamasin. "He used not to want to know what was in his letters."

"He had too few for him to realise the point of them," said Sarah.

"A thing should not lack interest, because it is rare," said Horace.

Avery regarded him with questioning eyes. Bullivant dropped his glance as he moved about the table, and drew a deep breath in a manner of anticipation fulfilled. The children were visiting their elders at breakfast, a recent custom that aroused Charlotte's misgiving on the ground of the threat of the hour.

"I don't read writing properly yet," said Jasper. "I don't think I ever shall."

"I wonder you like to say so," said Horace.

Avery looked again at his father, and Bullivant walked to the door, with an unconscious air of turning his back on what could not be avoided or helped.

"Anyone can read letters for me," said Jasper, "and I still hardly ever have any."

"So you are content to be on Avery's level. And you should not put people to the trouble."

"They always seem to like to read them."

"People do like to read letters," said Marcus, "especially those that are written to someone else."

"They do that sometimes when they are not supposed to," said Tamasin. "They must like it very much."

"That is a serious piece of wrong-doing," said her father. "They might come on something they were not supposed to know, and that might have grave results."

"Do people have so many secrets?" said Sarah. "And if they are wrong ones, wouldn't it be wiser not to write them down?"

"It does seem that letters ought not to be so private," said Charlotte. "The rules about them should never have had to arise."

"Or anyhow to be so solemn," said Marcus.

"People say things about each other," said Tamasin. "That would be the trouble more often than real secrets. I don't think there would be so many of those."

"No. Life is hardly on that scale," said Charlotte. "People ought to admire each other more. That is the root of the matter."

"And of many others," said Sarah.

"We talk of reading letters," said Emilia. "It might be better if no one could write them."

"It hardly seems worth while to learn to read them," said Jasper, "when the only ones we may read, are those we can have read to us."

"People may have secrets that are innocent," said his father. "Someone might want to share one with you. We do not owe everyone our confidence."

"People might want to hide the good they were doing to someone else," said Jasper.

"Trying not to let the left hand know what the right hand was doing," said Tamasin. "But I don't think that is the reason for not reading letters. The right hand does not do as much as that. Even if it really does not let people know about it."

Emilia and Charlotte laughed, while Horace remained grave.

"It is the left hand that has made the rule necessary," said Sarah. "It seems to be the more active of the two."

"I think the nature of man must be left-handed," said Tamasin.

Marcus broke into laughter; Tamasin did the same; and the pair rocked about on the verge of losing self-control.

"No, leave them alone," said Horace, as Charlotte rose to shepherd them to the door. "They must learn to behave like civilised beings, without being protected from themselves."

"It is Cousin Mortimer's writing on the letter," said Jasper.

"You should not have looked at it," said Horace. "And if you saw it by accident, you should have said nothing. He was obliged to show the writing, and you took advantage of his being helpless in the matter."

"He could have got someone else to address it for him," said Marcus.

"But we should not like people to be put to such shifts, to protect themselves from our prying. We should have too much respect both for them and for ourselves."

"Then shouldn't we ever look even at envelopes?"

"Never," said Horace. "No more than at anything else that is not your concern. Jasper has found out that my letter was from Cousin Mortimer, and that was nothing to do with him."

"But we knew Cousin Mortimer would write," said Avery, "because he promised he would."

Sarah gave him a warning frown.

"Do not exchange glances with people, Sarah. It is not a thing that is done. And there was nothing in what I said to cause any alarm."

Horace eased his tone and smiled as he ended, and rose and went to the fire with the letter. The children left the room, as though at his word, with something perplexed and dejected about them.

"My dear Horace,—You told me not to write to you, but I am never so malicious as to take people at their word. It is almost like telling them that they have made their bed and must lie on it. Thank you very much for your letter. It has broken my heart, but that is the natural result of the use of words. When human speech developed, it was a foregone thing. It allowed people to communicate their thoughts, and what else could come of that? And putting them on paper renders it a certainty. People can keep on returning to them.

"I am in homely and comfortable rooms, as I knew from a card in the window. The card has been taken down now, which may be a mistake. It is best to keep a thing like that before your eyes. My landlady is an acquaintance of Bullivant's and has had a letter from him. I should not have thought he would write letters. What occasion can he have for breaking hearts?

"You are wondering how I spend my time, which is kind of you, considering everything. I just wait for it to pass, and I find it is true that all things come to those who wait. Five weeks have gone beyond recall, which seems very nice and thorough. I cannot understand why people want to recall the hours. I could not bear to have my time back again.

"It is nice of you to miss me so much, when I wronged you under your own roof. But it was not my fault that I had no roof of my own, and had to do things under yours. And roofs seem to give rise to situations. Whenever anything happens, there is mention of them. As a child I always wanted to be a gipsy, and they are known to be such a moral people. I think it does show that my heart is in the right place. And I only had the one thing to hide, when most people have so many. And such petty things, that really take from them. My sin was single and great; I could not have borne not to be worthy of you, Horace. I am homesick and solitary and suffering with a man's simplicity, but I do not talk about myself. And I know I deserve everything, which is a great comfort. I have not that bitter sense of injustice that is so hard to bear. Of course it is satisfactory to have the due reward of your deeds.

"I have had a letter from Magdalen. She sent it for me to keep for always. And she asked for one from me, for her to do the same. I did not make several attempts and tear them up. I made one attempt and read it aloud until I knew it; I did admire it so much; and then I posted it. And I felt quite glad that someone was to keep it for always. Magdalen's letter did quite well to tear up, and I know she would be glad for it to serve any purpose of mine. How I should hate to be like other people! It might mean writing so many letters. But I have your letter, and of course I will keep it for always.

"I am just going out for my lonely walk, before I settle down at the fireside, to feel I have nothing to look forward to. I cannot live in the past, because that must be as if it did not exist.

"My landlady brings me regular meals, which somehow sounds to her credit. But why are meals described as regular, when we don't talk about other things as if they ought to be haphazard?

"Of course you must not shed a tear for me, as I am not worth it.

"God bless you, my dear boy,

"MORTIMER."

Horace sat with the letter in his hand, and a look on his

face that seemed to call for its words. He missed his cousin in a measure he could not confront or confess. His sense of wrong was sunk in the depth of his need. This was where his bitterness had its real source. Mortimer might deceive him in his home, might scheme to break up his life, but must not take his heart from himself.

"Has Mortimer anything to say?" said Emilia, her voice calm over her courage.

"Nothing that will help him," said Horace, in a cold tone. "And his name was to be forgotten."

"Not after fifty-five years. The future shortens too much for words of that kind. They can be only words."

"You must face the truth, Horace," said Charlotte. "You are not so much the master of your own fate, and we are none of us the masters of our feelings. You cannot spend thirty years in waiting for the end. Your life must be adapted to your nature, possible for you to live."

Horace left the room without reply, looked back at the fire as though to throw the letter on it, but kept it in his hand. He set out on a walk by himself, meaning to face and sort his thoughts. He passed his two elder sons, employed in the garden, and suppressed an impulse to ask for their company. He felt he had nothing to give and little to take, and that the intercourse would carry its danger.

"What are you making?" he said in a pleasant tone. "I shall be back in an hour or two to see what you have done."

"Jasper is making a hutch, and I am helping him," said Marcus. "When we come to the skilled part, I shall read to him while he does it. It will not be finished to-day."

Horace crossed the park and mounted the hill that rose in front of the gates. The boys worked on without a word, now and then lifting their eyes to scan the rising road and their father's figure.

"Father has gone to the ravine," said Jasper, after some time. "He took the road that leads across it by the bridge."

"He will know that the bridge is broken."

"How will he know? Was he there when the message came?"

"You know he was not. But he will see it is not safe."

"How will he see?" said Jasper. "The man said the damage did not show. The boards were shivered by the storm, but they had not broken. They would give way under anyone's weight. But if they did, he could save himself; he is a grown-up man."

"He is not a person anything could happen to," said Marcus, with a laugh. "It is not as if anyone else were going to the bridge."

"Anyone else would be killed. No one has lived, who has fallen down that cliff."

"Why did we not tell him?" said Marcus, as though he wanted an answer to the question.

"He walked away so quickly; there was not much time."

"Why did we not run after him? We could have caught him up."

"He might have been cross," said Jasper. "It startles him to be overtaken, and you know what he is like when he is startled."

"It is better to be startled than killed. He would be less safe than we should. He would put more weight on the bridge."

The brothers looked into each other's eyes, found that their lips were unsteady, and let their eyes fall.

"It seemed that the other times might come back," said Jasper.

"If they did, we could not bear it. And Mother could not bear it either. It would be better for him to die, if it was the only thing to prevent that."

"And his soul would be safe," said Jasper. "He is so good now."

"That is more than can be said of us. We are worse than we have ever been. We are not meant to kill people, whatever the reason. We might meet him in a future state, and know that he knew about it. It would be what is called poetic justice."

"That would not be for a long time."

"It might be soon. Some people would die of remorse."

"I think we should go on living," said Jasper.

"We want to live ourselves, and we have not let Father live; and he has never been as bad as we are, and he was trying so hard to be better. Even when he could hardly do it, he went on trying. It is not fair that he should die, and we should not."

"He has had a good deal of his life."

"But people want it all. And he has been so kind lately. The last thing he said to us was kind, and the last thing we did to him was this."

"He was always rather kind sometimes. He gave us things even when he wanted to save them. And he did not have so very much himself."

"When he might have had everything," said Marcus. "There is not enough time to run after him. Can we tell people, so that he can be saved?"

"He is dead by now, if he has crossed the bridge. We both know that nothing can be done."

The brothers looked at each other and broke into weeping. They threw down their tools, paced the paths with clenched hands, scanned the steep and deserted road, and abandoned themselves to grief. Charlotte, walking in the gardens, heard the sounds and hastened to the spot. Her sons threw themselves upon her and poured out their tale, protecting themselves by incoherence from the full truth. She gathered that Horace had gone to the bridge, and that they had remembered the warning too late. She rushed to the house to send aid to the spot, and returned to share the vigil.

"He must have reached the bridge," said Marcus. "He was walking fast. They can't get there in time."

"He may not have gone to that place," said Charlotte.

"The road leads nowhere else. And he has not come back. And there has been quite enough time. Father is dead, when he did not want to die. And no one has ever done anything for him. And lately he has done all he could for other people."

"The bridge must have broken under him," said Jasper. "The man said it would not bear anyone's weight. He said it when you were there."

"And I did not think to pass on the message. Your father has not gone that way for a long time. He used to go sometimes when he had been upset about something, but all that belonged to the past."

"It seemed rather like that again to-day," said Jasper.

"He was not in good spirits this morning, and I knew he was out by himself. But it did not cross my mind that he might take that path. It is more my fault than yours."

Jasper and Marcus clung to their mother, wringing their hands and watching the hill that seemed to lie more bleak and steep. She returned to the house to await the men, and they followed her, without the will to be different. Preparations were made for an accident; the men had taken a mattress; the doctor was in the house. There was nothing to do but live the hour and face the possible truth.

The brothers stayed in the hall, crouched in its darkest corner, acquiescing in their mother's word that the trouble should be kept from the house. They felt it was on them that the weight must lie, that it was right it should lie there. When a sound came, they hid their faces and pressed closer to the wall. Their father's voice, faint and unreal and incredible, came as a threat from a ghostly world. As it steadied and swelled, they trembled and clutched each other. Then they sprang up and flung themselves upon him in an ecstasy of joy, shaking and weeping in their first experience of utter relief. Horace was startled and bewildered and looked at his wife.

"They remembered that the bridge was broken, after you had gone. It was too late to run after you. They have been in such a state. So have we all."

"My poor little sons!" said Horace. "And they were not so far from the truth. When I reached the bridge I found a board marked 'Danger', and climbed up the cliff above it and walked, clinging to the slope, until I reached the road. If I had known the effort it would be, I would have returned. I am in a state of exhaustion. And it was only by chance that the board was there in time. I do not wonder at your feelings. It is one of those cases when it is better not to think of what might have been."

"You might have been dead, and it would have been because of us," said Marcus.

"We will never do anything like it again," said Jasper. "We should have killed someone who knew us and lived with us. We should always have thought about it."

"What you did, was to forget an important message. It was a serious thing and might have had tragic results. But there was no question of anything more. It was quite by chance that it involved the safety of your father. No one can completely guard against forgetfulness and coincidence. You need not imagine too much."

The boys relaxed and stood in exhaustion, taking deep breaths and looking about them in their return to ordinary life. Their eyes looked as if they were surveying a new world.

The men with the stretcher came to the door, and entered to say their word.

"It was a bad hour, sir. The mistress will be the worse. The work was done sooner than we thought. The board is fixed to block up the bridge. There is no longer any danger. No one can pass."

"The trouble is over," said Horace. "But the message should have gone through the house. In future such messages must be brought to me. It does not do to depend on their being passed on."

"We gave it in the kitchen, sir, and saw that it was taken upstairs. And we saw the young gentlemen in the garden just before you passed them. We thought you were going to the bridge to inspect the damage."

"Then you could do no more," said Horace. "Thank you. That is enough."

The men went on to the kitchen, and Horace looked from his wife to his sons.

"So this is how it is. This is the reason of the scene. This is the meaning of the talk and the tears. They were not old enough to carry the project through, but it was their nerve that failed them, not their will. The truth is clear."

Charlotte looked afraid, and Emilia so grave that gravity seemed a new thing. The boys stood pale and shaking, looking at the ground.

"So I am placed like this. My children desire my death. That is their feeling for their father. I have escaped from it to find it is what is wished for me. And I can honestly say that I have never wished it for anyone else. I have never grudged anyone the right to live."

There was silence, and Horace's voice went on.

"I may be a dour and difficult man, but I am not sunk to this. I have done nothing that means a hard heart. I have had much to contend with, and have found it too much, but no failure of mine has been on this scale. I may have clouded people's lives, but I have never tried to destroy them. I have never grudged a fellow being breath. And this is done to me by creatures who would be called my innocent children."

"It is their childishness that accounts for it," said Charlotte. "Their minds are less ready than ours. The moment passed before they knew it. They could not have been more distressed than they were, when they grasped the truth."

"They protected themselves throughout by falsehood and evasion. Their own safety was their thought through all the well acted scene. Yes, they acted it well; I grant it to them. I was deceived by them, and so were you. Or were you in league with them against me? It would not be the first time you had planned my undoing with someone supposed to hold me dear. What is the reason of that look, Emilia? How would you feel in my place?"

"I could not be in your place. A failure on my part, such as yours this morning, would not take on the guise of a threat too great to be borne. Your trouble is that the past is still alive. It is a thing that dies hard."

"It is no good to try to live it down. I had better go back to my old ways. I see they were more wholesome. They did not lead to this."

"This is what they led to," said Emilia.

"Then every time I am weary or distraught, I may look for a plot against my life! It is a strange way to live, a strange way to go on from day to day, always walking on a quagmire, always in danger. I have walked much on one in my life. Charlotte, will you send your sons away? I do not feel I can speak to them myself. I must think what is to be done, think if I can keep them in the house, if I can leave them with their sisters. Their fate is at their own door. There it must be laid. I have not brought it on them. I have altered their lives. I have tried to alter myself, and few human beings have done that. But it has been to no purpose. They are not of a character to take understanding and kindness. The old methods were the best."

The brothers crept away, Marcus crying, Jasper trying to consider their course. They felt they were in greater trouble than they had ever conceived. The earlier clouds and constraints did not exist.

"What are we to do with them?" said Horace.

The women gave him no answer; they could not give one to themselves.

"We cannot go on as if nothing had happened."

"We could not, if only this had happened," said Emilia.

"It is no good to take the stand that this is the natural result of the past. Of anything you like in the past. This is no doing of mine. It was something in the nature of the boys, whom we have seen as innocent and helpless. Who was the helpless one? They or I?"

Emilia was silent, trying to weigh the words.

"What line are we to follow? How are we to regard them? Can I regain my feelings as a father? Can we treat them as simple boys? Have we to be always on our guard against them, lest they harm us or harm others? Have we to protect them against themselves, to protect them against other people's knowledge of them? How are those questions to be answered?"

"Can I be of any help, my dear boy?"

Horace turned and started forward, and almost fell on his cousin's neck before he recalled himself.

"You do not know how I am placed, Mortimer. You do not know of this last threat that has assailed me."

"Yes, yes, I do. I have been paying great attention."

"You have been a witness of this, the saddest scene in my life?"

"I have not taken my eyes off it. I have never met one like it before."

"What would you do, if you had my part in it?"

"There does not seem anything to be done now."

"How would you bear yourself in my strange place?"

"Well, we are all the victims of circumstances. I suppose as a victim. And I think that is what you are doing."

"Would you cast off your sons and never again utter their names?"

"That would mean that the truth would emerge. And people tend to think that we deserve what happens to us. I suppose they know they always deserve it themselves. Of course I do not mean that you deserved it, but people never know how exceptional we are. They themselves are so commonplace."

"Can I see them day by day and watch them grow up, as if nothing had happened?"

"I hardly know, my dear boy. No, I should not think so. I hardly expect you will do quite that."

"Is it not strange that the pair of them acted with one accord? You would think that one would put a check upon the other."

"I think you would. But the moment passed quickly and the chance with it. And children regard grown-up people as masters of their own fate. They know how easily they are masters of other people's. And they were really glad that you were not dead, and that is a great thing, when you think how readily people can spare each other."

"You have not a high opinion of human nature, Mortimer."

"No, I have not. And it is not because I judge other people by myself. That is a thing I never do."

"It is a strange and sinister thing that has befallen me. And I was already in a sad enough place. It is indeed a case of woe upon woe."

"It must be because it never rains but it pours. People should not say such things; it helps to establish them. And really I think it always rains a little."

"Why have you come back?" said Horace.

"Because I heard your voice saying: 'Mortimer, Mortimer.'"

"I suppose you are only staying for a few hours."

"Horace, I do not think you are speaking the truth."

"You have come back for your own sake?"

"It is odd how bad that sounds, when it is true of almost everything that is ever done."

"Why did you choose to-day of all days?"

"Horace, do you not listen when I speak?"

"You did not know you were coming, when you wrote that letter. Or you gave no hint of it."

"No, my dear boy. Hints are so often taken. I suppose if they were not, they would not be worthy of the name."

"I had no thought of your returning."

"Then the cry from your heart must have been unconscious. It was the deeper sort of cry."

"You have not brought your luggage with you?"

"Only a very little. Bullivant only packed things for a few weeks."

"You have not my permission to remain in my house."

"Horace, I do hate to stay without it. But what am I to do? One cannot disregard a voice."

"The voice was not mine."

"Then surely you would not have me disregard it."

"Mortimer, if only you had not betrayed my trust!"

"Then you would not have had the chance of betraying mine. That letter would not have been written, that you found and read. You would not have amended your life and won the hearts of your children. I think you would be in a worse place."

"What letter?"

"Horace, this is unworthy of you."

"I did not know that you knew I had read it."

"This is at any rate open and above-board."

"It was a small thing indeed, compared with the wrong you did me."

"Yes, one of those little, petty things that are so hard to forgive."

"A wrong on a large scale is harder. That is the truth."

"It does seem to be," said Mortimer.

"I am not going to ask how you know that I read the letter."

"Well, it is a dignified course, and a little dignity does improve the position."

"No doubt you left it about and could not find it."

"It must be nice to have no doubt. Then of course questions are superfluous."

"It was addressed to Miss Buchanan's shop."

"I know it was. Not that I ever saw it. Does my taking that precaution look as if I should exercise so little care?"

"You deal in mysteries," said Horace.

"I do not think either of us has been quite open with the other. You must understand it, if it is too late to change now. On one point my lips are sealed. I rather like the slight importance of that."

"Mortimer, I must ask you one thing. Can you meet Charlotte hour by hour and day by day, and remain master of yourself?"

"Horace, it is nice of you to welcome me back."

"You have not answered my question."

"It is a difficult subject, my dear boy."

"You mean it will be beyond you?"

"Must you know exactly what I mean?"

"You mean that your feeling is too strong for you? Do not talk to me in riddles."

"I really must talk in them."

"You do not mean that it is weakening?"

"You ought to give me the opportunity of putting it in a riddle."

"Mortimer, this is a good word. When did you realise the truth?"

"When Charlotte returned, and showed me how far the children came before me in her heart. It was at the moment when you came in. Your words were late. The matter belonged to the past."

"How does Charlotte feel on her side?"

"My dear boy, I think you guessed the riddle."

"Has she ever put you first in her heart?"

"Horace, I believe that is hitting a man when he is down. One so seldom meets an example of it, as it is so strictly forbidden. That almost suggests it is the natural moment to choose. Hitting a man when he is up, does have to be strongly recommended. You must always remember that when I hit you, you were up."

"Why was my position different from what it is now?"

"It was not. You are always up. So you ought not to wonder at the blows of fate. You are a suitable target for them."

"Well, let us put the matter behind.'

"Yes, let us. It is hard to think of so many riddles."

"It is sad to remember all that is between us."

"Yes. All my years of penniless dependence, my long feeling that fate has not dealt fairly with me, my long effort not to grudge you what you had."

"You know I did not mean that."

"Then what did you mean? You said you had put the other matter behind."

"I did not know you had that sort of bitterness."

"I did not either. But it seems that I must have had it. I suppose my better nature has always triumphed."

"Can I do anything to ease things for you?"

"You can maintain the allowance you have made me in my exile. You meant them both to go on for ever."

"But now you will be living in my house."

"Yes. So I should keep the allowance for myself instead of giving it to my landlady."

"But your old allowance will be enough. You have always found it so."

"You may know me better than I know myself, Horace. I think my better nature has triumphed so much, that it is forgotten I have a worse one. So we will keep the dear, little allowance that carries me back to my boyhood, indeed could not carry me away from it. No wonder it is said that there is something childish about me."

"My expenses increase with every day. I seem to spend more on every member of the house, including those boys who desire my death. I hope you do not think that I grudge you what you asked."

"It has been so stupid of me to get a false impression. Of course I should take the will for the deed. Or what is the good of a better nature? Well, Bullivant, the landlady sent you messages, and said she never had a lodger who gave less trouble. And I think that was nice of me, considering I had so much myself."

Horace felt Bullivant's desire to talk to Mortimer, and suppressing the same desire in himself, left them together.

"Has the house been the same without me, Bullivant?"

"It has lacked a vital spark, sir."

"Did you expect me to-day?"

"I did not know on what day or at what hour, sir. But that it was imminent seemed to emerge."

"And is George glad to see me?"

"Well, sir, for one less rooted in the house, the same thing applies."

"Will you have my things unpacked?"

"Everything is in its place, sir."

"Do lodgings always lurk in the memory?"

"Well, they served their purpose, sir. It was a short chapter, if not a merry one, and it is behind."

"Have there been many guests lately?"

"Miss Doubleday has not been here, sir."

"Has she gone into a decline?"

"Not to my knowledge, sir. She has been seen at church and she is going away for a change."

"I think it sounds like a decline."

"Perhaps that would be the fitting tribute, sir," said Bullivant, with the flicker of a smile.

"Has Mrs. Doubleday been here?"

"No member of the family, sir, save the tutor in the mornings, as was the original situation. We seem to be subsiding into it."

"Had I better see him, in case he wants to call me out?"

"I do not think the initiative need come from our side, sir. And I hope it would resolve itself into a war of words."

"I did not mean it to be anything but that."

"In which case it is easy to foretell the victor, sir."

"I am not sure. Tutors are good at words."

"Well, sir, I suppose they are in a manner their stock-in-trade."

"And they are not mine?"

"Well, sir, perhaps we may say the stock without the trade," said Bullivant, not raising his eyes.

"Bullivant, do you not know that teaching is the highest work?"

"Well, sir, I have heard it said, but it does not seem to be recognised as such."

"But the highest things do not win recognition."

"Well, sir, in that sense I should be prepared to yield it priority."

Mortimer went upstairs and waited at the nursery door,

and when Gideon appeared, exchanged with him a smile and handshake.

"You must be glad we are not to be brothers."

"Must I?" said Gideon, frowning in an effort to recall the position. "Yes, I dare say it is a good thing."

"You would not like me as a brother?"

"Well, it is said that the husband enters the wife's family, and I cannot imagine you in ours."

"So it was best for me to be jilted. But it was a dark moment."

"Poor Magdalen! I suppose it was."

"Have I not served a purpose for her? There is a romance in her life, and surely that is better than I am myself."

"You may be right," said Gideon.

"We all say belittling things about ourselves, but I have never known anyone agree to them as you do. Of course I shall never hold up my head again. I have not behaved like a man. Or rather I expect that is what I have done. The words, 'behave like a man,' seem to have assumed the sense of behaving like a god."

"You have not done that," said Gideon.

"There you are again. How do you know that I do not think there is something godlike about me? There is supposed to be about every human being."

"What made you propose in the first place?"

"I was in someone else's power. You do not know what it is, never to earn any money."

"I wish I knew what it was, ever to do anything else. What is the matter with those two boys, Jasper and Marcus?"

"They have behaved like men, or rather they have behaved in such a way as to show that the child is father of the man. God bless the dear children," said Mortimer.

CHAPTER X

"MASTER JASPER AND Master Marcus are wanted in the library," said George, in a tone that suggested a triumphant attitude to the situation. "They are to go down at once."

"Who wants us?" said Marcus.

"The master, sir; he is by himself," said George, with full enjoyment.

"The library?" said Jasper.

"Yes, sir. The dining-room is too ordinary for the occasion."

"That will do, George. The young gentlemen will come down," said Nurse.

"I expect they would rather be coming up again."

"That is how you feel, no doubt, when you are sent for."

"Shall we run away?" said Marcus to his brother.

"It would be my work to run after you, and my legs are longer than yours," said George, actuated less by malice than by satisfaction in seeing other young males in merited trouble.

"Father can't hurt us by what he says," said Jasper. "We need hardly let ourselves hear. Only just enough to answer."

"I can't bear it," said Marcus. "It will always be like this. I would rather be dead."

"You would rather first of all that the master was," said George, with a suggestion of a nudge.

"George, you will be summoned to the library yourself, if you do not take care," said Nurse.

The brothers went downstairs in the wake of George, who advanced with a free step, and going to the library door, held it open for them, giving the guise of duty to his curiosity. They stood in the room that was hardly known to them, and Horace waited for the door to close, aware that he was not contributing to anyone's comfort.

"Well, my sons," he said in a tone that seemed to stress the relationship, and therefore its discrepancy with the situation.

"Well, Father," said Jasper, in an uncertain manner.

Horace looked as if he had not expected a reply.

"I have been wondering if I could speak to you. I felt that somehow I could not. But I have forced myself to do so. It will be an effort to me. I do not disguise it."

There was a silence, as his hearers did not dispute his words.

"Do you feel you could speak to two boys, who had done by you as you have by me?"

"No, Father," said Jasper, almost with a note of suggestion.

"I felt I could not; I felt that the gulf between us was too great; that I must remain on one side, and you on the other. And then I remembered that you were my sons, and that you owed me life."

The boys felt this was the last debt that they should have owed to their father.

"I have tried not to dwell on the truth of the matter. I have not harboured bitterness. I have tried not to see my own life as a great thing. But life is what we have; it was my all that you would have taken. The truth stands between us, stark, staggering, strange. What would you do in my place? What if sons of yours had dealt thus with you?"

"It was only for a minute that we waited," said Marcus; "and then we wished we had spoken. It did seem that, if you did not come back, the other times could not come back either. It had seemed that they might be coming. And we felt we could not bear it."

"So you would have no father, rather than the one you once had," said Horace, sadly, looking into their faces. "But was that a fair way to deal with him? Just to do him to death? Could you not give him a chance? Could you not say a word of help? What would happen to you, if I took the line with you, that you take with me?"

"We are afraid of you. You know we are," said Marcus. "Your being different for a little while has not altered all that went before. Nothing can alter it. You did not let us have anything; you would not let us be ourselves. If it had not been for Mother, we would rather have been dead. It was feeling like that so often, that made us think dying an ordinary thing. We had often wished to die ourselves. It is not the same with you as with other people. If anyone else did something, we should just see that thing. If you do it, it adds itself to all the rest. We cannot help it. Neither can you help it now. It is something that cannot be changed."

"Well, I will take up my life," said Horace, after a pause. "I will go forward, feeling that every little stumble must be a crime. I will walk warily, feeling I must indeed guard my steps. But there is one thing that I must say. I will not countenance evil. Any evil thing must be uprooted, plucked out, cast from us in the face of any feeling of yours, of any risk to me. It will be done at any cost to either. You have shown me your capacity for evil. I shall carry it always in my thoughts. I shall not be able to help it, as you would say. You are not the only people who cannot forget. You know in your hearts that nothing base has ever come from me."

There was silence.

"You may go," said Horace. "I will not visit your sin upon you. I will take it upon myself, even as you put it upon me. I will remember that you are my sons, though you forgot that I was your father. But the thing will remain between us, the hidden, unspoken thing. We shall not speak of it, but it will be there. May it work you good rather than harm."

"He cannot understand," said Marcus, as they went to the stairs. "Nothing will make him."

"Well, it is over now," said Jasper. "It will never happen again. He said so himself."

"It will always go through everything. It will not be over any more than our lives."

"Well, it was short and sharp, was it?" said George, coming from a private lurking-place. "It was not likely to be one without the other."

"Why did you not listen at the door?" said Marcus.

"I can take better care of myself than that."

"You could have jumped away when the door opened. No doubt you have plenty of practice in doing it."

"I do not walk into trouble," said George, with an airy confidence that was hardly justified.

"You would have been disappointed, if you had heard," said Jasper.

"You don't look as if things had not come up to the mark."

Marcus said nothing, knowing that both spoke truth.

"What penalty are you to have?" said George, in a zestful tone.

"None," said Jasper. "Why should we have one? We only made a mistake."

"I hope the master called it that. I know that any mistake of mine, that did not half come up to it, would not be given the name."

"It would not deserve it," said Marcus.

"So you and the master are to be as thick as thieves again," said George, on a baffled note.

"Well, the thing will pass off. There is nothing in it."

"Nothing in it! There is something in being the sons of the house and not a servant. A good deal would be put into it, if I had done anything of that kind."

"Do the young gentlemen wish to enter upon a discussion of yourself, George?" said another voice, as an obstacle looming in the shadow of the stairs showed signs of life.

George started and wheeled round and sped towards the

kitchen, and a pair of small, steady eyes watched him out of sight.

"It would be as well, Master Jasper, not to foster in George any disposition to terms of equality," said Bullivant. "It is not a suitable tendency, and would not be to his ultimate benefit."

"We don't often talk to him. To-day he brought us a message from Father."

"That was a transaction within his sphere, sir. It is any impulse to move beyond it that I deprecate."

"He seems to know everything that happens in the house and out of it," said Marcus.

"Well, sir, that kind of knowingness would go with the type. It is the knowledge of what to know, and what not to know, that is a further step and at present beyond him."

"I wonder he stays in this house, when he could go somewhere else. I wonder anyone does."

"Well, sir, what would be his choice? The position of indoor lad is what it is; there is no great scope. And what is there in him to respond to it, if there was? His limitations must be taken into account. Indeed it is sometimes difficult to see him for them, if you understand me. And in your case, sir, it may be an instance of familiarity breeding contempt."

"Certainly the more you know about things, the worse they seem."

"Ignorance may be bliss, sir," said Bullivant, with a smile. "But its being folly to be wise is not a thing in which I concur. The folly in such as George consists in something very different."

The two boys laughed, and at the moment Horace came from the library and paused with his eyes upon them. Bullivant, unconscious of the cry in their hearts, left them and moved down the passage.

"So you are amused by something," said Horace.

"Bullivant said something rather funny," said Jasper.

"And you were in the mood to be entertained?"

There was silence.

"Tell me," said Horace, in a gentle tone. "It throws light upon you, and I am glad of light."

"We laughed before we thought," said Jasper.

"Do not be afraid of laughing, my sons. Do not be afraid of the light heart of youth, because you have belied its innocence. Do not fear to appear as other children, because your hearts are not as theirs. Do not think I wish for that sort of atonement. That I wish for any kind. Indeed atonement is not possible."

"You said you were not going to speak about it," said Marcus, "and you keep on all the time."

"You cannot bear a word?" said Horace, in the same tone, looking into his face. "Well, then, you shall not hear one. You will not hear another from me. There will be silence on the matter for ever. But there is one thing that I will ask of you, before we put it off our lips and out of our minds, or rather into our minds' darkest place. I am going to-day to the bridge, to face what would have been my fate, if you had had your will, and to give thanks both for you and myself that your purpose was frustrated. I will ask you both to come with me. Together we will stand and face the truth. Together we will lift our hearts in gratitude that we are saved, I from you, and you from yourselves."

"I shall not come," said Marcus. "We should not be facing the truth; we should be facing something that was in your mind and not in ours. We are far enough apart in our thoughts already, and that would only take us further."

"And the board was there in time, Father," said Jasper. "None of us is really saved from anything."

"Then I will go by myself," said Horace. "I will go to the place where you willed that I should lie alone, with the breath battered out of my body. If the bridge is restored, I will make my solitary round, will make it as I have often made it, with troubles dragging at my heart, alone with this last and greatest trouble. And I hope to return, purified of personal feeling. It is true that my conquest of self has not been complete. It was much that I had to forgive."

Marcus turned and went upstairs, signing to his brother to follow. When they reached the nursery, they flung themselves on the ground in open abandonment to grief.

"We know how it was," said Sarah, coming up to them. "Mother has told us everything. She said it was no good to guess and get away from the truth. We know how the thought went through your minds, and how by the time you understood it, the chance of speaking had gone. You could not help having the thought after all those years. Your both having it is a proof of that. We have all had thoughts of that kind; I have had them myself. I don't mean that I should have done anything; I mean that it makes me understand."

"And you did not do anything either," said Avery. "Nothing has happened. Father is not dead."

"Mother will not say a word about it," said Tamasin. "She told us to tell you. She says that Father has done it, and that things lose force, if they are done twice. And she does not think the same as he does. So you have nothing more to dread."

"I have often thought it might be best to die," said Marcus, "and now I know it would."

"Then you would have done Father a kindness," said Tamasin, "and have no reason for remorse."

"He is going to the bridge this afternoon," said Jasper. "He wanted us to come with him, but Marcus refused."

"That was right," said Nurse, in a tone as unexpected as her words. "It would be wrong to impress the thing on your minds, as different from what it was. You would never have harmed your father, and you must not make a false memory. We cannot always control our thoughts, but they need not pass into action. We all mean to do things that we could not do, good things as well as bad. Have you not imagined yourselves heroes or martyrs or some other sort of great man?"

"Yes," said the boys together.

"And you know in your hearts that you will never be any such thing?"

"Yes," said the boys, who certainly felt no likelihood of it at the moment.

"That is how it was with this. Your minds ran on beyond yourselves. You would never do a wicked thing any more than you would do a great one."

"It is like making Father out of a candle," said Avery, who had paid earnest attention. "You mean him to feel things, but you do not make him feel them."

Horace came to luncheon, pale and aloof, conscious of himself, of the eyes of others, and at a deeper level, of his personal joy that his cousin was again at his board. As he took his seat he glanced towards the door that led to the kitchens.

"What is the noise in that passage? No one should be there. See what it is, Bullivant."

Bullivant opened the door and disappeared, and as no sign or sound ensued, the family rose and followed. He was standing still and silent, shaking his head and breathing deeply. Before him stood George, equally still and silent, with the shaking in his case extending from head to foot, and the breathing hardly taking place at all. The cupboard was open between them, and a selection from it, representative of George's tastes, was on the table.

"So this is what it is," said Horace. "What an odd thing that no one heard the sounds but me! Am I different from other people?"

No one threw doubts on the suggestion, but Horace was not the centre of interest at the moment.

"George! After all this time," said Bullivant. "So a leopard does not change his spots."

"It is the first time for a long while," said George.

"What a thing to say!" said Horace. "As if it were a natural thing to happen at intervals!"

"What were you going to do with the things?" said Mortimer, with a note of interest.

"Take them to my friends, sir. It is my afternoon out, and it is nice to take them something. They often do things for me."

"Do you make a practice of doing so?" said Horace.

"It appears to be a case of accumulation, sir, both of feeling and other instincts," said Bullivant, looking at the table.

"Have you no wages?" said Horace.

"They do not go so far, sir."

"They will have to cover your presents in future. This is an easy kind of generosity."

"George," said Bullivant, in a grave tone, "do you really take pleasure in offering these things to people innocent of their source?"

George did not describe his glow of feeling on the occasions, or say that the innocence was a necessary condition of them.

"Suppose I had to give you a character!" said Horace. "What should I say? That you were a thief?"

"Suppose you had to give your own sons characters!" said George, on a desperate impulse. "What would you say? That they were—worse than thieves?"

There was a silence that seemed as if it could not be broken. The family looked at Bullivant, who did not fail them. He saw that it was not broken by George, by stepping up to him and laying a hand on his mouth, and then broke it himself.

"George, you are making things no better for yourself."

"He has made them a great deal worse," said Horace, with a cold vibration in his tone. "I will see him by himself later."

"It is my afternoon out, sir," said George, voicing any objection to the interview that came to his mind.

"George, is that on the point?" said Bullivant.

"No, I know it is not," said George, weeping. "I did not mean to say what I did, sir. I did not mean you to hear."

"Get him out of the way," said Horace to Bullivant. "I

do not wish to have him in my sight. I will see him when he comes back to-night. I will not interfere with his enjoyment of his afternoon."

George turned his eyes on his master at his incredible assertion.

"He can take the things to his friends, and give them what account he can of them. I shall ask him, when he returns, what account he gave."

George was not troubled by this prospect, indeed hardly concerned with it, as he knew what Horace did not, that he would not return. His sensation was one of triumph, as he imagined his master hearing of his lifeless body lying in the ravine. The feeling was certainly tempered by one of regret that it was not Horace who lay there.

"George!" said Bullivant, indicating the array on the table and then pointing down the passage.

"I don't want the things," said George.

"It is a pity, George, that you did not come to that conclusion earlier."

George did not explain that it was only at the moment that he had found himself beyond such needs. He began to gather up the things, and did not find the situation eased by his being unable to take them all at once. Bullivant signed to him to remove them by instalments, and the third journey saw the process complete, and the withdrawal of the spectators from a scene with nothing more to offer.

Bullivant addressed himself to George's tasks, recognising the infeasibility of the latter's presence, and the double duty took him from the room and left the family.

"How wicked everyone is!" said Mortimer. "There does not seem to be a single exception."

"Do you feel that you provide one?" said Horace, in a cold tone.

"No, no, my dear boy. And I was dreadfully afraid that George would refer to it."

"I wonder what George is doing now," said Charlotte.

"Why did you postpone your interview with him, Horace?"

"I am taking a walk by myself this afternoon, and it will not hurt him to look forward to it."

"You mean that it will," said Emilia. "Well, a lesson may not come amiss."

"Do you like to look forward to it yourself?" said Charlotte.

"He does at the moment," said Mortimer. "Anyone likes to rehearse a speech and imagine himself delivering it. But he will like it less as time goes by, and then will begin to dread it. George has no idea how his prospects will improve. I never know why procrastination is the thief of time, but it is certainly the thief of other things."

"The prospects are already better," said Horace with a smile, willing to serve his own character. "I fear he will get off without his deserts."

"We like people to do that," said Mortimer, "but it is not as nice of us as it seems. It is because we can so easily imagine ourselves in their place. We say quite openly: 'Think what would happen to any of us, if we got what we deserved.' But really we deserve so little; so few things are really wrong."

"Think of George," said Charlotte, "carrying gifts to those who show him kindness, and when he cannot afford them, taking them from someone who will not miss them! It can hardly be seen as a repulsive course."

"He did not continue to behave in an appealing way," said Horace.

"That is the unlikeable thing about him," said Emilia, "his habit of making trouble for people more helpless than he is."

"He likes to see someone in trouble besides himself," said Charlotte. "And people who are not helpless do not get into it."

"He does not know the truth about himself and his destiny," said Mortimer. "I am sure Bullivant was born with the knowledge."

"Did you address me, sir?" said Bullivant, coming to the table.

"I was saying that George did not know the truth about his destiny. Did you know it at his stage?"

"At his age, do you mean, sir? His stage is a thing that I think passed me by. I think the elements of my obligations were dawning. It seems to me that not only poets are born, not made, but that it applies to the members of other callings."

"And what was George born?" said Mortimer.

"Well, sir, we know," said Bullivant, with a condoning shrug. "A workhouse lad."

"But that is not a calling."

"It almost seems to be, sir, in George's case."

"You do not think a thief?" said Horace.

"Well, no, sir, I think it is all comprised in the first description."

"You do not think he will leave it behind?"

"Well, sir, the process does not seem to be set on foot. We have been awaiting it for some time. And the heart grows sick with hope deferred, to use rather too telling a term."

"I did not like the way he spoke to me, or what he said."

"No, sir, it was not a thing to regard with tolerance. And he will not fail to know my opinion of it."

"Does Cook do what she can for him?" said Charlotte.

"Mrs. Selden has always exerted a salutary influence, ma'am. How far it is efficacious must depend partly on George. A quarrel is not the only thing it takes two to make. It is applicable also to other dealings."

"How will George carry all those things to his friends?" said Mortimer.

"He has gone, sir, carrying nothing," said Bullivant, with a faint smile.

"But how would he have carried them?"

"I suppose in some sort of receptacle, sir, probably borrowed."

"George seems to have the world at his feet," said Emilia, "and to have only to choose."

"That seems to be too much his own opinion, ma'am."

"Where has he put the things?" said Mortimer.

"I am unable to say, sir. There is no sign of them to meet the eye."

"Would not Cook have missed them from her stores?"

"Mrs. Selden only broaches that cupboard at intervals, sir, as George was doubtless well aware. And he may have felt that sufficient for the day was the evil thereof. And indeed may have found it so."

Bullivant walked to the door with his lips again unsteady. He was on his way to deposit the tray in the scullery, and to find the articles in question disposed upon the floor, in such manner as to suggest an utter indifference to them.

"Where are you going, my dear boy?" said Mortimer.

"For a walk by myself. I shall be back before long, and we can go round the farm together," said Horace, who had resumed his relation with his cousin to the extent of disposing of his time.

Mortimer, left alone in the dining-room, leaned back in his chair and addressed Bullivant.

"Did you ever ask Miss Buchanan to pay you a visit?"

"Yes, sir, and I may say that the experiment was quite a little success. And it made a slight diversion for us all. Mrs. Selden was observing the other day that we might repeat the occasion."

"I suppose no problem arose?"

"No, sir, thanks to your forewarning. There was no hint of any, or nothing that went beyond. I had the situation in my hands."

"You remembered what I told you?"

"It was not a thing to be forgotten, sir, if the occasion was not to be more of a peril than a pleasure. More than once I was enabled to steer clear of pitfalls. There seemed a tendency for them to arise. Indeed I understood how Miss Buchanan's path must be beset."

"But you think you will be able to manage for her?"

"I must make the confession, sir, of having extended our confidence to Mrs. Selden. So much penetration was better enlisted on our side, indeed was enlisted of necessity, as he who is not with us, is against us. It lifted my own situation from between the horns of a dilemma."

"Well, I dare say there was no alternative, but tell no one else."

"There is no one else to invite the confidence, sir."

"She will realise the necessity of silence?"

"Mrs. Selden's answer would only be 'Yea, yea,' or 'Nay, nay,' sir. But it is not the less to be depended on."

"Are you fond of George, Bullivant?"

"Well, sir, my impulse would be to give a negative reply. But I believe I am more concerned for the lad than he deserves."

"Is he fond of you?"

"Well, no, sir. He regards me as existing to thwart his instincts, which indeed call for frequent check."

"Is he fond of Cook?"

"Any other boy would be in his place, sir. That is all that can be said."

"Does she find him ungrateful?"

"She finds the approval of her conscience enough, sir, and looks for nothing further."

"Is he fond of Miriam?"

"Well, sir, he is thrown with her, and his talk finds an ear. But I have had to instil into him the elements of proper conduct, and to watch for signs of falling away, which are not wanting."

"Is he without natural affection?"

"Well, sir, he was brought up without it," said Bullivant, lifting his shoulders.

CHAPTER XI

"R<small>ICE</small>?" <small>SAID</small> M<small>ISS</small> Buchanan, with the hint of a smile, looking over her counter.

"No rice to-day. A letter, if you have one, and anyhow some macaroni," said Gertrude, who had come with her daughter to meet Gideon after his morning's work. "You see me surrounded by my family."

"How much macaroni?" said Miss Buchanan, not actually meeting this sight, as she did not turn her eyes upon it.

"I usually have a packet."

"You usually have rice," said Miss Buchanan, by means of keeping her eyes on Gertrude's face for an extra moment.

The door of the shop opened and George entered, and won a half-smile from Miss Buchanan on the ground of their private acquaintance. He could make no response, as he was never to smile again.

"Sweets?" said Miss Buchanan, in a low, deep aside. "I will attend to you in a moment."

George had regular recourse to this refreshment, and was in need of it on his way to self-destruction, as although bodily nourishment had lost its point, the plan itself called for stimulant. It had even occurred to him that he might have resorted in this degree to his master's stores. But his desire to stand well in the world, as is the manner of genuine feeling, did not desert him in his last hour.

"Some tobacco please," he said, as he saw the Double-days.

Gertrude turned to him with a smile.

"Are you not Mr. Lamb's young footman? I am sure I remember your face."

"Yes, ma'am, it is my free afternoon."

"Then get your tobacco and do not waste any of your precious time. My afternoons are always free, so I have not the same claim on attention."

"I cannot put my hand on a knife," said Miss Buchanan, not swerving from her course of supplying customers in turn. "And I must cut the string on these packets."

Gideon and George produced their knives, and Miss Buchanan took the first without a word.

"What a remarkably pretty knife!" said Gertrude, looking at the one held by George.

"It was a present, ma'am. I have had it for some time."

"Well, mind you do not lose it. It is a beautiful possession. I think I have never seen one like it before."

"Mine is a very workaday relation," said Gideon.

"Yes, yours is the one for cutting string and other blunting purposes. I am glad it was here to save this one."

"What is the use of a knife, if it may not cut?" said Miss Buchanan.

"My son's would certainly have no use, if it had not that. But this one is a different matter. It has an ornamental purpose; it is a thing of beauty."

"What do you use it for?" said Miss Buchanan to George.

"I generally just carry it."

"You put it to its right use as a precious possession," said Gertrude.

"It is a strong knife, ma'am; it could be used for a good many things."

"Yes, yes, I see it is not a toy. I dare say it is often in requisition for delicate purposes."

"I think I have seen it before," said Gideon, and found himself prevented from seeing it again by George's putting it into his pocket.

"Is your household complete now?" said Gertrude.

"Yes, ma'am. Mr. Mortimer has just returned."

"Has he? You must be glad to have him back. I hope he is in good spirits?"

"Yes, ma'am; he is always the same."

"Mr. Lamb must have been lonely without him. They spend so much time together."

"Yes, ma'am," said George, in an uncertain manner, hardly attributing ordinary human feeling to Horace.

"I saw Mortimer Lamb yesterday," said Gideon to his mother.

"And why did you not mention it? Was there anything sinister and secret about the meeting?"

"I dare say there was; there is about things in that household. The family curse seems to be over the boys at the moment."

"Upon my word, I think that would be the last household to be connected with," said Gertrude, speaking in a more distinct tone and glancing at George. "Much as I respect them all, I am glad that any threat of that kind has been withdrawn from me. We had better call this afternoon —a formal call to recognise this last return—and then retire from their orbit. And I hope the breath of outside influence may do good."

"I cannot go, Mother," said Magdalen, in a low tone.

"And why not, my dear child?"

"It would be a breach of faith with Mortimer. It would destroy something about our parting, that we undertook to keep intact. He gave me what he could, something he will never give to anyone else, and I cannot spoil his conception of it. It is all we have."

"Well, stay at home, my dear, and your brother will come with me. That will do as well."

"Lamb will be out this afternoon," said Gideon. "He is going to inspect that broken bridge. The boys were talking about it. It seems to have made an odd impression, and to have caused trouble of some kind. I know nothing more. But it will be no good to pay one of your early calls."

"Then we will pay a later one; that will present no difficulty. But I want to be back for tea. I prefer to eat and drink in the wholesome atmosphere of my own home."

Miss Buchanan handed a parcel to Gertrude, and Magdalen immediately relieved her of it. She then put a twist of tobacco on the counter, and added a packet of chocolate with a flicker of a glance at George. He pocketed both, though with a feeling that they strengthened the ties that bound him to life, at the moment when he was about to sever them. He was sustained by the knowledge that the tragic discovery was to be made by Horace himself. He dwelt on the scene, unconscious that he was imagining himself a witness of it, but in no doubt that he would have some knowledge of it, as he would have all knowledge.

"What a very nice young man that young footman is!" said Gertrude, who found this true of any young male, who was not actually engaged in wrong-doing, indeed saw the circumstance in itself as a tribute to him. "He looked as if he were escaping from something. Poor boy, he must need his free afternoons."

"He is earlier than usual," said Gideon. "He generally waits at luncheon. I think there must be something wrong."

"It seems that we shall be putting our heads into a hornet's nest this afternoon," said Gertrude, with a note of enjoyment.

"Then why do it, Mother?" said Magdalen.

"Oh, I do not care for these imaginary troubles. They are not real. They are the manifestations of too much leisure and too much luxury and too much of everything. A person who has known real trouble can only snap her fingers at them." Gertrude showed that she could play this part.

George, to whom it had not occurred to deal with the troubles in this way, was speeding towards the ravine, with a view to fulfilling his purpose before it failed. He looked at the sky and the shadowy slopes, and drank in their beauty for the last time, without any idea that it was also the first. His plan was to displace the board, advance upon the bridge, fall to an instantaneous death, and lie in readiness for his master's eye to discern him from above. A written warning that the bridge was yet unsafe, was included in his scheme, and he dwelt on Horace's words of him in his death, though he was facing it to avoid hearing what he had to say of him in life.

"Poor boy, poor, noble boy!" murmured George, as he mounted the hill. "So I brought him to this. And in his death he thought of me. That was his real level. Do I myself live on it?"

As the hill grew steep, George realised for the first time that it was the measure of the depth of the cliff. His breathing quickened, impeded, as it was, by exertion and the consumption of the sweetmeat. Waste was not to be a feature of George's last hour. Bodily nourishment was not to be a feature of it either, as seen by survivors, as the wrapping paper was to be concealed in a bush.

"Greater love hath no man than this, that he lay down his life for his friend," said George, as he reached the summit, now under the impression that this was his relation with his master. And indeed, as it was imperative that only one of them should survive, he was taking the self-effacing part upon himself.

The tobacco was to remain upon him. The persons of the dead were searched, and he imagined Horace's tender smile of fellow feeling.

"After all, we were both men at bottom," murmured George, or rather murmured Horace in George's mind. "And it is I who am to carry the burden of remorse and gratitude. May I be a better man; may it be yet another thing he has done for me. I must not shrink from my debt."

Horace returned from the hill at the hour that George had foreseen, his face bearing as many signs of emotion. He muttered to himself, as the former had imagined, and his whole person radiated powerful feeling. He hastened down the slope, gaining impetus from its incline, and entering his hall, pealed a bell that rang through the house, and was a recognised summons in moments of stress. He faced his household, as it hurried from all quarters to his aid.

"I desire everyone to come to the library. I will not pollute the scenes of our daily life. I have to stage a shocking and degrading scene. To stage it is the word; it is melodramatic and incredible. I cannot escape from it. You will see it, when you hear the truth. That your minds should have to be besmirched by the mean and miserable thing! But you will see that I am helpless and beyond help."

The family drew together, seeking support in their nearness. Emilia's face suggested that it showed but a fraction of her feeling. Charlotte looked sceptical and angry, Mortimer curious and perplexed, the children simply afraid.

"You are all here?" said Horace. "Everyone whom I summoned? None of the servants but Nurse? All the children but Avery?"

"We are all here," said his aunt.

"Then hear what I have to say. Hear this wretched and crushing thing. I went to the bridge this afternoon; I went by myself; I went to look the truth in the face, before I put it behind me for ever. I asked my elder sons to come with me, and they denied my request. They sent me on my way alone. You will see their reason. When I reached the bridge, the board with the warning had gone. I had the narrowest escape from setting my foot on it and being dashed to my death. But something warned me; something held me back. Perhaps it was the evidence of boyish handiwork; perhaps it was a sinister current from my sons' souls to mine. I paused and looked about me; I stayed my step; and behind some bushes on the slopes there lay the displaced board. I approached and examined the bridge, and found the damage unremedied, the danger what it had been; and I knew that evil lay about me, the intent to lure me to my end. I put the dark thought from me. I tried to think some accident had taken place, some mistake or

misunderstanding. I clung to the belief in the boys' innocence, though in the face of what had gone before, the case
was dark. I looked for some trace of a human hand, in the
natural human hope that I should find another guilty, and
not my sons. I found the trace I sought, that I hoped and
dreaded to find. Near the board I found this knife, the knife
that I gave to Marcus as a Christmas gift. I took it up and
carried it with me, and I carried a burden at my heart.
What more can I say to you? What more is there to be
said?"

"Why did you not tell the matter to me alone?" said
Charlotte.

"I could not expose other people to the peril. The danger
in the house threatens us all. My warning is not only for
ourselves. It cannot even rest within our walls. We are
encompassed by sin and shame."

"You have no real proof."

"Have I not?" said her husband.

"I have not had the knife for months," said Marcus.
"It was lost soon after I had it."

"You told me a few days ago that it was safe."

"I was afraid to tell you the truth. You make an accident
seem like a crime. Or you used to, and it was one of those
times when things were like they used to be. It was the only
thing I dared to say. It was Jasper's knife that you saw. I
could not show you mine."

"I will return it to you, Marcus. Take it for the second
time as a gift from me."

"No, keep it in your hands," said Mortimer. "It is a
proof that you found it, proof that it was on the cliff when
you were there."

"What have I to gain by all this proof?"

"You have nothing to lose," said Emilia.

"Marcus has not had his knife for months," said Jasper.
"He always has to borrow mine."

"He did not have to to-day, Jasper," said Horace. "Perhaps you borrowed his, or perhaps you used it together."

"Marcus has often looked for the knife, Father," said Sarah. "Each time you asked about it, he made a search. Sometimes we all helped him, but it was never found."

"It is found now, Sarah; it is found by me. And if it was lost, someone found it before I did."

"What have the boys been doing to-day?" said Charlotte.

"They could have reached the bridge before I did. There is no hope there. My thoughts rushed on to that point, as well as yours. I did not fail to clutch at the chance. I did not give up hope before I had to."

"It seems a poor proof, just to find something belonging to someone," said Mortimer. "Anyone may carry a knife that has been lost."

"If it was lost," said Horace.

"You have Sarah's word that it was. And you know that only means one thing."

"If I have known her," said Horace, who had no idea that he had not done this, "I have not known my sons. And the knife is not the only thing in point. Something had happened before this. You know the truth."

"I know very little, and I feel I know less and less."

"We would be less likely to do this, because of what we did before, not more likely," said Marcus.

"It would make it more natural for people to suspect us," said his brother.

"You have thought it out, have you?" said Horace, in a sad tone. "You did not think enough. Or you thought too much. I do not know which it was."

"They did not think of it at all, sir," said Nurse, rising to her feet. "They were too upset about the first trouble to think of anything else along that line. They would not have dared to frame the thought; their minds would have shrunk away from it. And I do not talk of my own opinion; I do not talk of hope; I talk of certainty. Of course I do not watch them every minute of the day; they are past the age for that; but I know them as only a woman can, who lives with them hour by hour, and of whom they have no fear. Better than you do, sir, better than you ever can. I have a right to say what I know, and a right to expect a hearing."

"Mrs. Doubleday," said Bullivant's voice at the door. "Mr. Doubleday."

"I have come in to welcome Mr. Mortimer, and to say how glad I am that your family circle is complete. You must all be in high spirits," said Gertrude, her voice wavering as she perceived how far this was from the truth.

"That we cannot claim to be, as you may see," said Mortimer. "My return has not done so much. We are in the throes of a family trouble, that it does not help."

"There must be troubles as well as joys in family life, as indeed in all life. It is especially true of family life, dear though it is to us. Where things go deep, all things are involved in the depth. I will leave you to yourselves, feeling it is the best I can do for you, trusting that the happiness will soon reassert itself, sure that it will."

"Why are you so confident?" said Gideon. "It appears to me a matter of doubt. I am glad we did not know of the trouble, or we should not be here. And I always feel I can do something. I cannot see anyone fumbling with string, without snatching it from his hands. I have an interfering nature. I wish someone would tell me the whole."

"What made you show people in at this moment, Bullivant?" said Mortimer, in an aside. "You must have known it was not the time."

"I thought any break would have its results, sir," said Bullivant, not mentioning that one of these was his own presence at the scene.

"Father thinks that Jasper and I took away the board from the bridge, so that he should cross it and be killed," said Marcus, looking at Gideon. "He thinks it because he found my knife at the place. And I had not had the knife for months. I lost it soon after he gave it to me."

Horace was holding the knife in his hand, and stood silent with his eyes upon it.

246

"That is George's knife," said Gideon, "the knife he had in Miss Buchanan's shop an hour or two ago. We all looked at it. There cannot be two so much alike."

"Be careful, Gideon," said Gertrude, coming forward. "Such things are easily said, and mistakes are soon made. And it was more than an hour or two ago; an error has already crept in. And of course there can be two knives alike. There are lines in manufactured things."

"These knives are not a line," said Horace. "There are no two the same."

"There is no mistake," said Gideon. "There is the broken place on the handle, that I noticed in the shop. And that paper sticking to it comes from the sweetstuff that George bought. I get that stuff for Magdalen. Two packets of chocolate may be the same, but it all points the same way. How have the things got here?"

"By way of the ravine," said Mortimer. "It sounds a roundabout course, but the thing is clear. It is George who has plotted against your life, Horace. You had that trouble with him, and you were to see him on his return. He felt there was nothing for it but to get you out of the way."

"How did he know I was going to the bridge?" said Horace.

"I spoke of it in his hearing," said Gideon. "The boys had said something of it, and I mentioned it to my mother in connection with the time of her call."

"So George stole my knife," said Marcus. "I could never think where it had gone. I can have it myself now."

Emilia came forward.

"Can there be any danger of George's having made an attempt on his own life?"

"No, ma'am, we may say there cannot," said Bullivant.

"Was there any sign of anyone's setting foot on the bridge?"

"None," said Horace. "I did not fail to think of that. I examined the bridge and looked down the ravine. Not that

I thought of George in the connection. It was hardly a solution along his line."

Bullivant walked rapidly to the door, and in a minute returned.

"My little sons!" said Horace.

The boys flung themselves upon him, breaking into tears. Nurse wept freely; Sarah and Tamasin strove in vain not to weep; Charlotte advanced to say a word to the guests; Gideon gave an account of the scene in the shop. Gertrude's voice, deliberate and distinct, pierced what seemed to be a tumult.

"Now what did I say about happiness being soon to reassert itself? You see that I was right. Indeed I do not often find myself wrong in the intuitive sphere. My instincts in some ways are true."

"Nurse, I must thank you for what you said," said Horace.

"I had the right to say it, sir, and I am glad I used the right. And I should like to thank Mr. Mortimer for the same thing."

Emilia again spoke.

"Should not someone be sent to remedy things at the bridge? At present there is danger to everyone."

"I have attended to the matter, ma'am," said Bullivant.

"We should also thank Mr. Doubleday," said Charlotte. "If it were not for him, we should still be in darkness and seeing no glimmer through it. We were indeed strangely placed."

"It was a sad little trouble, and I do sympathise with you in it," said Gertrude, with a note of saying what had to be said, before coming to her main point. "But I hope you will let me say a word on behalf of your young footman. I feel he had no intention that cannot be explained on some ground of health or nerves or personal situation. I am sure it is a case where to know all is to forgive all; I feel it in a way that I can trust. It can be seen in the very face of the boy, in the straight way he meets the eyes. I ask for sym-

248

pathetic dealing with him as a personal favour, and I should like him to know that I interceded for him."

There was silence, while people faced the demand, which in Horace's case seemed considerable.

"I will see that he hears of it, ma'am," said Bullivant.

"Thank you," said Gertrude. "I know I can depend on your word. And now I must hasten home, leaving only happiness behind, and so glad to leave it."

"Mrs. Doubleday speaks as if she had conferred it," said Charlotte.

"Her coming led to it," said Emilia. "Well, there is no joy like relief."

"My dear children, your path is clear," said Mortimer to the boys. "And your previous stumble has become a comparative success."

"Shall we be as we were before?" said Jasper to his father, seeking to use the moment to establish the future.

"You will be more to me than before. I see how far you are from being what I feared. This has cleared my sight."

"Of course it was what we did, that put it into George's head," said Marcus, with his eyes on Horace's face. "But that will not be said to us?"

"George had no need to do it," said Sarah, "and he is years older than you. It would be very wrong to connect you with it. No one could be so unfair."

"Certainly not their father," said Horace. "My wise little girl is right. I do not think she is often wrong."

"You all have great courage," said Mortimer, looking at the brothers and sisters. "May it do as much for you, as it demands of you. May it always give as well as take. God bless you, my dear children."

"They will be better in the nursery, sir," said Nurse. "What they need is to become children again. They have been forced too far forward by this suspicion of something beyond them."

"You must forget it all," said Charlotte to her sons. "You need not feel you have escaped from something. You simply had nothing to do with it. No more than I had, or Cousin Mortimer or the girls. You must put it out of your minds."

"What will happen about George?" said Tamasin.

"Forget him with the rest," said Horace. "We will not let the thought of him cloud our peace. He has worked us enough harm."

"Now remember that Avery knows nothing about it," said Nurse.

Avery came running towards them, alight with question.

"Has there been anything bad downstairs?"

"No, it all turned out to be nothing," said Sarah.

"Tell me all about it," said Avery, in a coaxing tone.

"No. It was a silly, grown-up thing. You would not want to listen. Shall I read aloud to you all?"

"Yes," said Marcus and Jasper, feeling that this would meet their need.

"The Book of Job, the Book of Job," said Avery, running for the Bible. "Then I can say it all to myself, before you come to it."

The children took their seats about their sister, and Nurse surveyed the familiar group and sank into surreptitious tears.

"Bullivant," said Horace, "did you not hear me say that none of you was to be present but Nurse?"

"I admit, sir, taking matters into my own hands. But it occurred to me that if opportunity should arise of my being of service, it would hardly operate if I were not present. And the exception being made of Nurse told me that the matter was not of a family character, and indeed it turned out to be otherwise."

"And what help can you be?"

"Well, sir, I would suggest taking the onus of dealing with George off your shoulders. It is unfit that you should be dragged down further by him, and I am myself inured to coping with those below me, in the endeavour to raise their level. And the case of George is the usual one on a larger scale; indeed we must say unprecedented."

"I should be glad for the ladies to hear no more of the matter. It is not fit hearing for them."

"Nor for any woman, sir. But as regards Mrs. Selden, it may not be amiss for her to bring her influence to bear on George, as the benefit conferred will outweigh the sacrifice, and self is never her foremost thought. And that brings me to the point of Miss Buchanan's being with us to-night, sharing our slight collation. As this matter must become public, will it not be best for it to become so in its correct form, free from addition and embellishment? Her shop being a nucleus of talk in the neighbourhood."

"You will do your best in the matter. But what of the other servants?"

"The housemaids will be out of the way, sir. And the kitchen girl, knowing nowhere to go, and being so much an appendage of Mrs. Selden, would be too much under her guidance to take any harm. And her knowledge of George may render it expedient for her to know likewise the consequences of his tendencies, and Mrs. Selden may so regard it."

"What are the consequences to be?" said Mortimer.

"Well, I must know that, sir," said Bullivant, looking at Horace.

"I do not seek revenge," said Horace. "The cost to me and mine remains, and cannot be undone. I ask nothing more than repentance and an effort to amend. But I must rely on you to see that both are on the right scale."

"You may leave it to me, sir," said Bullivant, opening the door for his master and following him out of the room.

"So it is true that people forgive a real injury more easily than a slight one," said Charlotte. "Horace takes an attempt on his life better than one on his household goods. I suppose George is too old to take things to eat, and no one is too old to take a life. People can only be too young for it. When they are young enough, they do not pay the penalty, as though they cannot really have done it. I suppose

Horace's thought took that line. But it was not a case for such extremes. George should have found a middle course, one just bad enough to bring out Horace's nobler side."

"What an innocent creature I am!" said Mortimer. "Simply planning to break up Horace's life, when no one else thought of anything but destroying it! Poor boy, I suppose he did deserve to die."

"What an event to break the daily life of a household!" said Emilia. "What a meeting of the little and the great in one thing! It brings near so much that lay at a distance."

"I suppose a good deal happens in daily life," said Charlotte. "We only have to look at what is near to us, to find the drama of existence. It seems such a pity that that is so."

"What was George to do?" said Mortimer. "He could not face his interview with Horace; he had nowhere to lay his head but under his roof; a method of disposing of him had been suggested, and he resorted to it."

"He should have made an end of himself," said Emilia. "I shall always wonder if that was his original purpose. And it would have punished Horace better."

"But it would have punished George as well," said Mortimer. "People do not like to lose their lives. That is the reason why they should not take other people's. It really was unkind of George."

"He did not want to punish Horace, merely to be rid of him," said Charlotte. "If he could have had him translated to a higher sphere, it would have served his purpose. Indeed I dare say that was the method he was taking."

"Would you like to be a witness of the scene between him and Bullivant?" said Emilia.

"I could not even refer to it in cold blood," said Mortimer. "I do not dare to think of it. I cannot understand how Bullivant can have so much rectitude and confidence and lack of compassion."

"It is Horace who has my pity," said Emilia. "Why should we not sympathise with the innocent as well as the guilty? The victim of a crime is a sadder figure than the criminal, though it seems to be an unusual view. Perhaps it is too obvious for people to like to take it."

"Can Horace really be innocent?" said Mortimer.

"Bullivant is so used to reproving George," said Charlotte. "It will only seem to him the usual thing on a larger scale."

"I hope it will not seem so to George," said Emilia. "How about the theft of the knife? Will that be dealt with? Or does the greater include the less? I do not suppose Bullivant will overlook it."

"George really does covet his neighbour's goods," said Charlotte. "It may come from having too few of his own, but he does do all he can to remedy the position."

"And to avert the consequences from himself," said Emilia. "I hope Bullivant will do his work well. George has gone too far this time. Horace had done no harm to him."

"He really had not," said Mortimer. "I am proud of the poor, dear boy."

CHAPTER XII

"Mᴀʏ ᴡᴇ ʙᴇ guided, Mrs. Selden. May words be put into our mouth. Before this the other encounters with George take on a mild aspect."

"And they failed of success. It does not offer much promise."

"Perhaps we tried to manage in our own strength."

"Anyhow we did not succeed," said Cook, perhaps hesitating to depend on higher aid, for fear of the same result, George being a tax on any force.

"Hark!" said Bullivant, raising his hand. "There is the step. The moment is upon us. May I be led to the opening words."

His air of abstraction suggested a feeling that heaven helps those who help themselves, but as often happens, preparation was in vain. It was hardly to be thought that heaven would help George, but the opening words were spoken by himself.

"The master said I was to see him when I came home."

"Did he, George?" said Bullivant, looking into his face and finding that a simple word met his need.

"And are you concerned for the master's wishes?" said Cook. "Are you concerned for him in any way?"

"I can't not do what he said," said George, in a miserable manner, twisting his hands together.

Bullivant looked at the twisting hands, and glanced at Cook to see if she estimated the duplicity.

"You are not to see the master at the moment, George."

"Why, has anything happened to him?" said George, widening his eyes.

"Why should you think anything has happened to him? What do you conceive the thing to be?"

254

"Nothing. I don't know. Nothing. But you said he could not be seen."

"Those were not my exact words, George. You read into them the meaning in your own mind," said Bullivant, rising and looking again into George's face. "Shall I take you to see your master?"

"No, not just now. I will see him presently. To-morrow. Not just at this minute."

"And what makes you think you can choose your own time? Has the master no say in the matter?"

"I don't suppose he is in a hurry to see me."

"Perhaps you do not suppose he will ever be in a hurry again," said Cook, unable longer to repress speech.

"And why will you not see him, George?" said Bullivant. "What is the picture in your mind?"

"Nothing. I don't know. Nothing. There is no picture. What do you mean? What has happened to him?"

"Nothing has happened to him," said Bullivant, coming close to George, with his mien ominous and his finger shaking towards the latter's face. "What has happened is in your own mind, the guilty mind that conceived the thing that you assume has taken place. It has not done so, George. Other forces were operating about the master; the powers of intervention were at work. He is safe. And what are you? What word can be used to describe your situation?"

"Certainly not that one," said Cook.

"I did not do anything. Who says I did? Nobody can know anything, and there is nothing to know. And if the master is safe, what is the trouble?"

"The trouble is yours, George. It touches no one else. And many people know the whole, and their number must increase. You will move about, a marked man, for the time remaining to you."

George cringed at the suggestion in the words.

"And that time should not be long," said Cook, not confining herself to suggestion. "And it is doubtful if moving about is the correct term."

"What is the matter? What is it all about? I have no idea what you mean. You seem to be insinuating something, but you can't tell me what it is."

"Let me tell you, George, what I can," said Bullivant, in a rhythmic manner. "The telling can be soon and swift. I tell it from a picture before my eyes."

"You are fond of pictures," muttered George.

"I see the picture, George," continued Bullivant, in the tone of one undeterred by irrelevant words, "the picture of a young man going forth to a hill, and coming to a chasm spanned by a bridge. Do you need me to go further? Is there a change in your eyes? I see the young man pause before a warning of danger. I see him lift the plank that bears it, conceal it close at hand, and go his way with furtive but rapid steps, leaving peril behind to assail him who must approach. Do you recognise that young man, George?"

"It was not me," said George, as though he would not suggest who it was.

"Is the picture graven on your mind?"

"It seems to be graven on yours. Perhaps it was an old man and not a young one. I dare say it was. Your life would be more your own without the master."

"Mrs. Selden, levity at this moment!" said Bullivant, turning round and using his ordinary tone. "And a plot against the master assumed as a matter of course!"

"I don't know why it is levity for me to accuse you, and not for you to accuse me," said George.

"Your description did not render Mr. Bullivant," said Cook, "as the prime of life calls for another term."

"Youth has its own ideas on such things, Mrs. Selden; we will not press that point," said Bullivant. "There are other matters in our minds."

This was true of George, whose thoughts were busy with his own predicament. He could not say that the picture was incomplete, as he was not prepared to supply the points omitted: his tentative effort to set his own foot on the bridge; his emotional stress, as his mind veered from one purpose to another; his vacillation as his better self strove with his worse, and was overcome; the minute on his knees, as he asked for tolerance towards the deed he had decided to do; the tears he shed for Horace, as he took his homeward way, alert to take cover at any sign of the former's approach. That Bullivant knew so much, without knowing the whole, was a sinister thing, disposing, as it did, of the possibility of watching eyes. He felt, as he put it to himself, that forces were at work, and sank into a chair, covered his face and began to weep.

"George, are these tears of repentance?" said Bullivant. "Or merely of self-pity and despair?"

George gave no answer, though the strength of his emotion suggested one.

"You weep for yourself, George," said Bullivant, seeming to have settled the point for himself. "You weep for the danger that threatens you, and indeed it is great. But what of the danger that assailed another? Did you weep for that? Was weeping the part you played in that drama?"

George might have said that it was, if he had felt it would help him.

"Who saw me? No one could have seen me. There was nothing for anyone to see."

"There was One that saw you, George. There was the all-seeing Eye. Did you think, as you plied your guilty task, that you were not seen? Did you forget your early teaching, the lessons you learnt in infancy?"

"You tell me to leave that part of my training behind."

"Do not indulge in trivialities, George, at this moment of your life. That can only mean what it does."

"And will mean it for himself," said Cook.

"But how did you know? You can't know anything. You are pretending to know," said George, not doubting the divine observation as much as the conveyance of its results to Bullivant.

"The exact method need not be divulged," said Cook.

"The age of miracles is past," said George.

"You think so, George?" said Bullivant, on his musical note. "Let me tell you that the process of events may at times deserve the name."

"A miracle may take its forms," said Cook.

"Now, George, let me have a full and free confession," said Bullivant, in an almost business-like tone. "That will be best for the expurgation of your sin, even though it may do nothing for yourself."

"You have no proof of anything," said George, not swayed by the motive suggested.

"George, do you need me to say more?"

"Yes, I do. You have not said anything."

"The matter does not call for elaboration," said Cook.

"No, it can be a simple statement," said George.

"George, have we to contend with arrogance, in addition to everything else?" said Bullivant.

"Why should I answer your questions, when you will not answer mine? If you want to know any more, ask whatever it was that told you the rest."

"So, George, blasphemy is your resource."

"And will leave him with no other," said Cook.

"I have done nothing. I know nothing. I came home to see the master, as I said when I came in. I don't mind seeing him, if he is alive and well. It is only about those paltry things from the cupboard. And he can have them back; I did not take them from the house."

"It is hard to see why you stole them," said Cook. "Perhaps you can illumine the point for us."

"If he is alive and well, George!" said Bullivant, taking a step nearer to him. "How you give away your case! Why should he not be alive and well? You can answer that. And before God, before you leave the room, you shall answer it."

"So blasphemy is your resource," said George.

Cook looked aside, as though fearing that her eyes might say the same.

"And paltry as the things may have been," she said after

258

a pause, "though it is hardly the way to refer to what is granted to us, it is not the term that renders sin."

"It is a word that hardly has its uses," said Bullivant. "As there is nothing to which it should be applied."

"And what of the young gentleman's knife, George?" said Cook. "Was that paltry? Have you some other word to refer to that?"

George put his hand to his pocket and withdrew it with a bewildered expression.

"Forces are hemming you in, George," said Bullivant, in a manner of sober triumph.

George did not dispute his words.

Miss Buchanan's knock was heard, and Cook and Bullivant composed their faces to admit and greet her.

"You see us in trouble, Miss Buchanan," said Bullivant, "though you do not know its nature."

"I shall know it soon. It will be about the place. Rumours of it are about already."

"It is the worst kind of trouble, the sin of another," said Cook.

"Trouble generally comes from that."

"But seldom on this scale," said Cook.

"Am I to know the truth? Or to wait for it to sift itself out?"

"Truth is what will be observed," said Bullivant, "and nothing but the truth. Names are involved and reputations are at stake."

"And only one name and one reputation need be that," said Cook, turning her eyes on George.

Miriam, who had been mentioned by Bullivant as an appendage of Cook, came from behind the latter in a manner that recalled the description, and he passed his eyes over her with an ease that supported it.

"I gather that no one has come to harm," said Miss Buchanan. "But has George anything to do with the matter? I saw him early this afternoon in my shop, and several other customers saw him too."

"And no one has seen him since, save the One that sees all things," said Bullivant.

"And has that One told tales?"

Bullivant, unable to suggest that Miss Buchanan should not blaspheme, said nothing. Cook was cast in a stronger mould.

"What has been seen will be revealed to those who should know it, and those who do not receive it in a certain spirit, are not among them."

"This is what has happened, Miss Buchanan," said Bullivant, unwilling to relegate the guest to this position. "George, that young man whom you see before you, cast in the ordinary lineaments of early manhood, went forth from this house to do his master to his death. Forth he went to the chasm that rends the cliff, tore up the warning that rested there, and left the bridge safe to the eye, but fraught with the last danger to his master's feet."

"I thought it was the boys of the house," said Miss Buchanan.

"That shows that the truth must be spread. George it was who did the deed. George it is who must suffer for it."

"And has not done so yet," said Cook.

"But how was it known?" said Miss Buchanan, giving another form to a question she had already asked.

"A pocket-knife disclosed the whole. On such a slight thread do issues hang. A knife was produced in your shop by George, produced, I believe, for some everyday, useful purpose, so like to other people are perpetrators in daily life. The knife was observed by onlookers; that knife was found on the cliff at the spot of betrayal. It was found by the master, mercifully guided to mistrust the signs that met his eye. On such a chance did the truth depend."

"Proving that chance is not the term," said Cook.

"It was Master Marcus's knife," said George, with an impulse that was not new to him.

"And in that case, George, why was it reposing in your

pocket?" said Bullivant. "Can you answer that? You see how one step leads to another. Petty theft it was, that started the downward trend."

"And petty was hardly the word, as matters gathered," said Cook. "And it is not a term to be so freely applied to theft. I am not in agreement with it."

"Why did George want to harm Mr. Lamb?" said Miss Buchanan.

"Theft it was again, Miss Buchanan, theft in this case from Mrs. Selden's stores. He was to answer to the master for it to-night. That it was, that led him to the act, the instinct to save himself. The instinct to save others was not at work."

"And I fear tends to be weaker," said Cook.

"It would have been dreadful to see the master," said Miriam, almost to herself.

"But you would not have sacrificed a human life to avoid it," said Cook.

Miriam was silent, reflecting that she would have sacrificed her own.

"George must be thankful that his plan was frustrated," said Miss Buchanan.

"Thankfulness is not a point that has been reached as yet," said Bullivant. "Nor is there any movement towards it."

"It is the master that I am sorry for in the transaction," said Cook. "The whole matter is beneath him and drags him from his place. George merits no compassion."

"Except that if we all got our deserts, Mrs. Selden," said Bullivant, in a tone that suggested a turning-point in his course.

"Well, the difference would stand as it does now. Our line is not parallel with George's, and there is no obligation on us to think so. As I said, it is the master who has my feeling."

"He has mine also, Mrs. Selden. So much so that I was moved to intercede with him, as it were, for himself. And my efforts were not unavailing. He has deputed me to take the onus of the matter off his shoulders."

There was a pause.

"So George is to answer to you?" said Cook.

"That, Mrs. Selden, is the case."

The hearers experienced various impulses, Cook to make some rallying comment, Miss Buchanan to exercise her dry humour, Miriam to congratulate George, and George to cast himself at Bullivant's feet and embrace his knees. The last was the only one to be fulfilled.

"So, George," said Bullivant, with a gentleness felt to be great in every sense, "you have come at last to repentance. That may be at once the beginning and the end. All things are possible to him that repenteth."

"I should never have done it of myself. It was the young gentlemen who put it into my head. And the master is not my father; it was worse of them than of me. I have never done a thing like that before."

"Well, I should hope your way has not been punctuated by attempts on human life," said Cook. "And the master has a right to live, even if he has not the honour of relationship with you. And it is not a privilege that would be likely for him."

"George, this taking refuge behind those younger and weaker than yourself," said Bullivant. "That is not the least of your failings. Shoulder your own burdens and carry them like a man."

George raised his eyes in instinctive protest that he had thought he was to cast them off.

"What is this about the young gentlemen being involved in the matter?" said Miss Buchanan. "The village has it in different forms, and I can't get at the truth."

"They saw the master on a previous occasion, setting out for the bridge," said Bullivant, "and remembered too late that they had heard it was not safe. And were greatly distressed, and naturally yielded to emotion on his return. And the second occasion called up the first, as was equally natural. That is the long and short of the matter."

George looked up to supplement the account, but felt Bullivant's eyes and was silent.

"Well, it is the short of it," said Miss Buchanan.

"It is best at times to be terse," said Cook.

"Rise, George," said Bullivant, making an upward gesture. "I am a man even as you are. Kneel to no one but your Maker."

The women kept their eyes on Bullivant, Cook in approval, Miriam in awe, and Miss Buchanan in a fixed and stony stare that was the precursor of other things.

"Forward, George," said Bullivant, his gesture now in this direction, as George gained his feet and seemed in need of further guidance. "Forward along the straight and narrow path. Do not look backward; there are depths behind. Fix your gaze on the pure and unsullied future."

"The past must cast its shadow," said Cook, who felt that these could hardly be the words for any part of George's course.

A sound came from Miss Buchanan, and Bullivant turned to see her sitting with clenched hands and tightened lips, fumbling for her handkerchief. He surveyed her, as the truth came home, and then suffered the revulsion of feeling that so readily succeeds an exalted mood. He took up a Bible within his reach, and held it as he continued to address George.

"From this book we will all read a passage in turn, that will help you forward. A word from the Book never comes amiss. Miss Buchanan, will you select your passage and render it? And then we will follow your example."

"No, I do not come here to take the lead in religious observances. I am a guest, not a conductor of your household ceremonies."

"As is indeed the truth," said Cook. "And reading the Bible is not quite the apposite thing at the moment. George has not quite reached that point, and we all tend to be in rather too secular a mood. And words regarding the Book

263

should be the true outcome of the heart. And what Miss Buchanan requires at our hands is a little refreshment, and not an assignment of duties, with which she is provided."

"That is so, Mrs. Selden," said Bullivant, in a contrite tone. "It was the impulse of the moment, that I see to be ill-advised."

George came to the table with his eyes down, embarrassed by taking nourishment to support a life so unworthy. Cook supplied him in the usual way, concerned simply with her household dispensation, and he felt an urge to get his future clear, before he set his face towards it.

"So I am not to see the master?" he said to Bullivant, in a tone that faltered both of his own will and without it.

"You have seen him, George. You see him now in my person. I am his deputy, authorised to carry out his task. I thought it lowering for him, George, and that I tell you plainly, to encounter you and sully his mind with things beneath him. So I offered myself as his proxy, and I hope I have done my part with sufficient firmness and at sufficient length. Of course I am not the master, and no one is more conscious of the fact."

"We are all equally aware of it," said Cook, keeping her eyes from Miss Buchanan.

"I have not said all I meant to say," continued Bullivant, "I have reminded myself at intervals that we all do wrong, and that to yield to temptation may be as bad in one case as another, though the issues involved may be less great. I have not said all the master would have said, being perhaps more in need of the reminder than he. I have made the cost to you light, as I hope the cost to us all may be. But I trust this course will not prevent your vowing your life to atonement. Were I to fail to bring home this need, I had failed indeed; failed the master, failed myself, failed you, George."

George made a murmur meant as an assurance that Bullivant had not fallen short in this way.

"And so we will leave the matter, George, leave it to

your sense of gratitude to One above, to the master and to me. Together we have striven to serve you—and I use the word advisedly—and to lead you to the best use of the life you might have forfeited. And to mark my sense of the gravity of the moment, I will ask you to remain silent during this meal. Miss Buchanan will excuse any breach of convention that it may entail, knowing there has been a breach of greater things. And now, Miss Buchanan, allow me to attend to your needs."

Miss Buchanan permitted it, with a sense of guilt as pressing, if not as grave, as that which lay on George, and the latter sat in the enjoined dumbness, feeling himself beyond the point of being brought lower. After the meal he glanced about him, uncertain if he was to resume his normal intercourse with Miriam, and as nothing was said, followed her to the scullery.

"I will do your washing-up as well as mine."

Miriam relinquished it and stood in an attitude of ease.

"What do you think of what I have done?"

"Well, I see you were afraid to meet the master."

"Would you have done it?"

"Well, I should not have thought of it."

"Neither should I by myself; it was knowing about those boys. Would you have done it, if it had been put into your head?"

"I could not make anyone die instead of me. I might have killed myself."

"I meant to do that at first," said George, eagerly; "that is why I went to the ravine. But then it seemed——" the eagerness failed as he came to his decision that it would be more expedient to kill his master, and found it hardly supported the maxim that second thoughts are best.

"I have never met anyone who killed anyone."

"People used to do it in history," said George, illustrating another saying, that a little learning is a dangerous thing.

"Not ordinary people like us. Kings and people of that

kind. And people did kill other people in those days."

"If the master had been killed, I should have been discovered just the same. The knife would have been found."

"You need not have stolen the knife," said Miriam, seeing no excuse for this.

"Have you never stolen?"

"I did at the orphanage, but only things to eat. And not enough to be found out. Here we have our own money and have no need to steal."

"We can't buy things as good as we see them."

"We can buy a good deal," said Miriam.

"I wonder if I shall go on getting worse and worse?"

"I should think you will, if you don't soon begin to get better."

"I suppose I ought to compare myself with you, and not with those above me."

"Well, what difference is there between you and me?"

"George can answer that," said a familiar voice. "Answer the question, George. What is the difference between you and Miriam?"

"She is better than I am," muttered George.

"Which may not be saying more than may be assumed," said Cook.

George stood with the air of someone who had borne much and was prepared to bear more.

"I suggest, Mrs. Selden," said Bullivant, "that we make it a rule not to refer to George's past from this moment. It will be fairer to him, and perhaps fairer to ourselves, as bringing forward the weak points of another is not uplifting. Let him start with a clean sheet, and if he besmirches it again, it is on his own head."

"And whose affair was it that he besmirched it this time, and on previous occasions? A clean sheet hardly seems to be at his disposal."

"George, there is another question for you to answer."

"It was my own fault," murmured George.

"And the question now arises whether he should associate with Miriam," said Bullivant. "George, what is your own opinion?"

"She does not follow what I say."

"And whose fault is that, when you are her senior and of the leading sex? Why does she not follow you? What is her reason?"

"Her ways are better than mine."

"Do you feel she is safe with you, George?"

"It is the woman who wields the influence," said Cook.

"And are you amenable to it, George? Do you gain what you can, as you can give nothing?"

"There is not much to be gained from anyone in Miriam's place."

"George, here is your old mistake! Can you not see that a candle may shine as bright in an obscure place as in a prominent one? And even brighter from the contrast."

"Though it may not shine at all," said Cook. "It does not do to depend on it. Do you bear in mind, Miriam, that there should never be a word from a woman's lips, that it would debase anyone to hear?"

"Words come from the other side, surely, Mrs. Selden," said Bullivant, "those of the tendency to which you refer."

"George is not given to words," said Miriam.

"That is something," said Cook. "But there are things that speak louder."

"Have we settled our point?" said Bullivant. "Are George and Miriam to continue in undisputed intercourse? What does Miriam herself say?"

"I don't see how it can be helped," said the latter. "We must both of us talk sometimes."

"I had gathered that you were under the compulsion," said Cook.

"If I did her any harm," said George, with a glance at the door, "her candle would not burn as bright as you say it does."

"That statement was not exactly made," said Cook.

"George, is it for you to point to our words?" said Bullivant.

"If that is the result of lenience," said Cook, "the course must be discontinued. I am at a loss to know what leads George to think he can dictate."

"I don't see so much lenience," said George, in an uncertain voice.

"George!" said Bullivant. "When you should by rights have been handed over, and might even now be in charge!"

"When does the rule of silence come into force?" said Miss Buchanan. "Or was the promise like pie-crust, made to be broken?"

"Mrs. Selden, we are losing sight of our guest," said Bullivant; "and for the sake of George, which is not the fitting order of things."

George, at the touch on a sore spot, had sunk into tears.

"George, I am glad of this sign of emotion," said Bullivant, meeting the episode in a way that relieved his hearers. "It was what I was in a way expectant of. There has not been too much."

"It is not a case for assurance," said Cook.

"Fear will drive anyone to anything," said Miss Buchanan. "George did not know he would not have to face his master, and if he had not gone so far, he might have had to do so."

"It was indeed a length," said Cook.

"I should hardly have been deputed," said Bullivant; "that is the case. But it seems that George's proceeding to extremes has worked out to his advantage."

"Which is not the desirable sequence," said Cook.

"People may be more affected by escaping expiation than by making it," said Miss Buchanan.

"That is the principle on which I was acting," said Bullivant, "when I was assailed by doubt."

"George, thank Miss Buchanan for her intervention," said Cook. "And the principle of silence can begin to work. And it will be to everyone's benefit. We cannot touch pitch and not be defiled."

The elders withdrew, and George sat down by the sink, as if his strength failed him.

"I suppose the village will talk to me about this."

"Perhaps they will not like to speak about it," said Miriam.

"Oh, they will touch pitch and be defiled," said George, in a tone hardly warranted by his own contribution to the situation.

"I don't think Cook and Mr. Bullivant will speak any more."

"They could hardly find any more to say. I am unfit to associate with you, Miriam. I am beneath even such as you now."

"You were never above me. It was wanting so much to be, that made you behave as if you were. That made yourself believe it."

"The wish was father to the thought?" said George.

"Yes," said Miriam, looking surprised by the exact interpretation of her words.

When the rising of Cook's voice marked the departure of the guest, George went to the door and listened for Bullivant's accompaniment. As it did not come, he tiptoed across the passage and edged into the kitchen. Cook rested her eyes on him while she completed her song, not grudging to any verse its full chorus.

"Well?" she said in a neutral tone.

"You have lost your opinion of me, Mrs. Selden."

"It was never so much that it called for deterioration."

"But you used not to look down on me."

"Well, only from my position of being older and wiser and more conversant with things. And there was no reason to look up to you on other grounds, that I can remember."

"Do you think I shall ever rise above this?"

"I am not entitled to an opinion," said Cook, moving her hands about her tasks. "I have been mistaken once, and may find myself so again."

"You think I am beneath your attention?"

"You are a long way below what you were, when I was moved to interest and guidance. The effort has not been repaid. Failure does not often cross my path, but this time I have encountered it."

"But if I improve from this moment?"

"The impetus downhill is not so easy to check. It depends on how far it has gained the ascendancy, which in your case you may be to an insuperable extent."

"You think Miriam is better than me?"

"It is not a matter of my opinion; there is no room for doubt. Not that it is necessary to harp on her superiority."

"Is character the only thing?" said George.

"It generally is, other things not often being forthcoming, if it is brain and ability to which you refer."

"Does just not doing anything wrong count so much?"

"Not as much as it ought to, people being as they are. But nothing counts without it. Of that we can rest assured."

"You do not think I can ever rise?"

"That hardly seems the word to call in question, when the tendency has been so much the reverse. And you will have to rise a great deal, to attain your original point."

"I see you have no hope of me."

"Hope cannot spring eternal, as is sometimes said," said Cook.

Bullivant entered with an easy gait and his hands in his pockets, marking the transition to ordinary life, and the rule of silence upon certain things.

"Well, Miss Buchanan is an easy and pleasant guest."

"And does not create an atmosphere because it is possible to do so," said Cook, believing herself to be observing the rule.

George noiselessly left the room, not holding the opinion.

"Not that she might not have been involved in embarrassment herself," said Cook, not pausing in her work. "It was owing to her own resource that she escaped it, guest or no guest."

Bullivant began to hum, with his head moving up and down, and his hands behind him, to indicate that his mind did not happen to be on Cook's words. She did not reprove him for inattention, as a glance at him told her that he was not guilty of it.

CHAPTER XIII

"It is said that cold deadens sensation," said Mortimer. "It seems to make an exception in the case of itself. Why such a mean fire, Bullivant?"

"We are economising in fuel for the moment, sir. Something in the nature of a relapse, as is to be expected at intervals."

"Is it likely to be a long one?"

"I trust it may not be protracted, sir, if only for the master's own sake. He is not in a condition to withstand this onset. It is to mild cold that he is impervious. And his resistance is impaired by the vicissitudes of our life of late. 'All's well that ends well' is not always a reliable maxim. Things leave their trace."

"I would give anything for a real blaze, and I will give anything. My place in his home, any hope I have for the future, and I have no other hope. Give me the shovel, Bullivant; this is the action of a brave man and a gentleman."

Bullivant obeyed, in agreement with both the claims.

"Shall I replenish the scuttle, ma'am?" he said to Emilia, recognising the unscrupulousness of an appeal to Mortimer at the moment.

"Well, it will have to be filled at some time."

"And a full scuttle looks better," said her nephew; "it does not suggest that we have emptied it. Do not fill it too full, and it will look as if only a little had been used. I want it to act a lie."

"And to follow its example," said Emilia.

"The master may be glad to be assisted back to his standard, ma'am, the normal one for him now, as it is fair to see it."

"You are very much attached to the master, Bullivant," said Mortimer. "I never quite understand it."

"Perhaps, sir, I might say the same to you. We cannot account for these things, and perhaps it would lessen their meaning."

"We don't seem to see George in these days."

"No, sir, I hope it is not a loss to you."

"I have only just realised it. You have not parted with him?"

"No, sir. We should be put to it to place him at the moment, as his character must depend on his living down what is behind. And I should think the saying of the proverbial bad penny might apply."

"Then why is he in hiding?"

"He has shown a reluctance to appear in the dining-room, sir. And I welcome the sign of dubiousness about himself. It is greatly better than assurance. I have accordingly evinced understanding, and taken his work upon myself at the necessary points."

"I suppose he will recover in time?"

"It is not a matter of doubt, sir. His confidence asserts itself; it is one of the things we have to contend with in him. He seems to regard it as an asset, which is not a tenable outlook. It is something of a relief to see it in abeyance. And the best way to ensure that, sir, is for him to be in abeyance himself." Bullivant ended with a smile.

"How does Cook feel about him? He cannot always follow that course."

"Mrs. Selden judges not, sir, that she be not judged."

"And judging George would be a life work?"

"There would not be much respite, sir."

"How did Miss Buchanan take the matter when she was with you? You were not very fortunate in your day."

"It was not the most auspicious occasion, sir. But Miss Buchanan was little affected. There seems to be a sort of lightness in her, a something that is almost levity, that carried her through, and that would hardly be suspected.

Indeed there was a danger that her attitude to the issues might lessen George's sense of their gravity."

"It sounds as if a little society had done her good."

"We may flatter ourselves that it has served that purpose, sir. And it being a cause that is its own reward, I ask no other."

"You do not enjoy her company?"

"Well, yes, sir. It makes a break in our routine, that may have become a little rigid. It was only on this occasion that her buoyancy did not strike the note."

"She had come in a social spirit, and found the atmosphere at variance with it."

"You are right that there was a discrepancy, sir, and one that was not to be laid to her door."

"It might be well to ask her again quite soon."

"I believe Mrs. Selden has put that on foot, sir, with a view to compensating for anything that may call for it."

"Was George grateful to the master?"

"Well, sir, grateful! George! He is glad to have his own future clear, glad in a high degree; that is to be seen. But how far gratitude comes into it! I may misjudge him, sir, being so much involved with his failings and their correction; and indeed they were not wanting on this occasion."

"Do he and Miss Buchanan take to each other?"

"Well, sir, yes and no. I had hardly thought of their mutual feeling. But nothing human is below consideration, as I concur. I should say that she turns a kindly eye on him, on the ground of youth and curtailed opportunity. Whether he turns an eye on her at all, sir, is open to doubt. Youth tends to pass over middle age, or to consign it to the past."

"I like what I hear of Miss Buchanan."

"Yes, it has been a good fight, sir, a persistent standing up to circumstances. It cannot but win respect. It would be sad to think of its perhaps meeting the opposite."

"You do not feel any personal liking for her?"

"Well, I am approaching it, sir, as may also be said of Mrs. Selden. There is more that makes up Miss Buchanan than misfortune, and we may not have been prepared. It does not do to think of an unfortunate person as a mere unfortunate. It was you, sir, who detected the human heart beneath the exterior."

"We can always depend on that."

"Yes, sir, as applies to the case of George. And I have done my best to act upon it, in the face of little evidence."

Horace entered and came to the fire, his face lighting at the sight. He sat down and leaned forward, holding his hands to the blaze. Bullivant exchanged a glance with Mortimer and went to fetch the tea.

"This cold seems to have no end," said Horace.

"We were on the verge of succumbing to it," said his cousin, "but I kept my presence of mind and we are safe, and in the mood of quiet thankfulness that follows danger. Bring the tray to the fire, Bullivant; it does not waste the heat to feel it."

Bullivant set the table by his master with a glance at Mortimer, as though the former were hardly in a state to deal with it.

"Something hot to drink makes people warm," said Horace, in an unfamiliar tone, speaking with a shiver and looking for a place to set his cup, as though he feared to spill it. Bullivant took it from his hand, as if he had been in readiness to do so.

"You are not well, my dear boy," said Mortimer.

"A chill, sir, consequent upon the protracted cold, imposed on other circumstances," said Bullivant, keeping his eyes from Horace.

"He had better go to bed," said Emilia. "That is what the mistress would say."

"As soon as the fire is kindled, ma'am, and has counteracted the chill of the room," said Bullivant, going to the door. "I will carry live coals from the kitchen."

"The fuel that would have averted the trouble, must now be used to deal with it," said Emilia. "It seems that it cannot be saved."

Horace gave an uncertain laugh, put out his hand to his cup and withdrew it, rested his eyes on the trembling hand, as if it were a thing apart from himself, accepted his cousin's aid, and sank back in his chair, an openly sick man.

By the time that his wife returned, his illness seemed to have left its first stages behind. It moved to the further one without haste or hope. It was known with feelings less of surprise than of foreboding fulfilled, that Horace was sick, it might be to death.

The house was hushed, vibrant with covert emotion, charged with fear and hope. The children were deceived, prepared for the truth, assumed to know it. They recoiled, shocked and disbelieving, and then simply faced it. Death was to them an unfamiliar but fundamental thing, that was not strange in itself because to them it was strange. They feared for their father, feared for themselves and each other, saw death as a real threat to their own lives, as a real thing in them.

The cold held, bound the earth, could not break. Fires through the house were piled and deep. Fear of cold had become a different thing; suffering from cold belonged to a past that was distant, strange, fraught almost with guilt.

Horace strove for breath, feared his end, faced it, prayed for its release. His illness took a course where crises followed each other, in lessening force but met by waning strength. Days passed, and nights with hours that were more than days. The dreaded collapse was held at bay, and the respite from death became in itself a ground of hope.

Horace felt that he was dying. With the abatement of the fever his weakness seemed all that was left, and he took it for the last weakness. When he heard his own voice, it came through a darkness and from a distance.

"I have gone too far to go back. I have reached the point where we cannot turn. We shall all reach it, though I have come to it soon. And it is no great matter; people do not need my life. I do not make things better for them; they dread that I shall make them worse. With all my effort, that is what I have done, and I have striven with my might. There is one thing left for me to do, and then I can go away alone."

There was resolve in the soundless tones, and Charlotte came to the bed. This change did not come from weakness. Was it the last strength?

"You must wait for a while. The time is coming."

"No, I cannot wait. I should wait long indeed. Bring the children to me, to hear my last words. They have not much to remember. They can have that."

"Wait for your real self to return," said Emilia, coming nearer. "You are suffering now, and will pass on your suffering to them. A word when you are better will be worth many now. Wait for their sakes."

"I will not be preached at in my last hour. I am not a dead man because I am dying. I have a right to say my farewell, and they have a right to hear it. I will be master in my own house until I leave it."

The truth in these words was heard, and Mortimer went on the quest. The five little figures stood at the bed, and the five pale faces looked at the suffering face, showing their wonder that it was still the face they knew.

"You are all there?" said Horace, looking past them as if he could not focus his sight.

"Yes, Father," said Sarah, and her voice seemed to release his own.

"My little eldest daughter, I have one thing to say. I do not ask you to deny it. The bond between a father and his first girl has not been between you and me. I know you have not felt it. But as I move away from life, I feel it straining at my heart."

Charlotte drew Sarah to her side and let Jasper approach.

"Jasper, my eldest boy, you have not had a friend in your father. If I were to live, we would go our way together."

"Yes, Father," said Jasper, in a quiet, natural tone.

"Marcus, my little son, I have done little to help and

277

guide you. I have not showed the pride in you that you deserved. I have left you to a life apart."

Marcus silently accepted the words. He did not think his father had done well by him, or that the truth should not be said.

"Tamasin, my dear one, you have known that you were near to me. If I were to live, others should know it. But it must lie between you and me."

"I don't want to hear," said Avery, looking up at his mother. "I don't want poor Father to say it. They are sad things; it makes him worse to say them. I don't want there to be one for me."

"Avery, my little one, I have not thought of your helplessness. It has not been sacred to me. But I was learning to see and protect it, and I would have striven to learn. When you remember your father, remember his saying that."

Avery drew back to Charlotte, almost smiling in his relief that the moment was past.

"My children, I bequeath to you the freedom and joy of life. If they depend on my leaving you, take them as your gift from me. I go willingly to give them to you. I mistrust myself, as you mistrust me."

Emilia led the children away, and Avery's voice was heard through the closing door.

"Is Father going to die to make things better? Will they be better because he is dead? He might have been alive and done it; that would have been the best. He was beginning to do it. Why can't he be alive and go on?"

"My little kind son!" said Horace, shedding tears. "What I have missed in my carelessness of him! But I might continue to miss it. I have no faith in myself."

"It is our turn now," said Mortimer to Charlotte, trying to strike a lighter note. "He cannot mean to miss us out."

The faint voice came again.

"Mortimer, I have not done much for you, and you have not done only good to me. But as I go away alone, the strangest part is to leave you behind."

Charlotte waited for her own word, but her husband was lying with his eyes empty, and the look of one who was apart, and she knew he did not hear or see.

"You will sleep now," she said, and Horace saw and heard.

"I shall," he said, smiling into her face. "And it will be a long sleep."

As yet it was not long. Horace awoke with a start and slept again, awoke again and slept, passed to more uncertain sleep and waking, and then to a stage where there was little difference between waking and sleep. No one knew if he would be asleep or awake, when he breathed more freely or drew his last breath. Everyone knew that each breath might be the last.

The silence in the room pressed like a weight. Were they to face the change or to repulse it in disbelief? The impossible might be upon them; he who moulded lives might pass from life. They stood aloof and unaware of each other. They did not feel that the head of the house was to die, that the husband and father was to die, that the friend of a lifetime was to die. Horace was to die, Horace who might drive others to their death, but was himself immune from danger. They knew they had imagined him weeping for themselves, weeping in remorse and grief. The trial, the bondage, the safety of their lives would be gone. They would be free, unprotected, dependent on themselves. The helpless lives they had defended, would be their own responsibility, their own burden.

They left the room at the doctor's word. The bedside must be still and silent. No step or breath must assail the sick man. They went to the dining-room to await the final word. The room where he and they had lived the daily scene, was their natural refuge now. Things would be as Horace had left them; his customs would die too hard for them to see their death.

"What do we feel?" said Charlotte. "What should we have felt ten years ago? This has come too late, or it has come too early. Having lived so long, he should have died hereafter. You and I will still serve him. The children will still have a father."

"It is a pity that speech cannot be printed," said Mortimer.

"It will be printed on our hearts. When we die it will be graven there. More than that, it will make our lives. They belong to Horace; they are his by right of usage. It is an accepted right."

"How about the children?" said Mortimer.

"I will leave them for the time. Emilia is with them. If I see them now, I shall press on them too hard. They will feel more emotion than grief, and that is quick to pass. But soon they will begin to serve their father. Their service will get lighter as the years go by, but you and I will serve to the end. It has been our life work, and it will last for our lives."

"It is a humbling thought," said Mortimer. "We are Horace's slaves in soul. We belong to him and not to ourselves. To think that we ever thought we belonged to each other! I wonder if he knew the inner truth. I find myself hoping that he did, and that is the last proof of servitude."

Bullivant entered and went about his work, though his face showed signs of emotion.

"Well, life has to go on, Bullivant," said Mortimer.

"And it is no sign of feeling to fail in duty, sir."

"This is not the least of the things we have faced together."

"It is the greatest, as you say, sir," said Bullivant, as if Mortimer might have used the words.

"We have to face the threat of the future."

"It may be an aftermath, sir. And in the meantime we may be carried on to the day that is before our eyes," said Bullivant, his thoughts overtaking a function that loomed large in his world. "The ritual may have to be enacted."

"You would be with us, Bullivant, if the day had to come."

"I should be in my place, sir, as need hardly be said. And

the boy would wish to show respect, being conscious of being held to have shown other things. And Mrs. Selden would be in her element, if such a phrase may be used. I do not see it as the woman's place to rally to such observances, but there is a vein in Mrs. Selden that sets her apart. The young women servants would remain at home, and have things in order for the return, as Mrs. Selden might enjoin upon them. And in the meantime Mrs. Selden asks to be allowed to say a word of feeling in person."

"We shall be glad to see her at any time, either now or later."

Cook entered the room, at ease in her working garb, her apron openly assumed at the moment, and the emotion on her face equally undisguised.

"Will you not sit down, Cook?" said Charlotte.

Bullivant placed an upright chair at a distance from the family, rendering to all their due.

"Thank you, ma'am," said Cook, as she took it.

"Take the other chair, Bullivant," said Mortimer.

"No, sir," said Bullivant, with gentle decision. "This is how I stood before the master; this is how I stand before his representative. And I do not forget that the ladies are present; he would not forget it."

"We are all in trouble together, Cook," said Charlotte.

"The emptiness is in every corner, ma'am, when a presence has been there. And that is how the master's penetrates."

"He always feels he can depend on you."

"He and I have a point of agreement, ma'am, that the kitchen is the foundation of a house. And it gives zest to effort to feel it is recognised. And the higher the person, the more he is enabled to see it, as to see all things. It is only at a point that such understanding begins, and that is the master's level. And as you would be his widow, ma'am, so I should remain his servant. There would be no break."

"You will give our sympathy to all of them, and tell them we feel for them, as they feel for us."

"I will dispense it in the different degrees, ma'am, as befits each one. And they desired their sympathy to you, each in his or her order, and in that measure I undertook to convey it."

"And the mistress has a duty to herself, Mrs. Selden, that should now be observed," said Bullivant. "And I can be the bearer of any word between her world and ours."

Cook returned to the latter sphere, to find it peopled as usual. Miriam was standing, mute and still, before a weeping figure in a chair. The chair was Bullivant's, and the occupant, as had been the case at other times of stress, was George.

"I tried to do wrong to him, and he never did anything to me. He never said a word to me about it, and he never knew I was thankful."

"He returned good for evil, George; that was his last dealing with you," said Cook. "It may well overwhelm you, coming from such a source. But it should also give a spur to resolve. It constitutes a memory."

"And if you were thankful, George," said Bullivant, "it probably penetrated to the master, as such things do. And he will now see into your heart."

George took his hands from his face and raised his head, uncertain if his state of mind actually invited such scrutiny.

"Go forward and follow in his steps, George, as far as anyone can, who must follow so far behind. Do not be discouraged by the distance. Follow in your own place."

"And you may as well vacate Mr. Bullivant's chair," said Cook. "What is unfit remains so, whatever the circumstances."

"Did the master do a great deal to make people happier?" said Miriam, seeing Horace's life as complete and to be viewed as a whole.

"Well, happiness is not the only thing in life," said Cook, "and laxness and liberty may not always be conducive to it. He took his stand for welfare in the true sense, especially after he modified his course."

"You see, George, even the master was not above self-discipline," said Bullivant. "There is an example for you from a higher plane."

"People placed above others must beware of pandering," said Cook, with some thought of herself. "They are seldom estimated correctly, and perhaps should not be. We must not adapt ourselves to win esteem."

"How does it feel to be so ill that you must die?" said Miriam.

"Well, I have never been down into the valley of the shadow," said Cook, in a practical tone. "It has not fallen to me to be led so far, though I should have followed unmurmuring. I have been called on to face more protracted onsets. But I can put myself into another's place. To omit to do that has never been my failing."

Miriam could not make the same claim and still looked her question.

"We forget that your health is uncertain, Mrs. Selden," said Bullivant, on a contrite note.

"It is no more than can be borne without adding to others' burdens. And I may have derived benefit. Things have been known to date from a sickbed."

"We take things too much for granted from you."

"As may be the truest compliment. Habits must be formed when things maintain their course. Change may be the salt of life to some, but for me it would lose its savour."

"And then wherewith would it be salted?" said Bullivant, in a reverent manner.

"We all have a summer holiday," said Miriam.

"The break is sufficient to enable me to face another year," said Cook.

"Where did you go for your last holiday, Miriam?" said Bullivant, in the tone of one showing interest in another's life at the time of the disintegration of his own.

"I did not go anywhere. There was only the orphanage, and it is better here."

"The girl is under my eye," said Cook, giving Miriam

no ground for disagreement. "And perhaps it is hardly the occasion for talk of holidays. Other things are foremost."

"That is so, Mrs. Selden, and they are about to gather upon us. The hour is at hand. There will be the sad word to pass, and the sad function will supervene."

"As I had not overlooked. But I suppose instructions will be forthcoming."

"And through my lips, Mrs. Selden, and perhaps the moment is hardly premature. The males of the household will attend, that is to say myself, Mr. Mortimer and George, in our respective place. The other sex will remain under this roof, but I put in a plea for yourself, as moving on a different plane, and it is accepted that you will be present."

"Well, plea is rather a strange term for a suggestion of such a nature," said Cook, in a rising tone. "But there are differences that cannot be passed over, as you imply. So I will not refuse to lift my voice, even though the occasion may pierce the heart."

"And have you mourning of a suitable character happening to lie by you?" said Bullivant, on his musical note.

"I am in a position to appear in black from head to foot," said Cook, with a touch of aloofness. "And more is not required. We do not go to have eyes turned on us. It is a good thing nothing is required of Miriam. I hope that George can be presented so that he does not appear to fail in respect."

"With the aid of what I have by me, Mrs. Selden," said Bullivant, putting his fingers together.

"I am glad I shall not have to go," said Miriam.

"Well, there would be no occasion for your presence," said Cook. "There is no ground on which it would be indicated. And gladness is rather a strange feeling for the moment."

"So the long chapter is ending, Mrs. Selden," said Bullivant. "Man and boy, I have served the master for forty-five years. Man and boy, I have looked to him,

worked for him, borne with him, if you will. And now he is
to lie straight and still, while I stand behind, a hale man. I
thought he would follow me to the grave, master following
man, as I know would have been the case. But I am to
follow him, as has no especial bearing. I feel it to be an
emptiness. Not even Mr. Mortimer has the mien of one
having authority, as the master had. Though I face it like a
man, I face it also with a man's feeling."

Miriam looked at Bullivant with tears in her eyes.
George looked up in awe and almost incredulity. So this
was the real Bullivant. How it was his lot to move amongst
noble men!

Cook paid the speech the tribute of a moment's silence.

"The mistress in her weeds will move the emotions," she
said. "And Miss Emilia will be a stately, even though a
somewhat remote, form. We can see it with the mind's eye.
I suppose the master will be borne by his tenants to his
grave?"

"That will be the course, Mrs. Selden. It is an observance to which he is entitled. He has rendered as well as
received dues, and it would be true to say that he has
extorted nothing. As to one above them in every sense they
will render the last service."

"I hope to be equal to my part," said Cook, bringing to
Bullivant a vision of her, abandoned to song, while other
voices swelled in her support.

"We shall follow the master in our time," he said,
"though we know not on what day nor at what hour."

"'I do not ask to see,'" said Cook, "'the distant scene.
One step enough for me.'"

A sound broke across the stillness.

"The dining-room bell!" said Bullivant.

Cook lifted her eyes.

"It hardly seems a fitting medium, if it is the word."

"Life has to be maintained, Mrs. Selden. As I obeyed the
master's summons, so I now obey what may be in a sense
his last. In a way it is what is left."

The bell rang again and Bullivant left the room.

"There are verbal messages," said Cook, looking at Miriam, as though in some doubt of her being a suitable auditor. "And there are occasions that point to their use."

"They couldn't come here themselves," said Miriam. "How could they have sent a message?"

"George should have been in the hall," said Cook. "We have been guilty of an oversight, as was pardonable under the circumstances."

"I wasn't told to go," said George.

"I have referred to an omission," said Cook.

Bullivant's step was heard, rapid and firm, and his hand on the door seemed to follow instantly upon it.

"The cloud has lifted, Mrs. Selden! The cup has passed from our lips. The future opens again. The master is safe! Natural sleep has supervened. With care and precaution he will be restored."

Cook rose to her feet, her glance at George and Miriam compelling them to do the same. Then she fell on her knees, exercising a similar compulsion by some other means, as her eyes were now closed. As Bullivant knelt, she lifted them once towards him, and he rose to the occasion as befitted the manhood that carried so much weight in his world.

"We give the thanks that are due, where they are due," he said, and gained his feet.

Cook remained for a moment longer, in some personal relation with what was undefined, and spoke with a note of approval as she rose.

"The words covered the occasion, and did not touch divergence of custom or observance."

"Mrs. Selden, we render our gratitude in the same spirit to the same power," said Bullivant, with a faint note of reproach, as though such summing up were hardly in tune with the moment.

"And we resume the daily duty also in the same spirit,"

said Cook, as she shook out her skirts. "And I recommend, Miriam, that you take a similar view of the position. An excuse for self-indulgence is too often found in an occasion of feeling, and should not be acted upon."

"So, George," said Bullivant, "here is a chance to atone. The opportunity we had thought wanting, is forthcoming. May you make the most of it."

"It seems that Miriam and I are the ones who are to respond to the demand," said George, who was in a state of consternation and foreboding that was unsuspected, as it was assumed that his master's life meant more to him than his own ease.

"George," said Bullivant, "I give you up. The gulf between us is too wide. Too long have I striven to bridge it, and striven in vain. I will strive no longer. I recognise my failure. Henceforth we go our ways apart. Though together in the flesh and daily task, in spirit we are divided. I had not measured our distance."

George, who had always thought it exaggerated, watched Bullivant leave the room, with a sense of having come to an extreme pass. He looked at Cook, or rather at her back, that remained turned towards him, and then at Miriam, who dared not respond, knowing that Cook had eyes at the back of her head, though they were not at George's service. He realised and resolved that in future he would depend on himself.

Bullivant returned to the dining-room and went up to Mortimer and grasped his hand.

"I did not say my word, sir; I was not master of myself. It came upon me and stayed my tongue, but I hope my silence spoke."

"I am not equal to these moments, Bullivant. I can only hope the same."

"The history of the change will be made known to us, sir, in your own time. As also the master's progress."

"I will tell you all I know, Bullivant. I hardly follow it myself as yet. We are waiting for a word, but we have to realise our place. All attention is for the master. But the tale will come to be told."

"And may be passed on to Mrs. Selden, sir. She is much engaged with illness, both on the physical and spiritual side. Nothing fails to arrest her interest, and in the case of the master it will be redoubled."

"We will see she has the full account. It must be a strange and unusual one. Hope was almost gone."

Horace had lain in the stillness and silence demanded by the balance of his state. It was expected to sink to one side, but sank to the other. The unconsciousness was different and deeper; breathing was again perceived; the nameless condition took on the guise of sleep, and then its nature; and Horace awoke to weakness and wonder and the dawn of his body's health. For some days he lay still and silent, content with the abatement of pain, with the promise of continued life, with his awareness of the movement of the house. Then the illness sank into the past and became a memory, and gathered to itself other memories.

One of these was the scene with his children. It seemed to depend for its reality on his death, and in his life to have lost its meaning. He hoped it would fade from their minds, knew it was rooted there, and left it to the future, at once a threat to his ease and a basis for his life with them. It would serve its own purpose, though it would impose its pain.

The time came when he lay on the sofa in the dining-room. It was the room where he chose to lie, the scene of his future and his past. He had had his fill of solitude and silence. The draughts and the smoke and the passing figures drew him to the life he knew, and strengthened the bonds that had nearly broken.

One morning George followed Bullivant, bearing a tray for his use, and feeling it a frail ground for his own enforced appearance. As he passed Horace, he threw him a furtive glance.

"You need not be afraid of me, George. I am not a ghost, though I nearly became one."

George stopped, tray in hand, and stared at his master, relating his words to a previous occasion to which they would apply.

"Have you never seen anyone who has been very ill, before?"

"Yes, sir. No, sir. No, not quite so ill."

"Did you feel you would be happier without me?"

"Yes, sir. No, sir," said George, again referring the words to the earlier episode. His master's experience had made little impression on him, compared with his own.

"I am no more likely to harm you, than you are to harm me."

"No, sir," said George, grasping his tray and speeding to the door, uncertain of the exact threat in the words.

"He behaves as if he had seen a wraith," said Horace to Bullivant.

"Well, sir, he was connecting your words with the occasion when he had it in his mind to do you harm, as we know."

"Oh, I see. Poor boy!"

"Well, sir, you may use that term."

"I frightened him too much about his little thefts."

"Well, sir, it was hard to see how the mean was to be struck. It was not an occasion for encouragement."

"I expect he feels it hard that I should have been threatened with death three times, and each time escaped."

"As master with nine lives, sir," said Bullivant, smiling. "I don't know that he is quite such a worthless lad. Not that I retain any hope of moulding him to my own pattern."

"You have given him up in that sense, have you?"

"Yes, sir. Those words have passed my lips. In that sense, as you say."

"And is he affected by your decision?"

"No, sir, not perceptibly. He is chiefly affected by any threat to himself, or to the idea of himself that he harbours."

"And what is that idea?"

"Well, sir, something much beyond the reality."

"I did not know he had so much self-confidence."

"No, sir, there is no ground for supposing it."

"You have no definite impression of it?"

"No, sir, I have not troubled to acquire it. What would be gained? It is no good to imagine some great advance, and then to shirk the common daily steps that may lead towards it. Things can only ensue in course."

"He does not want to take some place such as yours in the end?"

"To take my place, sir? The old generation passeth away and the new generation cometh; but the one does not always step into the shoes of the other, and it might not be so in this case."

"It would not indeed. Some places cannot be filled, and yours is one of them," said Horace, almost welcoming the weakness that released his feelings and the words to express them. "You are an old and tried friend, Bullivant."

"Thank you, sir. That is my feeling towards you, in addition to those that accompany my calling."

"We must leave George to himself and his own future."

"Indeed, sir, that is a good way of putting it. It contains the truth."

Bullivant went to the door, the traces of pain and its assuagement passing from his face. As he approached the kitchen, he came up with Cook, also on her way to it.

"So, Mrs. Selden, we resume the common round. We may feel a touch of flatness after the rise and fall of the last days, but it is the sound and wholesome change, and so we must regard it." He broke off, the flatness passing from his bearing.

On either side of the fire, in the chairs peculiar to their elders, George and Miriam were seated. They did not perceive the former's approach, owing perhaps to the quality in it that Bullivant recognised.

"Well, are we to stand at your pleasure?" said Cook.

The young pair regained their feet, and the others

regarded the chairs as if some harm had befallen them.

"Well, will the chairs never be the same again?" said George.

Neither Cook nor Bullivant appeared to hear.

"Do you think, Miriam, that the master's facing death and being restored in some way constitutes your promotion?" said Cook.

Miriam had felt that her late association with her elders, through extreme experience, had lifted her towards them, but had not known that she felt it. She looked at Cook in recognition both of the fact and the latter's perception of it.

"And I do not know if George's new attitude is contagious," said Cook.

There was a pause for Bullivant's word to George, but none came.

"Was it in your mind that the late vicissitudes had lifted some obligation off you?"

"No," said Miriam.

"Then what was your object in esconcing yourself in a manner that was the prerogative of another?"

"A case of the mentioned contagion," said George.

"So an upward trend is the thing for you both," said Cook.

"'Manners makyth man', Miriam," said Bullivant, in a grave tone. "My passing over of George is not a sign of blindness to the gulf between us."

"Rather of the opposite," said Cook. "And I am in no doubt concerning the parallel distance between myself and Miriam. I think I am aware of its extent."

Miriam was unaffected, being certain of it.

"There is a figure passing the window, Mrs. Selden," said Bullivant. "Can it be Miss Buchanan?"

"Who else could it be?" said George. "There is no chance of anyone else."

There was the sound of the back door bell.

"That answers the query," said Cook, looking at

Bullivant, to indicate to which question she referred. "I should recognise her ring out of a thousand."

"Which is not a necessary effort," said George.

Bullivant went to the door with the rapid step of one who welcomed any break. The guest seemed uncertain of her purpose in coming, and he resolved her doubt.

"You bethought yourself of our situation, Miss Buchanan, and came to say the word of a friend."

"And so did the action of one," said Cook.

Miss Buchanan sat down, as if doing so meant consent, as in her case it did.

"You might have seen a changed household," said Cook, "and one changed to its depths."

"But happily you see it otherwise," said Bullivant. "The angel of death paused at our door, but mercifully passed on."

"I should have missed Mr. Lamb myself, though he might not suppose it," said Miss Buchanan. "In church he is such a constant figure."

"He observes the outward sign," said Cook, "as is fitting when there are those to be affected."

"I have often thought he must have the service by heart," said Miss Buchanan, who knew this was a possible accomplishment.

"You know it yourself, don't you?" said George. "People say that you never use a book."

"I wonder that anyone needs one after a time."

"My own destination being chapel, I have not used similar observation," said Cook. "But the loss would have operated; there would have been the pang, when I made my plans for one less at the table."

"And for me, when I moved about it, there would have been the empty place," said Bullivant, "and one corresponding in my heart."

"Mr. Mortimer would have been a father to the children."

"No, Miss Buchanan, he would not have been that,"

said Bullivant, gently. "He would have known his duty to the master and to them. He would have been their guardian and protector, as the master appointed."

"He would not have sullied a memory," said Cook.

"A distinction without a difference," said George.

Miss Buchanan looked as if she agreed, and Cook and Bullivant as if they had not caught the words.

"I suppose we should have called him Mr. Lamb," said Miss Buchanan, whose thoughts pursued Mortimer rather than Horace.

"Mr. Mortimer he has been; Mr. Mortimer he is; Mr. Mortimer he would always have been," said Bullivant. "As Mr. Mortimer he will pass to his grave; I know him well enough to say that."

"And he is not any less for being what he is," said Cook.

"We keep on imagining situations that do not exist, Miss Buchanan," said George. "We have no interest of our own to occupy us."

"Our minds have been lifted from the world as it is," said Cook. "It was a natural going forward."

"We shall have forgotten the master's illness in a few weeks," said George. "It is not going to leave any change."

Neither Cook nor Bullivant replied. Cook indeed had only responded to the former speech by an oversight.

"I am under a cloud, Miss Buchanan," said George, in an equal manner. "I have not the mind of a slave."

"And what kind of mind have you?" said Cook rapidly. "The master-mind?"

"So you can speak to me?" said George.

"It arose from the moment. And there is no obligation upon us to be on our guard."

"We do not want the preoccupation," said Bullivant; "it might entail effort."

"And that is the last thing you want," said George.

"There are objects of endeavour," said Cook, "and this does not happen to be one of them. Or it does not strike us in that light."

"You are certainly not sending me to Coventry."

"Well, that was avowed."

"Why not let bygones be bygones?" said Miss Buchanan. "This is a good moment for a fresh start."

"It is, Miss Buchanan," said Bullivant, "and I did not fail to see it in that light. But response was not forthcoming."

"Such things may take their time. The leaven must have a chance to work."

"I don't want your offices," said George. "They don't cost you anything. And I don't care to be interceded for by a person who cannot read."

There was silence.

Miriam raised her eyes and rested them on Miss Buchanan. Cook turned to the stove and appeared to be involved in some sudden predicament. Bullivant stooped and adjusted his boot, and then worked his foot, as though pursuing some cause of discomfort.

"You all seem preoccupied," said George. "But I know your thoughts. You are wondering how I found that out."

"We do not engage ourselves with your methods in the underhand sphere," said Bullivant, putting his fingers down his collar, as though mainly concerned with the attainment of complete ease. "We prefer to keep ourselves aloof from them."

"It is more on our level," said Cook.

"I will relieve your curiosity," said George, in a lofty manner that hardly heralded his words. "Your voices came to me through the kitchen door."

"And had not far to come, as I should infer," said Cook.

"That does nothing for our curiosity, George," said Bullivant, sadly. "Indeed curiosity is not the term. We are under no uncertainty as regards your dealings at doors. They have been brought to our notice."

"And I wonder you like to bring them further," said Cook, in the tone of one still engaged.

"And Miss Buchanan is now in no doubt about them," said Bullivant, feeling that the victim could not longer be left out of the issue.

"I suppose it is all over the village," said the latter, facing the position and voicing her main thought.

"Miss Buchanan," said Bullivant, "I will tell you the truth, the whole truth, and nothing but the truth, as is due to anyone on a level to face it. Mr. Mortimer it was, who suspected it, who gathered it, I should say, from some occurrences at your shop. He mentioned it to me under condition of secrecy, in order that your intercourse with us might be safeguarded, and we later extended our confidence to Mrs. Selden. That is all I can say. George it is, who can go further."

"Confidences are always extended. That is how trouble comes," said Miss Buchanan, looking at George in a helpless manner that went to Bullivant's heart.

"Was it the action of a man, George, the action of one who knew what was due to a woman and a guest?"

"You are fond of satisfying curiosity," said Cook. "Satisfy it now on this point."

Miss Buchanan looked at Bullivant.

"Did you know of it before my other visits?" she said, her eyes becoming retrospective, as memories came into her mind.

George looked up, paused for thought, and sat up straight.

"Was it the action of a man, Bullivant, of one who knew what was due to a woman and a guest?"

There was a pause, and Cook turned from the stove.

"Satisfy my curiosity on this point," said George.

"Have you been in the habit of addressing Mr. Bullivant in that manner?" said Cook.

"Was it the action of a man, *Mr.* Bullivant?" said George, his emphasis suggesting a discrepancy between Bullivant's claims and conduct.

Bullivant and Miss Buchanan met each other's eyes;

there was a highly charged moment, and the sound of their joint laughter fell on unexpecting ears.

"There is a something in me, Miss Buchanan, that runs away with me at times," said Bullivant, in a tone of self-abasement. "There seems to be an imp lurking within, that renders my actions at variance with myself. I have been led into predicaments by it all through my life."

"And led other people into them?"

"Well, Miss Buchanan, I had hoped I stopped short of that. Recollection came in time."

Miss Buchanan leaned back in her chair.

"I feel like a criminal who has lived so long under fear of arrest, that he is relieved when it comes."

"You a criminal, Miss Buchanan! You of all others, who are more sinned against than sinning! That is a word to wound."

"A clear conscience is all," said Cook. "We find our-selves sustained by it."

"We like something else," said Miss Buchanan. "And being sinned against is not a recommendation, or does not seem to be so regarded."

"It was the concealment that was a mistake," said George, in a masculine manner. "It was that, that gave you a feeling of being a criminal."

"I am glad you realise that open methods are best, George," said Cook. "And that you feel yourself the right person to express the matter. And that you can broach the question of concealment without blenching."

"He had his own way of dealing with it," said Miss Buchanan, in a tone that told George that she was no longer his friend.

"Miss Buchanan," said Bullivant, in a tentative tone, "may I say that no one of our standing strikes me as so equipped with language as yourself? What may be called your disadvantage has not put you behind."

"And so need not be given that name," said Cook.

"Who knows how far I might have been in front?"

"To a considerable extent, as is easy to see," said Cook. "To a certain extent as it is."

"You do not ever feel inclined to remedy the position?" said Bullivant. "As might so easily be done in your case."

"Illiterate I have lived. Illiterate I will die. The time for remedying matters is past."

"What you desire to acquire is known to all," said Bullivant.

"No," said Miss Buchanan, shrinking at the suggestion in the words as well as at their truth. "Ignorance is enough in itself. There is no need to build upon the foundation."

"There is no call to parade it to acquaintance," said Cook. "It is an individual concern and would be treated as such."

"I used to teach the letters and the first words to children at the orphanage," said Miriam, in the easy tone of one to whom such things were among the other domestic arts. "It was because I was slow and patient. The backward ones learned with me."

There was a pause.

"Well, that reason does not apply to Miss Buchanan," said Cook, in a light tone.

"Who is a backward one, if I am not?" said Miss Buchanan, with equal lightness.

"I still have the alphabet book and the spelling book," said Miriam. "They told me to bring them, in case they were useful in a nursery. But I was put into the kitchen."

"It would be a good thing for you to be put through the rudiments again," said Cook, in a thoughtful tone. "I do not like you to go backward, because of your situation under me. It does not redound to my advantage. Miss Buchanan would so soon outstrip you, that it would be a good spur to your progress."

"And Miss Buchanan, being a neighbour, could make it convenient to come in at intervals," said Bullivant, "which would make a pleasant break for us, and would present that outward aspect."

"And it would soon result in her taking the lead, rather than Miriam," said Cook, "which is what I want for the girl, subject to Miss Buchanan's agreement."

"Miriam teaching Miss Buchanan!" said George. "That is rather a reversal of things."

"It has been made clear that it will amount to the opposite," said Cook. "That has emerged."

"George," said Bullivant, turning to him on an impulse, "is this weakness in me or is it strength? Shall I offer you another chance? The condition being silence upon Miss Buchanan's situation, both in this house and out of it."

"I had not told anyone," muttered George, in acceptance of the offer, which he ascribed to weakness. "Not even Miriam."

"Which, considering the method of your ascertaining it, was the natural sequence," said Cook.

"I had noted that, George," said Bullivant, thinking it best to continue on his own line. "And I had marked it to your credit in my mind."

A sharp sound came from the bell that served the dining-room, and Bullivant gained his feet.

"The master's ring! The sound I thought never to hear again! We can indeed lay aside all personal differences. The old days have returned."

"Bullivant, the fire is smoking," said Horace. "When did you have the sweep?"

"At the accepted interval, sir. He observes regularity, if no other of his obligations."

"It is nothing to do with the grate."

"Nothing at all, sir," said Bullivant, hastening towards it. "It could not draw as sweet as it does, if that were the case. There may be some slight obstruction."

"You need not jump back, as if a tiger had sprung at you," said Horace, as this incident occurred.

"No, sir," said Bullivant, sustaining a second onslaught without a sign. "It is a mild outbreak. Doubtless some vagary of the wind."

"The wind must be a woman," said Horace, with a smile.

"Yes, sir, but much of the world is that, as emerges in my calling. And indeed it is not a thing one would speak against."

Horace could only be silent.

Corduroy

Adrian Bell

Introduction by Susan Hill

In the tradition of Gilbert White, Francis Kilvert, and Flora Thompson, Adrian Bell in *Corduroy* has given us an unforgettable account of past life in the English countryside. In 1920 the city-bred author left London to work as a labourer on a farm in the depths of Suffolk. We see the country landscape and rural pursuits through his perceptive young eyes.

'Bell's writings are literature, and should be kept in circulation as part of the English heritage'–Q. D. Leavis

The Rock Pool

Cyril Connolly

Introduction by Peter Quennell

'A snobbish and mediocre young literary man from Oxford, with a comfortable regular income, spends the summer on the Riviera with an artists' and writers' colony. His first attitude is interested but patronizing: he tells himself that he has come as an observer and will study the community like a rock pool. But the denizens of the pool drag him down into it . . . The story, which owes something to *South Wind* and Compton Mackenzie's novels of Capri, differs from them through its acceleration, which, as in the wildly speeded-up burlesque, has something demoniacal about it.'–Edmund Wilson

OXFORD PAPERBACKS

Twentieth-Century Classics

Memoirs of a Midget

Walter de la Mare

Introduction by Angela Carter

'This book is an authentic masterpiece. Lucid, enigmatic, and violent with a terrible violence that leaves behind no physical trace . . . It may be read with a good deal of simple enjoyment and then it sticks like a splinter in the mind.' So writes novelist Angela Carter in her new introduction to Walter de la Mare's elegiac study of the estrangement and isolation suffered by the diminutive Miss M.

The Slaves of Solitude

Patrick Hamilton

Introduction by Claud Cockburn

'Mr Hamilton has the habit, the art, or the genius of writing in his novels, about the most familiar scenes, the most threadbare experiences, as if they were being observed for the first time'– Stephen Potter

A seedy boarding-house provides a wartime haven for Miss Roach, a lonely middle-aged spinster. Romance, glamour, and finally tragedy enter her life in the shape of a handsome American serviceman.

OXFORD PAPERBACKS

Twentieth-Century Classics

Elizabeth and Essex

Lytton Strachey

Introduction by Michael Holroyd

Lytton Strachey achieved fame with the publication in 1918 of *Eminent Victorians;* but none of his books brought him greater popular success than his last: this dramatic reconstruction of the complex and stormy relationship between Queen Elizabeth I and the dashing, if wayward, Earl of Essex

'a brilliant and insufficiently appreciated book'–A. L. Rowse

The Aerodrome

Rex Warner

Introduction by Anthony Burgess

Published nearly a decade before Orwell's *1984* shocked post-war readers. *The Aerodrome* is a book whose disturbingly prophetic qualities give it equal claim to be regarded as a modern classic. At the centre of the book stand the opposing forces of fascism and democracy, represented on the one hand by the Aerodrome, a ruthlessly efficient totalitarian state, and on the other by the Village, with its sensual muddle and stupidity. A comedy on a serious theme, this novel conveys probably better than any other of its time the glamorous appeal of fascism.

'It is high time that this thrilling story should be widely enjoyed again'–Angus Wilson

The Village in the Jungle

Leonard Woolf

Introduction by E. F. C. Ludowyck

As a young man Leonard Woolf spent seven years in the Ceylon civil service. The people he met in Sinhalese jungle villages so fascinated and obsessed him that some years later he wrote a novel about them. It is his knowledge and profound understanding of the Sinhalese people that has made *The Village in the Jungle* a classic for all time.

'*The Village in the Jungle* is a novel of superbly dispassionate observation, a great novel.'–Quentin Bell

Ethan Frome and Summer

Edith Wharton

Introduction by Victoria Glendinning

Edith Wharton (1862-1937) is probably America's most original and important female novelist. This volume contains two short novels, *Ethan Frome* and *Summer,* both of which outstrip their predecessors in the genre of American realism.